Integrated Landscaping
Following Nature's Lead

A new way of thinking about shaping home grounds and public spaces in the Northeast

REVISED AND EXPANDED EDITION

Lauren Chase-Rowell, Mary Tebo Davis,
Katherine Hartnett, and Marilyn Wyzga

University of New Hampshire Press
Durham, New Hampshire

University of New Hampshire Press
An imprint of University Press of New England
www.upne.com
© 2007, 2012 University of New Hampshire Cooperative Extension
and New Hampshire Fish and Game Department
Revised and expanded edition, 2012
All rights reserved
Manufactured in the United States of America

For permission to reproduce any of the material in this book, contact
Permissions, University Press of New England, One Court Street,
Suite 250, Lebanon NH 03766; or visit www.upne.com

Library of Congress Control Number: 2011943280
ISBN 978-1-61168-278-6

5 4 3 2 1

TABLE OF CONTENTS

Acknowledgments . . . . .Page v

Introduction . . . . Page vii

    How this landscape manual differs from others
    Ways you can use this manual

Chapter 1. . . . . .Page 2

Natural Landscape in Transition: The Consequences of Rapid Growth

    The consequences of rapid growth
    An overview of invasive species and their impacts
    Fragmenting landscapes: the wildlife connection
    Facing the challenges to the Northeast's disappearing natural landscapes

Chapter 2 . . . . Page 8

The Integrated Landscape: Philosophy, Benefits, and Principles that Guide Practice

    Integrated landscaping: A holistic approach
    Integrated landscapes imitate natural ecosystems
    Benefits of integrated landscaping
    Ten natural principles to guide your landscaping practices

Chapter 3. . . . . Page 20

Outside and Onsite: Taking Stock of What You Have

    Scope of the inventory
    Learn about your soil
    Assessing wildlife habitat through the seasons
    Taking stock: the inventory process

Chapter 4. . . . . Page 29

Designing Landscapes with Establishment and Care in Mind

    Creating the base plan: putting it on paper
    Adding layers to your base plan
    Develop a wish list of needs and desires
    Create a functional bubble diagram
    Your conceptual plan
    Designing for wildlife
    Designing for shorelines

Chapter 5. . . . . Page 46

The Plant Systems Approach

    Locating and creating plant systems for the integrated landscape
    Choosing plants for your system
    Dealing with invasive species

Plant systems for wildlife
The Plant-System Models
Matrix of Plant System Models
Plant-System Model Descriptions
Plant-System Model Illustrations
- Model 1 — page 66
- Model 2 — page 68
- Model 3 — page 70
- Model 4 — page 72
- Model 5 — page 74
- Model 6 — page 76
- Model 7 — page 78
- Model 8 — page 80
- Model 9 — page 82
- Model 10 — page 84
- Model 11 — page 86
- Model 12 — page 88

Plant Chart   page 90
The planting plan: designing the plant system and selecting plants

Chapter 6 .... Page 120
Establishing Plant Systems

Protect existing plants
Lay out your planting bed
Select healthy plants
Planting
Thoughts on lawns and mowing

Chapter 7 .... Page 133
Caring for Sustainable Plant Systems

A lower-maintenance landscape
Through the seasons
Care and maintenance tips for future years
Healthy plant systems grow and change over time
Now, get up and get out!

APPENDIX A: Best Bets: Woody and Herbaceous Plants .... Page 141

APPENDIX B: Plant Lists .... Page 142

APPENDIX C: Inventory Worksheets .... Page 146

APPENDIX D: Additional Resources .... Page 152

APPENDIX E: Selecting Woody Plants for Shoreland Landscapes .... Page 158

APPENDIX F: Landscape Practices Aligned with the Ecological Principles ... Page 164

APPENDIX G: New England USDA Hardiness Zone Map .... Page 167

About the Authors .... Page 168

ACKNOWLEDGMENTS

This manual is a product of the Integrated Landscaping Practices Workgroup begun in 2002 through the Jordan Institute to explore ways to incorporate ecological principles into landscape design and to address the issue of invasive species. The Workgroup is made up of individuals with diverse experience and knowledge in areas that include landscape design, installation and maintenance, wildlife and habitat enhancement, organic land care, permaculture, urban forestry, land use planning, geography, environmental education, art and illustration. Authors include:

Lauren Chase-Rowell, Outdoor Rooms Permaculture Landscape Design Services, Nottingham, NH
Katherine Hartnett, Consultant, Integrated Design and Development, Deerfield, NH
Mary Tebo Davis, Community Forestry Educator, UNH Cooperative Extension, Manchester, NH
Marilyn Wyzga, Wildlife Educator, NH Fish and Game Department, Concord, NH

Note: The views expressed in this manual are those of the authors, and may not necessarily be those of the agencies with which they're associated.

Illustrations by Lauren Chase-Rowell and Marilyn Wyzga

Plant System Designs by Lauren Chase-Rowell and Marilyn Wyzga

Additional illustrations used with permission from:
Linda Isaacson
People, Places & Plants Magazine
Society for the Protection of NH Forests
Shigo and Trees, Associates LLC
Victor Young, NH Fish and Game

Cover Design by Pam Doherty, UNH Cooperative Extension

Design and Production by the Secret Agency, Somersworth, NH

Editorial & Production Overview by Peg Boyles and Holly Young, UNH Cooperative Extension

Photographs by Mary Tebo Davis

Additional photographs used with permission from:
Nancy Berliner, Groundwork, Concord, NH
Lauren Chase-Rowell
Dick Hamilton, White Mountain Attractions Association
Katherine Hartnett
Joe Homer, Natural Resource Conservation Service
Steve Hundley, Natural Resource Conservation Service
Lynne Langley, Atlantic Heights Neighborhood Garden Club, Portsmouth, NH
Jane O'Donnell, UNH Cooperative Extension Master Gardener, Grafton County
Will Stewart, Greater Manchester NeighborWorks
Judy Tumosa, NH Fish and Game Department
Marilyn Wyzga

Special thanks to Kathy Boire, UNH Cooperative Extension Master Gardener, Hillsborough County, who spent weeks editing the text, creating the appendices, and entering the plant charts and lists.

Thank you to the authors of *Landscaping by the Water's Edge: An Ecological Approach*.

From UNH Cooperative Extension:
Lauren Chase-Rowell, Outdoor Rooms Permaculture Landscape Design Services, Nottingham NH
Mary Tebo Davis, Extension Educator, Hillsborough County
Margaret Hagen, Extension Educator, Hillsborough County
Dr. Catherine Neal, Horticulture/Landscape Extension Specialist
Amy Ouellette, Extension Educator, Belknap County
Sadie Puglisi, Extension Educator, Merrimack County
Dr. John Roberts, Turfgrass Extension Specialist
Dr. Jeff Schloss, Water Resources Extension Specialist
Dr. Stan Swier, Entomology Extension Specialist

Thank you to UNH Cooperative Extension staff Pam Doherty, Rachel Maccini, Matt Tarr, Robert Edmonds, Darrel Covell, and Mary West.

Thank you to NH Fish and Game Department staff James Oehler, Judy Stokes, Judy Silverberg, and Victor Young.

Thanks to Jon Batson, Jenesis Gardens & Design LLC, NH Landscape Association, and Natural Resources Steward Program; Debra Claffey, Artful Gardener Professional Garden Care; John Hart, UNH Thompson School; Catherine Neal, UNH Cooperative Extension; and Kelly Omand, Antioch University graduate student, for their thorough reviews of the manuscript and constructive suggestions.

Thank you to Millican Nurseries, Inc., for use of their catalogue.

Thanks to our collaborators, who helped build our Demonstration Sites, clearly showcasing integrated landscaping techniques as discussed throughout this manual. These sites are open to the public, and we encourage you to visit them:

Grafton County Complex, UNH Cooperative Extension's Integrated Landscaping Demonstration Site, Grafton County Complex, 3855 Dartmouth College Highway, North Haverhill, NH

Hislop Park Integrated Landscaping Demonstration Site, Atlantic Heights Garden Club, Atlantic Heights Neighborhood on Preble Way, Portsmouth, NH

Public Service of New Hampshire Energy Park, Integrated Landscaping Demonstration Site, 780 North Commercial Street, Manchester, NH

We also want to thank those people who gave us their early input and support to move forward with the writing of this manual: Karen Acerno, formerly of Audubon Society of New Hampshire; Brett Andrus, NH Plant Growers Association and Churchill's Garden Center; Carol Barleon, NH Office of Energy and Planning; Kiki Bean, Surfside Lands & Container Design; Glenn Caron, Scenic Nursery; Lionel Chute, formerly of the NH Natural Heritage Bureau; Lynne Hardy, formerly of Millican Nurseries Inc; Pam Hunt, Audubon Society of New Hampshire; Karen Johnson, formerly of Millican Nurseries Inc.; Deborah Lievens, NH Invasive Species Committee and NH Community Tree Steward; Cynthia May, formerly of CLD Engineers; Ken Michael, formerly of Millican Nurseries Inc.; Michelle Plourde, formerly of Loughton's Nursery; Mary Reynolds, NH Division of Forests and Lands; Colleen Thornton, landscape designer; Heidi Tyson, formerly of UNH Office of Sustainability; and Leslie van Berkum, Van Berkum Nursery.

Many people put countless hours into the development of this manual. We appreciate your thoughtful suggestions for improving this edition. Please email comments to mary.tebo@unh.edu.

INTRODUCTION

Although we think of our landscapes and gardens as our own, they are part of a larger regional environment. When we landscape around our homes, businesses, schools, and community centers, we are doing more than planting flowers, shrubs and trees, and moving soil and rocks. We're shaping the landscape of the Northeast and all who share in its future, including ourselves.

When we see ourselves as part of the whole, we then see that what we do in the places we live, work, and play has a ripple effect far beyond the space each of us calls "home." We may begin to make the kinds of choices that support native ecosystems and maintain the look and feel of our region. Our goal for this manual is to help you do that.

How this landscape manual differs from others

We take an integrated approach to the design, establishment, and ongoing care of a landscape, considering each element equally and continuously throughout the entire landscaping process.

We encourage you to follow nature's lead by thinking in terms of plant systems rather than individual plant specimens. Native ecosystems include multiple layers of vegetation, from the subsoil up to the canopy. By applying this holistic approach in gardens and landscapes, consider the importance of each layer to the next and how they function together with the environment to support wildlife habitat and human desires for beautiful surroundings.

We provide you with plant-system models that will serve as interesting and beautiful alternatives to common horticultural species that have been identified as invasive, rather than offering plant-for-a-plant substitutions.

Finally, we look to local ecosystems for clues and ideas to create functional and beautiful outdoor spaces. We look beyond property lines to what may have occurred naturally and to what may now be missing, and urge you to explore the land around you to identify features that help define your "sense of place" and to incorporate these into gardens and landscapes.

Ways you can use this manual

You'll find this manual especially useful as a tool for landscape design, plant selection, and planning. It will help you:

- Establish landscapes that look and feel as if they belong in the Northeast. (Although we write this from our home state of New Hampshire, we encourage you to substitute your state or region in the pages ahead, as the concepts and information presented apply to the broader Northeast bioregion—all of New England, New York, and into southern Canada.)

- Integrate principles of the natural world into beautiful, functional landscapes.

- Think in terms of plant systems, rather than mere collections of individual, aesthetically pleasing plants.

- Use and apply models for design and plant selection.

- Find alternatives to invasive species in the landscape that offer the aesthetic characteristics you prefer.

- Take a comprehensive inventory of the existing features of your site: its soils, plants, wildlife, and relationship to the surrounding environment.

- Select the right plants for a particular place.

- Create landscapes that benefit wildlife, both above and below ground.

- Create landscapes that sustain themselves with minimum cost, energy, and effort.

- Create plant systems that enhance an existing landscape, such as adding vertical layers to what is already there.

- Design a new sustainable/ecological landscape using our plant-systems approach.

- Adapt one of the plant-system models for your site, substituting certain plants from our plant lists to mimic nature's design.

- Locate (through our Appendices) many additional resources on a wide variety of landscaping topics not covered, or only lightly covered, in this manual.

Integrated Landscaping
Following Nature's Lead

CHAPTER 1

Natural Landscape in Transition:
The Consequences of Rapid Growth

When we think of our home state, New Hampshire, we picture forested hillsides, mountain vistas, granite boulders, snowdrifts, sugar maples lining back roads, fall foliage, white-tailed deer, moose, lakes, ponds, rivers, salt marshes, dragonflies, stone walls, open fields, wildflowers, migrating song birds and resident bald eagles.

New Hampshire's diverse natural landscapes provide the scenic backdrop that makes the Granite State such a great place to live, work, play, and visit. The sights, smells, sounds, and textures of nature make us feel good. They connect us to the history of this place and offer promise for its future.

These natural landscapes aren't only beautiful to look at, they provide habitat for wildlife, food for humans and domestic animals, and public health benefits such as clean air and clean water. They drive our state and local economies. Nearly five million acres of forestland sustain a thriving forest-products industry. Agricultural lands and products are another major contributor to the economy: farms, orchards, plant nurseries, and garden centers serve horticulture professionals, gardening enthusiasts, and the public. New Hampshire's natural resources also attract tens of thousands of tourists each year.

The consequences of rapid growth: loss of open lands, proliferation of invasive species, and threats to wildlife

Our natural landscapes help provide a quality of life that helped make New Hampshire the fastest-growing state in New England for more than four decades. Instead of changing gradually over time, many once-rural areas seem to change overnight as open land is converted for residential and commercial development.

FOUR DECADES OF DRAMATIC GROWTH

New Hampshire's population more than doubled from 1960 to 2000 from 606,400 to more than 1.2 million. As population densities rise, New Hampshire is being transformed from a largely rural state to a predominantly urban and suburban one*. By 2025 rural New Hampshire will be restricted to the North Country and isolated pockets in the west.

Another way to assess the pace of growth in New Hampshire is to look at how much forest and farmland are being converted to developed uses like buildings, roads, and parking lots. Land conversion rates closely mirror the pattern of population growth and housing construction. Moderate to high rates of land conversion are now found throughout the southeastern third—if not half—of New Hampshire. New Hampshire is losing its high quality farmland. Rockingham County alone lost one-third of its productive cropland from 1997-2002. Forest cover has steadily diminished since the early 1980s, totaling about 17,500 acres lost per year.

The map at right displays estimates of land conversion in New Hampshire towns. Land conversion is defined here as a change from underdeveloped land cover (forests or farms) to developed land cover dominated by buildings and roads.

* Rural: <36 persons per square mile,
  Exurban: 36 to 144 persons per square mile.
  Suburban: 144 to 1000 persons per square mile,
  Urban: >1000 persons per square mile.

Source: Society for the Protection of New Hampshire Forests, *New Hampshire's Changing Landscape*, 2005.

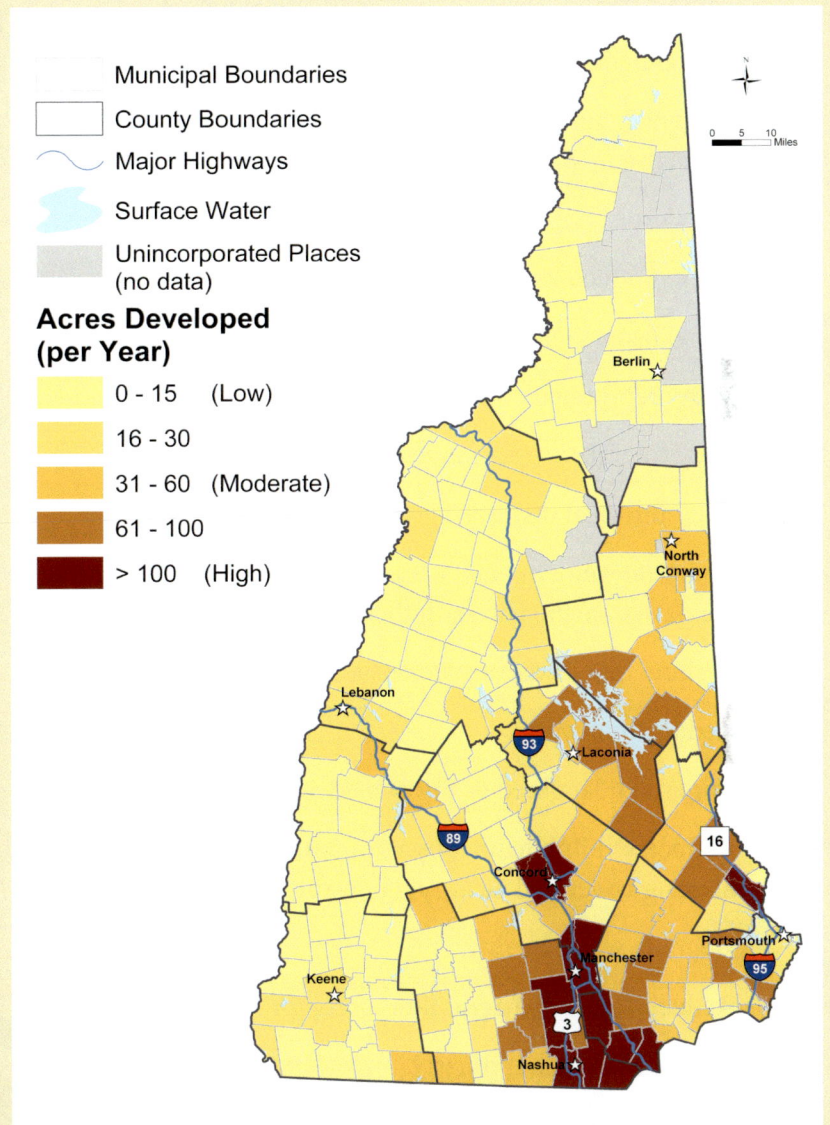

Acres Developed (per Year)
- 0 - 15 (Low)
- 16 - 30
- 31 - 60 (Moderate)
- 61 - 100
- > 100 (High)

Development often results in a one-size-fits-all approach to landscaping, in which the same few plants appear redundantly as sheared hedges, foundation shrubs, or linear arrangements along a walk or in a planting bed. In such landscapes, plants typically appear as static structures, rather than the growing, changing life forms they are. Such landscapes lack many key characteristics of natural communities, provide very limited habitat for wildlife, and have no connection to the surrounding natural or cultural environment.

These heavily sheared yews, commonly found in many commercial and municipal sites, no longer resemble their natural fountain-like growth pattern.

An overview of invasive species and their impacts

Another result of rapid population growth is the proliferation of non-native invasive species (these may be plants, or insects or other animals, but we limit our discussion here to invasive plants). Development results in considerable soil disturbance, paving the way for invasive plant species that readily colonize exposed soils.

Non-native invasive plants have become a serious problem, crowding out native species in natural and managed landscapes, not only in the Northeast but throughout the Americas and the world. Invasive species began arriving in North America with early European settlers. Many were brought here for ornamental uses, erosion control, or wildlife habitat. Others have hitchhiked in through international travel and commerce.

Invasive species typically possess certain traits that give them an advantage over most native species. Most invasive plants share these characteristics:

- They lack natural predators and diseases that keep their populations in check in their native habitat.
- They grow very rapidly.
- They produce large amounts of high-viability seeds.
- They disperse their seeds efficiently over long distances.
- Many reproduce both vegetatively and by seed.
- They tolerate a wide range of environmental conditions.
- They thrive in disturbed areas.
- They leaf out early and keep their leaves late, shading out the native species beneath them.

Studies show that invasive species can:

- Reduce biodiversity.
- Imperil endangered or threatened species.
- Reduce wildlife habitat by eliminating native foods, altering cover and destroying nesting sites.
- Degrade water quality.
- Reduce forest and agricultural crop production.
- Damage personal property.
- Reduce aesthetics.
- Cause health problems.

> **THE FUTURE OF BIODIVERSITY**
>
> New facts and figures presented in some recent books and articles debate the impact of invasive species on the environment. We maintain our emphasis on protecting biodiversity, which is the foundation of healthy functioning ecosystems. In inundated acreages, the benefits of invasive removals may be outweighed by the human energy and resources required. Conscious decision-making based upon wise resource use must be made. In manageable situations, early detection and prioritization are worth their weight in gold.
>
> *All plants are not created equal, particularly in their ability to support wildlife. Most of our native plant-eaters are not able to eat alien plants, and we are replacing native plants with alien species at an alarming rate, especially in the suburban gardens on which our wildlife increasingly depends. My central message is that unless we restore native plants to our suburban ecosystems, the future of biodiversity in the United States is dim.*
>
> Douglas Tallamy,
> *Bringing Nature Home*

Invasive plant species already cover more than 100 million acres of land in the United States and cost taxpayers billions of dollars each year in lost agricultural and forest crops, decreased biodiversity, impacts to natural resources and the environment, and the control efforts. For more information on invasive species see Appendix D.

IDENTIFYING THE BIG THREE INVASIVES

Left: Norway maple, *Acer platanoides*. *Middle:* Crimson King Norway maple, *Acer platanoides* 'Crimson King'. *Right:* Red maple/swamp maple, *Acer rubrum*, a native maple.

The leaves of the invasive Norway maple (now illegal to sell, purchase, and plant in New Hampshire and Massachusetts) are similar to those of the native sugar maple. One way to tell them apart is by picking a leaf off the tree and looking at the base of the stem or petiole. Norway maples have a milky white sap, while the sap of sugar maples is clear. Norway maple is also easy to recognize in the late autumn as the only maple that holds on to its fluorescent-yellow leaves through the end of October and even into November. This period of longer energy production gives it an advantage over native maples.

This Crimson King Norway maple is also listed as invasive, as it produces both green- and red-leafed seedlings which out-compete native plants. It is sometimes confused with "red maple" because of its leaf color. However, what most people commonly refer to as red maple or swamp maple, *Acer rubrum*, has a green leaf with three lobes and turns shades of red, orange and yellow in the fall. See Chapter 5 for non-invasive trees and plants that provide dark red foliage.

Left: Burning bush, *Euonymus alatus* in fall. *Middle:* Burning bush in summer. *Right:* Japanese barberry, *Berberis thunbergii*.

Although still one of the most common shrubs found in home, commercial and public landscapes, burning bush is illegal to sell, purchase, and plant in New Hampshire and Massachusetts. Chapter 5 of this manual offers many non-invasive alternatives that provide brilliant fall color.

Japanese barberry comes in many varieties, all of which are illegal to sell, purchase, and plant in New Hampshire and Massachusetts. The variety Crimson Pygmy Barberry was popular because of its size and leaf color. See Chapter 5 for several alternatives.

Fragmenting landscapes: the wildlife connection

Changes in land use have direct consequences for wildlife as well. For instance, in New Hampshire most land is currently held by private landowners. Most of the key wildlife species occur on these private lands, rather than on conservation land, which means that private landowners have a large impact on wildlife habitat throughout the region, depending on what they do with their land.

The landmass of the Northeast extends across two biomes: the eastern temperate forest and the northern forest. At one time, your site would have been forest that hosted waxwings and tanagers feeding on insects in summer and berries in winter. Owls would have nested in hollow trees, and salamanders hidden from predators in rotting logs. Deer would have drunk from pools of snowmelt, where wood frogs laid their eggs and announced the spring with their "quacking" calls.

Your site may have also seen dramatic changes over time. For example, in the past 150 years, New Hampshire has grown from 15 percent forest cover to approximately 84 percent forest cover, second only to Maine as the nation's most forested state.

All of these land uses and the changes they brought have had dramatic influences on the wildlife that use the land. Which wildlife occur on a given area of land depends on several factors, including the size of the property and adjoining lands, its location in the region, the site's characteristics and features, available habitat and its arrangement, and human activity on the site. With each change, we have seen a change in species mix and populations.

Most recently, development has fragmented much of northern New England land into small parcels bisected by roads. This fragmentation prevents wildlife from moving through an area to meet their survival needs. Roadways allow predators such as coyotes and foxes access to inhabitants of the deep woods, such as ovenbirds.

Development has also eliminated certain critical habitats such as vernal pools and other wetlands, essential breeding grounds for certain wildlife. As an area is transformed from rural forest to smaller, more fragmented suburban and urban landholdings, the mix of wildlife species that inhabit the area change. Some species adapt, while others are lost.

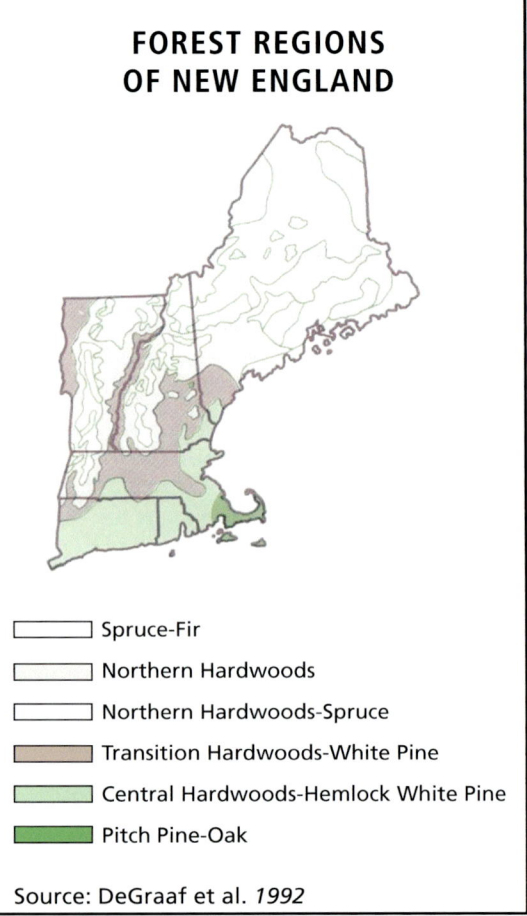

FOREST REGIONS OF NEW ENGLAND

- Spruce-Fir
- Northern Hardwoods
- Northern Hardwoods-Spruce
- Transition Hardwoods-White Pine
- Central Hardwoods-Hemlock White Pine
- Pitch Pine-Oak

Source: DeGraaf et al. *1992*

WHAT'S WILD?

The word "wildlife" often brings to mind large mammals such as the majestic moose or the elusive black bear, creatures we rarely see. In its broadest sense, wildlife means any non-human, non-domesticated animal. While wildlife can be as small as the smallest microscopic bacterium or as big as a blue whale, the term "wildlife" in its common usage includes birds, mammals, fish, reptiles, amphibians, and invertebrates (such as insects, spiders, and mollusks).

Natural Landscape in Transition: The Consequences of Rapid Growth

Facing the challenges to the Northeast's disappearing natural landscape

The loss of much open space and its native plant and animal communities due to rapid growth poses significant challenges, among them how to protect our region's life-sustaining natural resources and retain the unique aesthetic character around our homes, communities, schools, and businesses.

The Northeast's native ecosystems, with their unique geologic features, topography, soils, plants, and animals, offer lessons we can learn and apply to managed landscapes and gardens. Following nature's lead through the practices of integrated landscaping described in this book will help conserve the balance, beauty, and ecological services inherent in our region's native landscapes.

Integrated Landscaping is a holistic process that creates landscapes and gardens that are both individual in their composition and reflect the character of the native landscape. Landscapes diverse in plants and wildlife, both beautiful and highly functional, pique our curiosity about the world around us.

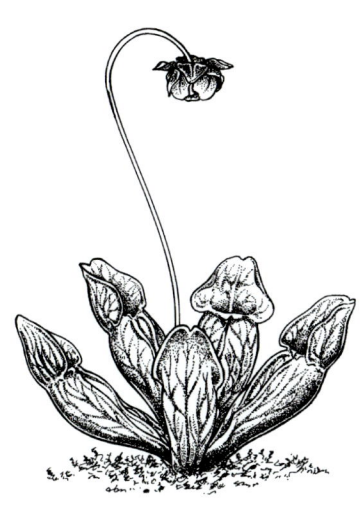

WE ALL NEED A PLACE TO CALL HOME

Wildlife, like humans, need food, water, cover, and space—what we know as home or habitat—to survive. Each wildlife species has unique habitat needs. Some are "generalists" that adapt to change and can live in human-built areas (e.g., skunk, gray squirrel, or coyote), while those we call "specialists" have more specific habitat needs and are more sensitive to disturbance (e.g., hermit thrush, spotted salamander, or bobcat). Specialists are most susceptible to the impacts of land use changes, and often are rare or endangered.

A TURNING POINT

We humans are at a turning point in our evolution. Though we began as a small population in a very large world, we have expanded in number and territory until we are now bursting the seams of that world. There are too many of us, and our habits are unsustainable. Having reached the limits of nature's tolerance, we are finally shopping for answers to the question: "How can we live on this home planet without destroying it?" Just as we are beginning to recognize all there is to learn from the natural world, our models are starting to blink out—not just a few scattered organisms, but entire ecosystems. A new survey by the National Biological Service found that one-half of all native ecosystems in the United States are degraded to the point of endangerment.

Janine Benyus
www.biomimicry.net

CHAPTER 2

The Integrated Landscape:
Philosophy, Benefits, and Principles that Guide Practice

Integrated landscaping: A holistic approach

Most landscape manuals address the functional, aesthetic, and budgetary goals of property owners by describing a linear sequence of processes: design, plant selection, installation, and ongoing maintenance. Integrated landscaping takes a nonlinear, holistic approach to these recognized practices, using natural ecosystems as models.

Integrated landscaping gives design, establishment, and care (long-term maintenance) equal consideration and importance throughout the process of creating a landscape. Each aspect is considered inseparable from the whole.

This holistic approach arises from the understanding that a decision made or an action taken at any point in the process of designing, establishing, and caring for a landscape carries its influence into every other point in the system. A constructive practice at one stage in the process will confer benefits throughout the landscape system. Conversely a poor choice (e.g., of plants), or an ignored step (in site preparation or planting), can add more work and cost to the long-term site maintenance, or even threaten the health of the landscape.

Integrated landscaping encourages us to think of and treat our landscapes and gardens as interacting systems, where a change in one part affects the other parts as well.

> **WHAT'S AN ECOSYSTEM?**
>
> An *ecosystem* is a group of organisms (the biota, or living aspects, including humans and other animals, plants, fungi, and microbes) interacting with each other and with the abiotic (non-living) aspects of the environment (such as water, soil, landforms, temperature, light, and wind). If you think of your landscape as a managed ecosystem, the abiotic parts can be thought of as site characteristics and conditions that influence the plants and animals that live there—but the plants and animals also affect such site conditions as soil chemistry, water quality, and even temperature. All components of ecosystems, both living and nonliving, affect each other and are in a constant state of change.

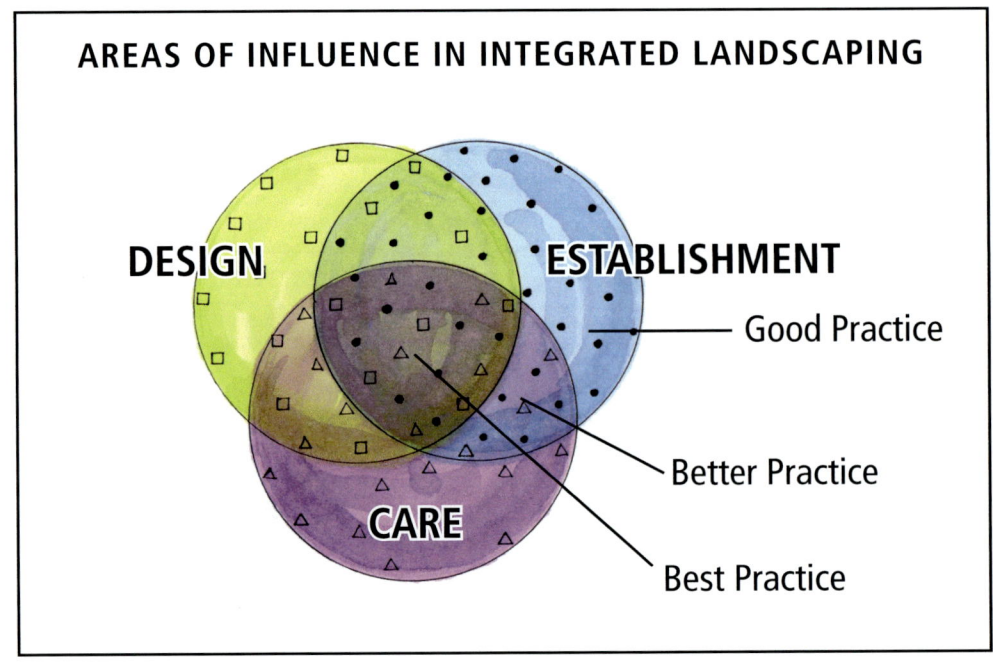

INTEGRATED LANDSCAPE PRACTICE

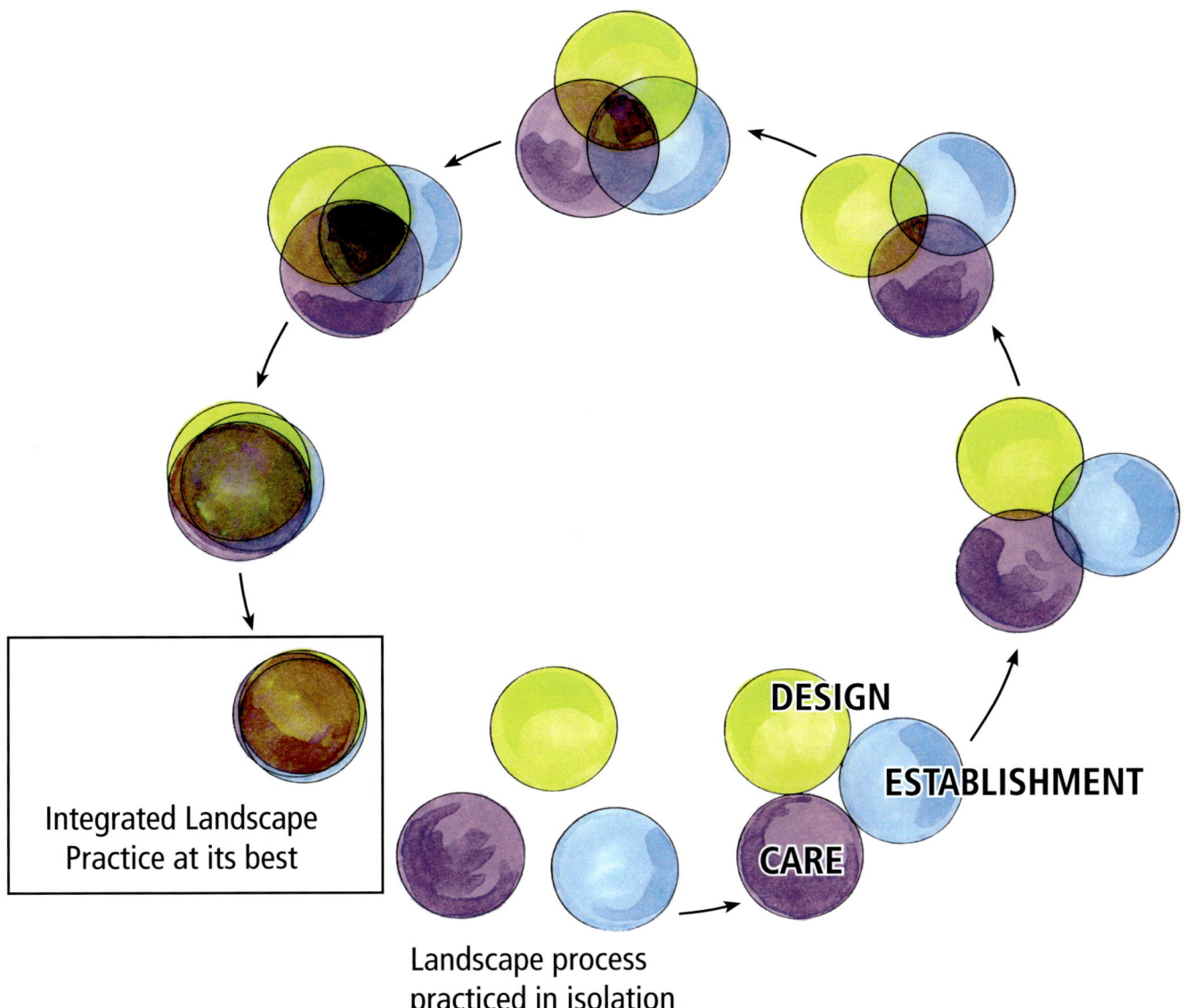

The three colors (green, blue, and lavender) standing on their own represent the processes of design, establishment, and care when practiced in isolation. This practice may be "good practice" but is often disconnected and problematic in the life of the landscape.

Where the circles overlap, the colors begin to blend and meld, representing how one process affects another. The central part of the circle, being an equal blend of all three processes, represents the most integrated landscape practice.

Ideas are filtered through the sieve of design, establishment, and care where no process is practiced in isolation. As the three spheres move in toward the center, the integrated "heart" of landscape practice becomes more predominant. The larger the center, the more relational and multidimensional the landscape processes become thus affecting all site values in a more holistic manner.

INTEGRATING LANDSCAPE DESIGN, ESTABLISHMENT, AND CARE

Street trees

The intent of a typical street-tree planting is to provide a shadier, cooler, more inviting, and aesthetically pleasing streetscape. Selecting appropriate species and planting arrangements (*design*), and providing street trees with enough soil volume when planted (*establishment*), will automatically lessen the need for future *care*, as the trees will remain healthier and less susceptible to disease and decline, thereby requiring less pruning. This increases the chance that the streetscape will thrive long into the future.

Median strips

A largely unused expanse of waist-high weeds between lanes of a major road is gracefully converted to a tough snow-and-salt-resistant perennial bed containing an array of seasonal flowers, ornamental grasses, and fruiting shrubs. This change increases winter interest and beauty, helps ensure that rain and snowmelt will filter down into the soil, and increases the soil's reserves of fertility, as spent flowers, twigs, and leaves decompose over time. The planting helps filter the surrounding air and increase species diversity. Community residents appreciate the aesthetic improvements in their neighborhood.

Steeply-sloped yard

A large tree stands alone on a steeply pitched lawn. Smothering a good-sized portion of turf beneath the tree and beyond the dripline creates a planting bed. In place of turf, the landscaper plants groundcovers tolerant of a dry root zone between the large-diameter tree roots, waters them, and spreads two inches of organic mulch over the new planting bed. This improves the landscape's aesthetics and protects the tree from mowers and weed-whackers. The lawn area is reduced and diversity added. By adding layers close to the ground, rainfall is slowed and captured. Such smart landscape choices may also increase property value.

Schoolyard

Meandering through a small woodland planting, carefully laid-out pathways encourage exploration in a well-designed schoolyard landscape. Perennials supply butterfly and hummingbird nectaries, a rotting log is left in place for salamanders, and a small circulating pond encourages frogs. A few boulders of varying shapes and sizes provide cover for snakes and toads, as well as interesting microclimates and places to sit and relax, or explore.

The pathways are mulched with four inches of wood chips provided by a local utility company for free. The children help maintain the pathway, adding woodchips where and when needed, using a small, lightweight wheelbarrow and bushel basket, which helps mitigate the compaction caused by so many little feet. The children use the pathways, allowing the remaining undisturbed soil to stay loose and friable. The healthy habitats thrive and the children and staff become an integral part of the ecosystem.

Commercial property

A design for a commercial property calls for a combination of meadows (the meadow seed is selected to match soil conditions), densely layered landscape plantings, and fields instead of lawns. The plan requires mowing the meadows every other year in the fall and the field every five years. By studding the densely layered landscape planting with native flowering trees, shrubs heavy with berries, and lush groundcovers, the designer eliminates the need for yearly applications of mulch and minimizes the costs of stormwater management, which can be largely handled through natural processes. The company enhances its reputation by its environmentally friendly landscape.

Protecting existing plants

Before site construction begins, arranging to protect existing native plants such as a hedgerow of gray dogwood, arrowwood viburnum, and highbush blueberry allows the proposed new design to feel and appear more mature. This decision retains wildlife habitat, prevents soil erosion, and aids water filtration. It greatly reduces the future needs for watering and fertilizing. The result is an aesthetic and integrated landscape that allows for wildlife viewing and observation.

Although planted in an urban Portsmouth setting, the largest catalpa tree in New Hampshire continues to add growth, as its root system has plenty of soil to expand.

This schoolyard landscape contains a variety of layers, which adds to human interest and provides habitat for wildlife, including songbirds and butterflies.

Integrated landscapes imitate natural ecosystems

Applied to managed landscapes in residential, commercial, and municipal settings, integrated landscaping practices strive to imitate an area's natural ecosystems, treating each site as a system of plant and animal communities, and considering their relationships to each other and their environment.

Following nature's lead, integrated landscaping creates welcoming habitats that support an astonishing variety of plants and animals. For example, landscapers can simulate a forest by retaining plant litter—dead and dying plant debris—which in turn helps build healthy soil. Including plant species that vary in form and habit creates structure—differences in heights and layers—that both humans and wildlife find attractive.

The holistic practices used in integrated landscaping include working with "plant systems" rather than individual specimens. A plant system unites diverse plants (some combination of groundcovers, grasses, perennials, vines, shrubs, and understory and overstory trees) and animals with nonliving components of the environment to interact and function as a whole. These plant systems imitate natural ecosystems by combining a group of plant species well-adapted to similar conditions.

Because they mimic combinations found in nature, the plant systems of integrated landscapes can:

- Offer year-round habitat and food for wildlife: seasonal components such as spring nectar, persistent fruits for fall and winter food, foliage for cover, and conifers for winter.

- Provide a variety of aesthetic landscape qualities, including sequential bloom, and year-round interest in habit, fruit, bark, and flower.

- Maintain a site's historical character.

- Resist pollution, drought, and other environmental stress.

- Minimize maintenance.

When creating plants systems, strive to imitate natural ecosystems.

Most of the Northeast's natural plant communities transition to forest land over time. Within a few years, an abandoned farm field will fill in with woody stemmed shrubs that then provide enough shade, allowing tree seedlings to sprout. Plant communities are always in transition and generally include plants of many differing ages arranged in both vertical and horizontal layers, incorporating some combination of trees, shrubs, an herbaceous layer of wildflowers, ferns, grasses and mosses, and a groundcover layer.

> **NATURE AS TEACHER**
>
> Thriving ecosystems, from large parcels left alone for a few generations to the smaller, recently disturbed fragments that abound along roadsides and unattended hedgerows, in ditch lines, and between developed tracts of land, can become areas where diversity flourishes and plant communities build over time. By implementing practices that apply plant-system principles (see page 16), a landscaper begins working in tandem with nature, intentionally incorporating naturally occurring processes into residential and commercial landscapes. Although plant systems mimic the inherent structure and function of natural ecosystems, nature does it better. Nature remains the teacher and inspiration.

Over time, such systems help establish soil layers (horizons). Creating plant systems by layering plants both vertically and horizontally and, whenever possible, incorporating plants of varying age, promotes biodiversity.

In general, the greater the number of layers and ages in a plant system, the more diverse the plant life. More diverse plant communities create a more diverse habitat available to support a more diverse array of wildlife (which we expand to include a multitude of insects and the microscopic organisms that live and interact within the soil).

Above: Plant systems include both vertical and horizontal layering.
Left: Densely layered plantings slow the force of rainfall, breaking droplets into smaller and smaller units until they soak into the ground. This reduces soil erosion and the movement of soil sediments.

To read more about this potential, refer to Eric Grissell's book, *Insects and Gardens: In Pursuit of a Garden Ecology*. For a fascinating glimpse into the world belowground, you can also read Yvonne Baskin, *Under Ground: How Creatures of Mud and Dirt Shape Our World*. Also check out the *Soil Foodweb, Inc.* and the work of Dr. Elaine Ingham at: www.soilfoodweb.com.

Plant systems provide habitat for a wide array of wildlife, including small animals such as this salamander.

Benefits of integrated landscaping

Integrated landscapes are sustainable.

Natural landscapes renew and sustain themselves. Throughout this manual we use the word *sustainable* to mean a system that largely perpetuates itself with few or no external inputs because it mimics natural principles. Whether applied in residential, commercial, or municipal settings, integrated landscaping involves practices aimed at creating sustainable landscapes. The benefits listed below all flow from or contribute to this essential sustainability.

Integrated landscaping is good for the earth.

Following nature's lead through integrated landscaping supports a wide variety of naturally occurring ecological services, including:

- Filtering pollutants from air and water.
- Preventing soil erosion.
- Creating microclimates that buffer temperature extremes, block or redirect cold winds, and extend the growing season.

Left: Trees and plants filter both air and water, helping remove many human-made pollutants.
Below, left: Correct placement of trees provides shade to buildings and can reduce energy needs.
Below, right: Trees and plants reduce carbon dioxide, absorbing it through their leaves.

- Moderating climate through shade and sunlight (cool in summer, warm in winter).

- Removing carbon dioxide (a greenhouse gas) from the atmosphere.

- Storing carbon (preventing its release into the atmosphere).

- Building healthy soil that supports healthy plants.

- Filtering pollutants.

- Decomposing organic wastes.

- Soaking up rain and snowmelt water to reduce the runoff that causes flooding and/or surface-water pollution.

- Buffering noise and providing visual screening.

- Supporting pollination and seed dispersal.

- Supplying food and fiber for humans and wildlife.

- Minimizing excessive damage from plant insects and diseases.

WHAT IS AN ECOLOGICAL SERVICE?

"Ecological services" is a human term denoting our recognition of how Earth systems work. Ecological services are the conditions and processes of natural ecosystems that sustain and fulfill human life. The services are generated by a complex of natural cycles all driven by solar energy.

Gretchen C. Daily, *Nature's Services, Societal Dependence on Natural Ecosystems*

Integrated landscaping supports biodiversity.

All living things, from soil microorganisms to insects, plants, fungi, amphibians, birds, and mammals, function together in a complex system of food webs and energy cycles. The greater the diversity within these systems, the greater the stability of the whole system.

Integrated landscaping promotes the greatest possible diversity of habitats, plants, and animals appropriate to a site's soils, moisture levels, exposure to sun, and slope. Besides providing stability and maximizing ecosystem functions, such diversity enhances a site's aesthetics and fosters a wide variety of human experiences within that environment.

A diversity of plants supports a diversity of wildlife.

The Integrated Landscape: Philosophy, Benefits, and Principles that Guide Practice

Integrated landscaping reduces the need for fossil fuel inputs such as fertilizers, pesticides, and gasoline-powered maintenance equipment.

Every year, people in the U.S. apply about 70 million pounds of mostly fossil-fuel-based fertilizers and pesticides to their lawns alone. Lawn mowers and other gasoline-powered yard-maintenance equipment produce several types of pollutants, including greenhouse gases and substances that harm human or environmental health.

Mimicking nature's principles and processes, integrated landscaping works to create a closed-loop system, where the landscape provides its own long-term fertility, moisture, and checks and balances to stress, and recycles its own wastes.

Integrated landscaping is good for human well-being.

Research by Drs. Frances Kuo and William Sullivan at the Human-Environment Research Laboratory, University of Illinois at Champaign-Urbana, shows that healthy landscapes help improve human health by lowering blood pressure, reducing stress, and speeding up the healing process.

Kuo and Sullivan's research also documents other benefits of greening your site:

- Green views and access to green spaces in urban areas reduce chronic mental fatigue, restore attention, and relieve the everyday pressures of living in poverty.
- Trees are valuable urban assets that can give people hope.
- The greener a building's surroundings in urban areas, the fewer reported crimes. Trees cultivate healthier, safer urban communities.

Kuo's and Sullivan's research confirms our intuitive understanding that New Hampshire's natural landscapes attract people to live, work, and play.

Richard Louv's groundbreaking book, *Last Child in the Woods: Saving Our Children from Nature Deficit Disorder*, is built on the research of Kuo and others. In it, Louv outlines the environmental, social, psychological, and spiritual benefits of children spending time in nature. He describes the growing body of research that reveals the necessity of contact with nature for healthy child development and for healthy adults, neighborhoods, and whole communities.

Above: *A fire destroyed a house on Auburn Street in Manchester, NH. The lot stood vacant for many years. The community worked together to transform the vacant lot into a neighborhood pocket park.*

Integrated landscaping is good for the local economy.

Landscaping with native stone, wood, and plant materials pumps money into local wholesale, retail, and service enterprises. This translates into economically vibrant communities and diverse "working landscapes," land-based enterprises such as forestry and ornamental horticulture that make open space profitable and less likely to fall prey to residential and commercial development. In turn, open fields and forests boost tourism, an important sector of the Northeast's economy.

By encouraging local plant growers to grow and sell a wider variety of native plants, integrated landscaping also helps diversify the look, feel, and functional utility of commercial landscapes.

Integrated landscaping is good for your pocketbook.

Integrated landscaping saves money and resources, in part because it minimizes "life-cycle" costs (extraction, production, transportation, maintenance, and disposal) of a landscape's components and reduces long-term landscape maintenance costs.

It can also reduce the costs of heating and cooling buildings, removing snow, screening unattractive views, and muffling noise. Property values also increase as both residential and commercial building areas are landscaped with sustainable planting systems.

Well-landscaped properties help attract more business.

Integrated landscaping connects people to where they live.

We shape the land and are shaped by it. People who take careful inventory, then work closely with the existing natural features of their site and the natural landscapes around them, feel connected to the place they live in. They develop a deep sense of appreciation for its natural character and history, as well as a desire to care for and protect it.

Integrated landscaping specifies using materials derived from on site or as local as possible. These materials not only save money, support the local economy, and reduce fossil fuel use, but connect our home grounds and public spaces physically and aesthetically to the wider natural/historical landscapes around us.

In New Hampshire's Manchester Millyard, the statue of the mill girl reminds us of the past and connects us to the present.

Integrated landscaping celebrates the practical and rewarding art of gardening.

- Making plant selection easier and more creative.
- Appealing to the senses.
- Building soil health, the foundation of a healthy landscape.
- Turning yard wastes into yard resources.
- Reducing maintenance over time.

Ten natural principles to guide your landscaping practices

Integrated landscaping relies on research in horticulture and other sciences, as well as on the everyday experience of landscape practitioners. It uses local ecosystems as models, studying the fundamental processes of nature and applying them to the landscapes we create around our homes, workplaces, and public spaces.

The following principles inherent in natural systems serve as both a framework and a justification for mimicking nature in our landscaping practices. We gleaned them from the works of great ecological thinkers such as Sir Albert Howard, Aldo Leopold and Janine Benyus, among others, as well as from the practical experience of local landscapers.

Because these principles serve as the foundation for all the actions that follow, we will refer back to them throughout the rest of this manual. Use them yourself, even if you plan only modest changes to your own landscape.

1. Diverse forms of life live and work together interdependently.

In natural systems plants are always found living together with animals. Plants growing in conditions that suit them well respond by producing abundant flowers, fruit, and dense vegetative growth. Pollen and nectar-feeders, birds, and other animals, driven by a desire to eat, or looking for nesting and shelter, are attracted to such resources, finding their niches within the multiple layers of vegetation and soils provided by the natural ecosystem. In turn, flowers get pollinated, seeds dispersed, and genes passed on. Feathers, hair, shed skins, and scat fall to the ground and decompose as animals move about, contributing to soil fertility.

2. Soils are covered and protected from the impacts of excessive wind, sun, and rain.

In natural systems, soils are typically covered and protected, with layers of vegetation serving as the first line of defense, beginning with the tallest canopy of overstory trees, followed by shrubs, herbs, and groundcovers. Canopy layers influence the amount of hot, drying sun reaching the ground. They also break falling rain into smaller and smaller droplets. Plant litter—leaves, twigs, fruit husks, and nut hulls—derived from the vegetative layers above, slowly decomposes on the landscape floor. Humus, the final stage of organic decay, remains in the soil layer, where it serves as a reservoir of plant nutrients and a source of energy for soil-dwelling organisms, helps create desirable soil structure, holds water, provides sites for essential biochemical exchanges, and reduces soil pathogens, among other important functions. Drying winds and air currents are slowed and sometimes humidified as they pass through layers of vegetation and litter. The canopy, litter layer, and humus all protect the underlying soil from wind, sun, and hard rain.

BIOMIMICRY

The core idea is that nature, imaginative by necessity, has already solved many of the problems we are grappling with. Animals, plants, and microbes are the consummate engineers. They have found what works, what is appropriate, and most important, what lasts here on Earth. This is real news of biomimicry: After 3.8 million years of research and development, failures are fossils, and what surrounds us is the secret to survival. The conscious emulation of life's genius is a survival strategy for the human race, a path to a sustainable future. The more our world looks and functions like the natural world, the more likely we are to endure on this home that is ours, but not ours alone.

Janine Benyus, www.biomimicry.net

LAND ETHIC

The land ethic simply enlarges the boundaries of the community to include soils, waters, plants, animals, or collectively: the land. This sounds simple: do we not already sing our love for and obligation to the land of the free and the home of the brave? Yes, but just what and whom do we love? Certainly not the soil, which we are sending helter-skelter downriver. Certainly not the waters, which we assume have no function except to turn turbines, float bridges, and carry off sewage. Certainly not the plants of which we exterminate whole communities without batting an eye. Certainly not the animals, of which we have already extirpated many of the largest and most beautiful species. A land ethic of course cannot prevent the alteration, management, and use of these 'resources' but it does affirm their right to continued existence, and at least in spots their continued existence in a natural state.

Aldo Leopold, *A Sand County Almanac and Sketches Here and There*

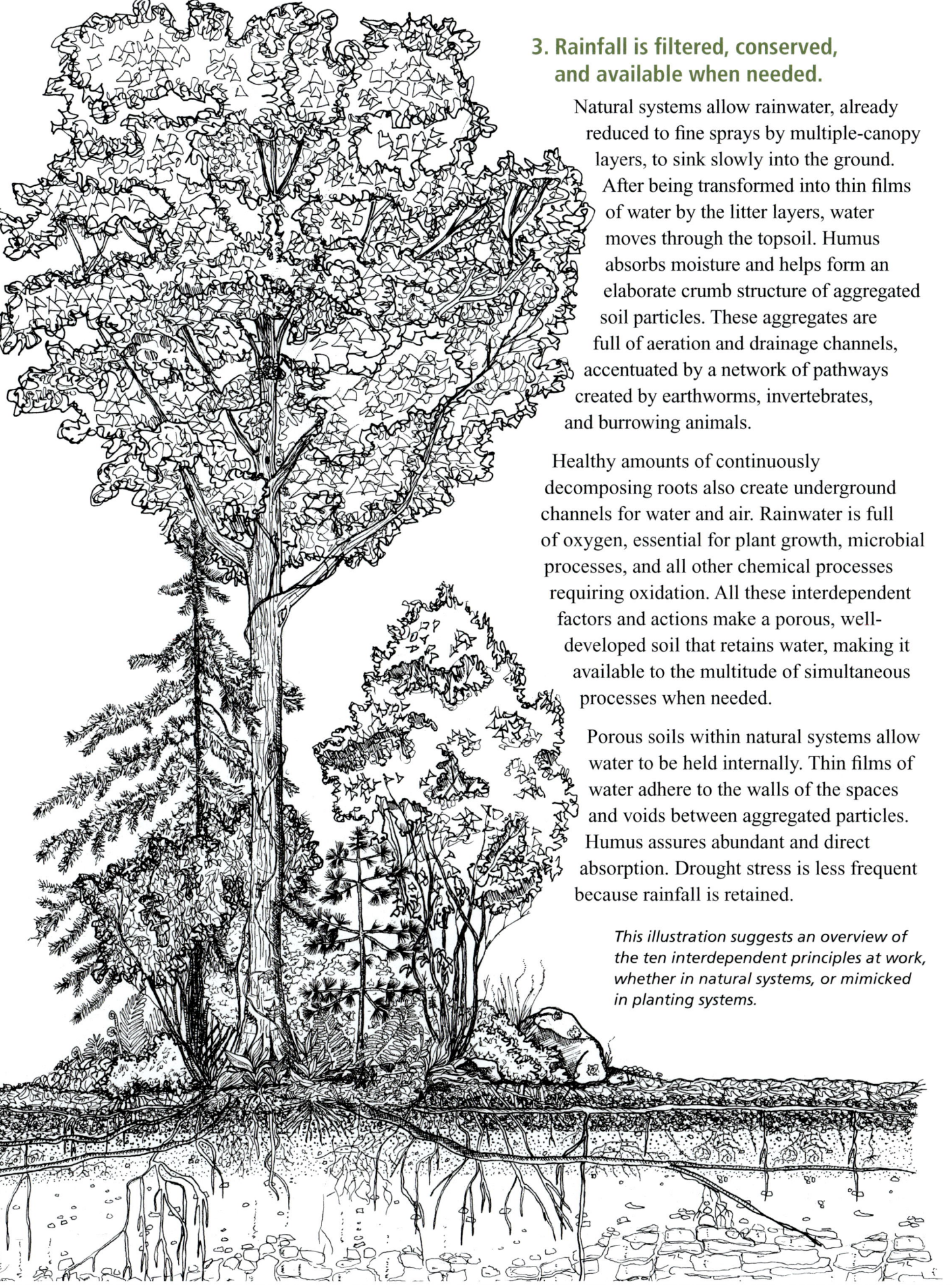

3. Rainfall is filtered, conserved, and available when needed.

Natural systems allow rainwater, already reduced to fine sprays by multiple-canopy layers, to sink slowly into the ground. After being transformed into thin films of water by the litter layers, water moves through the topsoil. Humus absorbs moisture and helps form an elaborate crumb structure of aggregated soil particles. These aggregates are full of aeration and drainage channels, accentuated by a network of pathways created by earthworms, invertebrates, and burrowing animals.

Healthy amounts of continuously decomposing roots also create underground channels for water and air. Rainwater is full of oxygen, essential for plant growth, microbial processes, and all other chemical processes requiring oxidation. All these interdependent factors and actions make a porous, well-developed soil that retains water, making it available to the multitude of simultaneous processes when needed.

Porous soils within natural systems allow water to be held internally. Thin films of water adhere to the walls of the spaces and voids between aggregated particles. Humus assures abundant and direct absorption. Drought stress is less frequent because rainfall is retained.

This illustration suggests an overview of the ten interdependent principles at work, whether in natural systems, or mimicked in planting systems.

The Integrated Landscape: Philosophy, Benefits, and Principles that Guide Practice

> **THE IMPORTANCE OF DECAY**
>
> Too much attention is focused on the exciting phenomena of growth and reproduction, too little on the processes of decay and dissolution. The odd thing is that properly examined these latter processes are as intense, as intricate, as exciting as any that precede them; that they are themselves living processes, life; there is not, in fact, any difference in principle between them and the birth and growth of the higher organisms. It is simply that one set of phenomena easily strikes our imagination and is commonly visually perceptible, the other is hidden and not generally perceptible to the eye, might, ignorantly, be termed secret.
>
> They are the other half of the Wheel; the half that revolves away from us, whirls round out of our sight, and emerges again at our feet to begin the upward sweep. The image of the Wheel is really very good and may well be kept in mind. A Wheel, moreover, can run true or can be thrown out of balance; on this also we may reflect.
>
> Louise E. Howard,
> *The Earth's Green Carpet*

4. Soil organisms are fed by the cycling and recycling of nutrients.

In natural systems, a great variety of decomposing organisms consume organic matter as a food source, leaving behind humus, the stable remnant (due to its chemical composition and chemical bonds) of decaying organic material. Sources of organic material come from plant litter: fallen leaves, twigs, spent flowers, and fruit. Another way of understanding this may be simply to say that what comes out of the earth—leaves, stems, flowers, fruits, bark, all made with solar energy captured from sunlight through photosynthesis—returns to the earth to nourish another generation of plants.

Organic matter improves the soil by allowing microorganisms to multiply. Larger organisms enter the picture. They all eat, grow, reproduce, and die, cycling and recycling nutrients into the developing food web. Natural ecosystems produce no waste; all waste products and dead bodies provide nourishment for other forms of life. Through these and other complex processes, organic matter is converted to simple inorganic forms that can be taken up by plants.

5. Humus holds fertility reserves within the upper layers of soil.

In the Northeast, plant litter doesn't accumulate but decomposes quickly with the help of decomposers such as earthworms and microorganisms. The volume of soil organic matter is maintained at the highest practical level, typically about five percent of the overall soil composition, by leaving seasonal litter on, applying mulches, and inviting in a diversity of life. The more organic matter left by humans to enter back into the system, the healthier and more diverse the soil life and structure becomes over time. The end product of organic-matter decay—humus—acts as reservoir of plant nutrients, held in the soil until needed.

6. Diversity builds over time, keeping plant insect damage and diseases in check.

Natural systems sustain themselves as organisms live, grow, die, and decay together. Plant diseases that attack the plants in that system may appear, and sometimes cause a species to weaken and die. When this happens in a diverse community, other species readily compete for the resources made available.

Healthy natural systems invite enough diversity to help ensure that wildlife populations stay in balance. (The arrival of an invasive species is one exception. Even healthy systems often can't accommodate invasives without being overtaken and out-competed.)

7. Plants supply fresh air, above and below the ground, as well as cool shade.

Both fresh air and cool, moist soil promote growth of root systems and populations of microorganisms. Healthy root systems take in nutrients that enhance plant growth, increasing the amount of biomass (leaves, stems, fruit, etc.) above and below ground. Increased biomass manufactures more food, giving plants energy to increase their overall size. This cyclical action supplies fresh air and shade, which in turn promotes continuous functioning of the natural processes described above.

The growth and decay of plant roots creates passageways through the soil, improving both air and water drainage. Nutrients, carried by rainfall and pulled by gravity, travel through this intricate network. In a loose, permeable soil, gas exchange occurs readily, while nutrients travel deeper into the soil, building soil fertility reserves.

In natural systems, dense layers of vegetation, from the canopy to the litter layers covering soils, provide fresh air and shade to the landscape. Water that infiltrates the soil is absorbed by roots and released through the leaves as water vapor (transpiration). Additional cooling occurs when water evaporates from soil, litter, and leaf surfaces.

8. The subsoil provides inorganic compounds required for living and nonliving processes.

In undisturbed natural systems, subsoil (C horizon) lies below the upper layers of soil (O, A, and B horizons). Formed by the weathering of parent material, the subsoil provides inorganic compounds (mineral matter) to the soils and plants above.

Systems with diverse plants and animals contribute to the upward movement of the subsoil's minerals. For example, the large mound of soil at the entrance of a woodchuck burrow and the much smaller mounds of ant hills are both examples of subsoil being brought to the surface where over time it will be incorporated into the litter layer and become part of the nutrient cycle.

9. Natural systems are dynamic and will change over time.

Natural systems undergo succession, the progressive change from one dominant plant community to another. For example, naturally disturbed soil gets colonized by lichens, followed by grasses. An old field becomes a forest. Both plants and animals co-evolve as a system, and both modify and are modified by their environment.

Plants and animals change over time in natural systems. For example, as the canopy of a young tree expands, the branch density provides safety for a nesting bird. Shade-tolerant plants such as ferns may flourish beneath and as the tree begins to flower pollinating insects arrive, fruit forms, and the fruit matures to feed wildlife. Sun-loving plants find their way to the outside edge of the canopy's spread, where they find plenty of light. All the while, soils keep developing and improving.

10. Humans experience sensory, intellectual, emotional, and spiritual stimulation, opportunities for learning, and insights into the wonder of complex natural processes.

Natural systems engage all our human senses:

- We hear the crunch of acorns and leaves rustling beneath our feet, water dripping, insects chirping, birds singing, and winds whistling through grasses.
- We feel the textures of bark and leaves, softness of a flower petal, coolness of shade or a warm pocket of sunshine, and soil in our hands.
- We see colors, patterns of light and shadow, shapes, depth, density, movement, and a myriad of plants and animals.
- We taste edible fruits, stalks, leaves, and flowers, the sour tang of a sorrel leaf.
- We smell the fragrance of mayflower and summersweet, of wet earth, of ripening fruit.

Nature stimulates our intuition by providing places to reflect, relax, imagine, inspire, hope, create, be still, be part of the great unknown, and fathom the mysteries of life.

Natural systems also provide innumerable learning opportunities by serving as outdoor classrooms.

In all these ways, we reconnect with nature and recognize our place within it. Our natural landscapes remind us that we humans depend on the natural world for our own health and wellbeing. (Appendix F includes a comprehensive list of landscape practices aligned with the natural principles.)

The Integrated Landscape: Philosophy, Benefits, and Principles that Guide Practice

CHAPTER 3

Outside and Onsite: Taking Stock of What You Have

Whether creating a brand-new landscape or making changes to an existing landscape, you'll first need to take stock of what is already there. Taking stock involves making detailed observations of the site and beyond (as far as the eye can see), its "landscape character," and your desired human uses and needs. Spend time taking inventory. This part of the process is the key that will help you understand the land, plants, and animal communities that inhabit or potentially inhabit the property and the surrounding area and help you make the best decisions for a sustainable landscape.

Scope of the inventory

The scope of the inventory may include the entire property or be limited by a specific planting site you have in mind. Either way, observation and study of the surrounding area will inform your analysis of specific planting sites. Look at maps, species lists, soils and zone information for your local area, and observe the plant communities, topography, and wildlife activity and human disturbance. Even though you may be working in a limited planting area, you need to consider the inventory in the context of the larger, surrounding area and human disturbance in an area can be the most important factor.

Learn about your soil

Soil is the foundation of plant communities and the wildlife a site will support. The more knowledge you have about the soils on your property, the better understanding you can have about the plants that will grow best within it and their needs over time. This section will help you understand:

- How soil is formed and its content.
- The soil on your property through exploring the soil profile and soil testing.
- The choices involved in choosing plants for your specific soil conditions.
- How to build soil over time.

How soil is formed

Several factors influence soil formation: climate, living organisms, topography, parent material, and time.

Living organisms
Soil life such as earthworms and burrowing animals aerate soil by tunneling, creating organic matter as food passes through their bodies. But their numbers are few when compared to the number of microorganisms in soil. In one teaspoon of soil there can be more microorganisms than human beings on earth!

Climate
Soils in warmer regions form more quickly than those in cooler places because higher temperatures accelerate the chemical and physical actions

When expanding freezing water finally crumbled the massive rock formation known as The Old Man of the Mountain, the monolith was reduced to all shapes and sizes of rubble, the parent material for future soil.

that break down rocks. Rainfall also weathers rocks; therefore soils form faster in regions with substantial rainfall. Ice, snow, and cold temperatures are also contributing factors (as the loss of New Hampshire's symbol, the Old Man of the Mountain, demonstrated).

Topography

A soil's composition is influenced by its location relative to the shape and slope of land around it. Soil located at the bottom of a slope tends to have finer particles, and be more nutrient rich and deeper than soil at the top of a slope where erosion has occurred.

The composition of bedrock also known as parent material influences the composition of the soil above it.

Parent material

The chemical and physical decomposition of parent bedrock forms the soil substrate. In New Hampshire schist and granite are common types of bedrock. This substrate then provides mineral matter to the layers of soil that plants grow in. Nutrient cycling occurs as plants grow, photosynthesize, and decompose through time.

Time

The time it takes for a soil to form depends on the four previous factors and their interactions with one another. It takes hundreds of years to form just one inch of soil. Unfortunately, just one misstep, such as leaving bare soil uncovered and exposed to rain, wind, and drying sun, can cause soil loss.

Soil: More than the sum of its parts

Soil is composed of minerals, organic matter, water, and air. The extent and types of these components influence the plant and animal communities that live within it.

Minerals derived from weathering of parent material make up the greatest percentage of any soil, 45 percent to 49 percent by volume. Sand is the largest of a soil's mineral particles, silt is medium-sized, and clay is the smallest. These **soil separates** are formed from minerals in weathered parent material. The mix of soil separates determines the texture of a soil.

Sandy soils don't hold much water because the large size of the particles allows water to move through without difficulty. The smaller particle sizes of clay and silt fit together so tightly that water can't flow through easily. Clayey, silty soils retain ample amounts of water; in some instances they become nearly impervious to water infiltration.

Sandy loam is made of about equal parts sand, silt, and clay, a mixture of particle sizes. Since sandy loam is made up of both small and medium sized particles, it holds on to enough water for plants to take up but it still drains well, allowing many different species of plant to exist within it.

Soil texture can vary a great deal from one location to the next. Soils high in sand or high in clay support a variety of plant life but it's important to know which plants can exist in a very well drained soil (sandy) or one that is highly saturated (clay).

Organic matter is living, dead, and decaying plant and animal material. It makes up a small percentage of any soil—typically 1-5 percent (depending on whether you're looking at a beach dune, turf, meadow, or forest)—but it contributes some of the most important qualities to a healthy soil and plant system. Animal manures and compost are good sources of organic matter used in landscapes and on crop land. Cover crops such as rye, buckwheat, and oats will increase organic matter when the residue is incorporated into the soil. Gradually decomposing organic mulches such as straw, leaves, or shredded bark add organic matter, while shading and protecting the soil surface from erosion. Adding organic matter to soil improves its water-holding capacity, promotes a diverse population of soil organisms and provides a source of plant nutrients. Soils rich in organic matter can absorb and hold more water, reducing the amount of runoff and leaching.

Soil water, about 25 percent of an average soil's volume, is a solution of water, microorganisms, and dissolved nutrients from minerals and decayed organic matter. Plant roots absorb water and nutrients from the soil solution.

Soil air, occupying another 25 percent of soil's volume, provides the gas exchange for organisms that live in the soil. Plant roots, microbes, and other soil organisms all use oxygen and release carbon dioxide during the essential process of respiration, just as we do when we breathe.

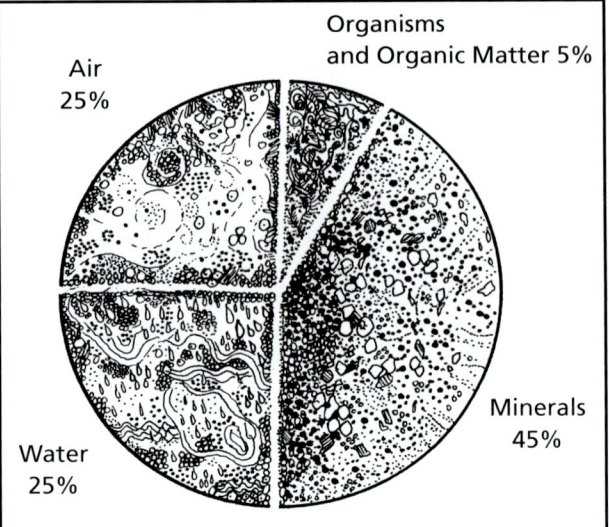

About one-half the volume of a good soil is solid particles (mineral and organic matter) and the other half equal portions of water and air space.

Gather regional soil information

To learn more about the soils in your area, start with the Web Soil Survey. Soil surveys are available through the Natural Resource Conservation Service at http://websoilsurvey.nrcs.usda.gov.

A soil survey will give the region's soil types and characteristics, which presents an overview of the soils found in your area. However, because soil surveys are regional in scale, they don't give exact information for individual properties. Soils naturally vary, even on a small property. On previously developed properties, site work (construction) often includes removal of topsoil from the property, followed later by the addition of off-site fill, changing the soil's characteristics.

Investigate the soil profile

To learn more about your soil, you will have to do a little investigating with a sharp spade or soil auger. As you dig down into undisturbed soil, you'll notice it is composed of different layers or horizons that vary in color, texture, and structure. These different horizons make up what is called the **soil profile**.

In developed areas where soil has been disturbed, the soil may seem more uniform and may have less organic matter. Quality soil is made up of layers, starting with a litter layer on the surface where plants drop leaves and twigs and animals and insects leave behind parts such as feathers, casings, hair, cast-off skins, and droppings, collectively forming a natural mulch. Below the litter layer is the "O" horizon where this natural organic mulch appears in various stages of decomposition.

Below the "O" horizon is the topsoil or "A" horizon, which tends to have higher levels of organic matter and is darker in color than the layer below. The topsoil varies in depth. Generally, the deeper the topsoil, he higher the soil fertility and overall quality.

Below the topsoil lies the subsoil, made up of more layers, including a "B" horizon and a "C" horizon. The subsoil is composed of sand, silt, clay, and gravel in varying proportions and little organic matter. The subsoil helps anchor plant roots and holds water. Below the subsoil lies the parent material, or bedrock, which continuously breaks down into smaller and smaller mineral particles, influencing all the layers above, including plant life.

Protect undisturbed soils

The most valuable soils on your site will most likely be those that are undisturbed by human impacts. They contain soil life and intact soil horizons. Before any construction begins on a site it is critical to protect the site's existing soil.

Disturbed soils are those that may have been removed or replaced during development and construction, often lack natural horizons, and may be poor for plants. These types of soils may contain large amounts of debris from building materials, sidewalks, and roads, any of which may have changed the soil's chemical, physical, and biological characteristics. In many sites where construction has taken place you'll find a thin dressing of topsoil added on top of the disturbed soil.

Disturbed soils are the most damaged and need more attention than soils that have remained relatively undisturbed. For example, disturbed soils can have a high pH near foundations and where construction debris is buried. Heavy construction equipment may have compacted the soil of disturbed sites. Compacted soils lack adequate pore spaces that allow air and water to move between soil particles. Compacted soils can be as impermeable as cement, making it very difficult for plant roots to get the air and water they need. The low fertility of these sites also makes it difficult for plants to grow because microorganisms cannot proliferate.

If the soils on your site are damaged, an integrated landscaping approach will help build your soil fertility and improve soil conditions over time. Your choice of plants that can tolerate such high-stress conditions may be limited at first, but as soil conditions improve over time, you can introduce more plant species.

Litter layer

'O' Horizon, surface layer of organic matter.

'A' Horizon, top layer of soil with darkest color and high organic matter content.

'B' Horizon, next layer of soil with intermediate color.

'C' Horizon, underlying parent material with light color.

A soil profile shows differences in color due to organic matter content and mineral make-up. Most root growth is in the top foot of soil.

Soils like these are common in urban environments and limit plant selection options.

How to test your soil

While investigating your soils, take some time to collect samples for soil testing. Soil fertility can be measured by testing for plant nutrients, soil pH, and organic matter. Observation and soil testing may save a great deal of money by helping you choose plants that fit the specific conditions of your site. Testing can also provide specific recommendations to improve soils, enabling you to invest in the long-term health of your plants.

University and commercial soil-testing laboratories produce more accurate results and provide localized recommendations, and are generally more useful than the do-it-yourself kits available in retail stores.

For a modest price, home gardeners and commercial landscapers can receive a detailed soil analysis through UNH Cooperative Extension. The test results will generate specific recommendations for soil improvements that will save you money, help you grow healthy plants, and improve your soil environment. Download soil test forms at www.extension.unh.edu/Agric/AGPDTS/SoilTest.htm or see Appendix D for more on soil testing.

Make sure to take separate soil samples from the highest and lowest points of the property, as well as from any unusual settings such as boggy areas or soils trucked in from offsite. Record where you take each soil sample, as you will include this information later on a base plan for your design.

DO A "PERC TEST" TO CHECK YOUR SOIL'S DRAINAGE CAPACITY

Choose plants that work for your soil conditions. These wetland plants don't mind having "wet feet."

Swamp Azalea
Azalea viscosum

Winterberry Holly
Ilex verticillata

A percolation test is one way to determine the soil's drainage ability and understand the type of plants that would best grow in existing soil conditions. This is best done after a soaking rain that leaves the soils uniformly moist. If conditions are dry, you'll have to soak the area thoroughly before you start; otherwise, dry soil will quickly take up any moisture and give false results.

In moist soil, dig a hole about 1½ feet deep and 1 foot wide. If the hole is dry, fill the hole with water several times until the surrounding soil is nearly saturated. Once the soil is thoroughly moist, pour enough water to fill the hole and quickly measure and record the depth. After 15 minutes measure the depth again to see how much water has drained. Subtract the second measurement from the first and then multiply that number by 4 to give you the inches of water drained per hour.

Source: Peter Trowbridge and Nina Bassuk, *Trees in the Urban Landscape: Site Assessment, Design, and Installation*

A few guidelines for your perc test:

- *Less than 4 inches per hour*: Poor drainage (soil may have high concentrations of clay particles or be extremely compacted). Choose plants that tolerate wet soil conditions or "wet feet" (plants with root systems that can be exposed to saturated soils).

- *4-8 inches per hour*: Moderate drainage (likely a mixture of sand, loam, and clay). Choose from the large selection of plants that grow well in soil conditions that aren't too wet or too dry.

- *Greater than 8 inches per hour*: Excessive drainage (soil has high content of sand). Choose plants that tolerate drought.

See system models' descriptions on page 58 and Appendix E.

These plants can tolerate droughty soils.

Russian Sage
Perovskia atriplicifolia

Blue Oat Grass
Helictotrichon sempervirens

Soil test results

The information you'll receive from your soil test will include soil pH and nutrient levels. This information will help you decide whether you need to amend planting areas or, using an integrated approach, choose plants that will tolerate your existing conditions.

Soil pH

Soil pH is a measure of relative soil acidity on a scale of 0–14, with 7 being neutral. Acidic soil has pH less than 7 and alkaline soil has pH above 7. Soil pH is influenced by many factors, including its parent material, management practices, organic matter, and water sources (including acid rain).

In New Hampshire much of the soil is naturally acidic. Most landscape plants grow best in a slightly acidic soil with a range of 6.2 to 6.8, although some plants, including rhododendron, azalea, holly and blueberry thrive in more acidic soil conditions. It may be easiest to choose plants that grow in your site's currentconditions. However, if soil tests reveal a very low pH, you can amend the landscape bed by adding alkaline substances such as limestone or wood ash to raise the pH. If you choose this option, remember:

- Test your pH once every two or three years.
- Apply limestone or wood ash only when the soil test results indicate a need for it, and at the recommended rate.
- Don't use hydrated lime, as it may harm soil organisms.

In other locations you may need to lower pH to a more acidic level, usually by amending the soil with elemental sulfur, iron sulfate, or aluminum sulfate, again only at recommended rates.

Soil contributes plant nutrients

A plant requires 18 nutrients to grow normally and complete its life cycle. Plants need large amounts of carbon, oxygen, and hydrogen. They get carbon and oxygen from air and hydrogen from water. The nutrients you hear most about, because they are commonly applied as fertilizers, are the so-called macronutrients: nitrogen, phosphorus, and potassium. You will see them listed as "N-P-K" or simply as a ratio such as 10-5-10, 5-3-4, etc. on bags of commercial fertilizer.

Calcium and magnesium are usually supplied in sufficient amounts by the soil or by additions of liming materials if needed. Sulfur, iron, manganese, copper, zinc, boron, molybdenum, chlorine, cobalt, and nickel are also usually present in adequate amounts in the soil if the pH is adjusted to the proper range. Excess amounts of these micronutrients can be toxic to plants. Building organic matter in soil is the best way to supply and retain many essential nutrients.

Rhododendron maximum (shown here) and other plants such as azalea, holly, and blueberry tolerate acidic soils.

> **THE EDUCATION CENTER: PROVIDING PRACTICAL SOLUTIONS TO EVERYDAY QUESTIONS**
>
> The Education Center at UNH Cooperative Extension provides practical help to everyday questions. The Education Center's professionals and intensively trained volunteers answer your questions about gardens, lawns and landscapes, fruits and vegetables, household food safety and food preservation, tree planting and care, backyard livestock, and more. The Center also offers written information, programs, or referrals on family finances, nutrition, parenting and child development, and 4-H youth development.
>
> For help, call the **toll-free number: 1-877-EXT-GROW** (1-877-398-4769) or email your questions to: answers@unh.edu

To amend or not to amend?

Healthy landscapes are based on healthy soils. Test results may reveal that soils already have adequate levels of nutrients and elements from organic matter and from weathered bedrock. Conversely, the results may indicate nutrient deficiencies. This is where you have to make a choice that will affect plant selection and later plant health; will you select rugged plants for existing soil conditions (possibly "poor" soil) and begin to build soils over time, or will you amend soil throughout the planting area to improve overall soil quality and permit a wider selection of plants?

Amending the entire planting bed

If you choose to amend the planting bed, be prepared to improve the soil over the entire planting bed and not individual holes. It's a good idea to add compost to a clay or sandy soil. An inch or two of compost tilled in with lime as recommended will increase the soil's water-holding capacity, improve drainage, and provide a slow-release source of nutrients. Till the area several inches deep to incorporate the amendments, unless doing so will destroy numerous roots from plants in the area. As a general rule, don't apply more than 2 inches of compost, and mix it into the soil as soon as possible to stabilize it.

Building soils over time

Building soils over time allows the integrated landscaping processes to unfold, but it requires patience and a little experimentation with plants suited to the site conditions. Adding layers of diverse organic mulches from onsite such as leaves, woodchips, and grass clippings will add nutrients for building the diverse populations of soil organisms. Another good source of information on building your soil can be found at: www.soilfoodweb.com.

Assessing wildlife habitat through the seasons

A careful seasonal inventory will help you make the best decisions for a healthy, sustainable landscape that supports a diversity of wildlife. Whenever possible, observe and record the property through the seasons. Spend time evaluating the land features for the habitat elements that already do and could potentially exist. Think like an animal: *Where will I find food, water, and cover?*

Note existing trees, shrubs, flowers, and vines, and make special note of natives. The more native plants, the more native wildlife is likely to be present. In summer, flowers, green plants, insects, and certain fruits make up much of the food base for wildlife, but as the weather cools in the fall, these decline. Look around for sources of fall and winter mast—fruits, nuts, and seeds—that help wildlife build winter fat reserves. Some fruits also persist through the winter, feeding the wave of migrating birds that return in spring. Photos will help record seasonal conditions, and you'll also find them useful during the design process.

Dead standing trees known as snags are highly valuable for many forms of wildlife and, if in an area not frequented by people, should be left standing.

Consider what wildlife and plant communities might have been present before development. Take a look at the bigger picture—the surrounding community—to help you figure out the role this property might have had and what role it could play in the future. A useful tool for inventory is *A Landowner's Guide to Inventorying and Monitoring Wildlife in New Hampshire*, by Malin Ely Clyde, with Darrel Covell and Matt Tarr, of UNH Cooperative Extension. For habitat maps, descriptions of habitat types, and information on wildlife species of concern, a valuable resource is the New Hampshire Wildlife Action Plan: www.nhfg.net/Wildlife/wildlife_plan.htm. (Check online for your state's wildlife action plan.)

When beginning your inventory look to the properties nearby to gather understanding of the natural communities that influence your site.

Taking stock: the inventory process

Some landscapers believe that plant identification is the most important aspect of an area's natural history, but we consider that understanding the basics of what makes up the community and the type of wildlife that lives there is more important. For the purposes of integrated landscaping it is probably more important to understand what layers of plants you have and which ones are missing on the site, rather than each individual name. Say, for instance, you identify in the overstory layer a large nut-producing tree, and notice that both squirrels and birds consume the nuts. It's probably less important to know that it's a red oak.

Having some understanding of the soil and the plants that grow within it can help you identify some of the wildlife present, but you can also follow the thread in the opposite direction. Understanding the wildlife can help you understand both the plants and soil. For instance, if you see lots of red squirrels, you probably have many evergreens (soft wood) trees nearby, while gray squirrels indicate deciduous (hardwood) trees. Another example would be that you identify pitch pine and small scrubby oaks naturally growing on the property, which indicate very sandy soils left 14,000 years ago by the glaciers. Plants are part of the natural history of the area, but so are the soils, fungi, and all forms of wildlife from insects and amphibians, to birds and mammals. They all live together as important forms of life within the ecosystem.

Several good resources can help you gain a basic understanding of the natural world around you. These include many different types of field guides. The National Audubon Society's Field Guide to New England offers basic information of both the different ecosystems and the plant and animals communities found within them.

> ### HOW TO OBSERVE
>
> *People who have lived or worked in the woods for a lifetime carry in their heads a search image for habitats—a mental laundry list of the wildlife they would expect to see there. When they step into a habitat, they notice the kinds of plants blooming underfoot and the type of trees spreading overhead. They have come to associate this vegetation with a certain community of animals. Under a ceiling of northern needleleaf trees, for instance, they know to look for porcupines, red squirrels, redbelly snakes, and brown creepers. They also know where in the habitat to look—on the ground for snakes, on the trunks for creepers, and in the canopy for porcupines and squirrels. If you haven't had the pleasure of living in the wild, take heart. Step outside and take a good look around. Are you in a forest, an opening or a wetland? Is the water fresh or salt? Are the trees broadleaf or needleleaf? In each community, thousands of plants, animals and microorganisms have evolved over eons to work together as one fantastic organism.*
>
> Janine Benyus, *Field Guide to Habitats of the Northeast*

Many organizations offer workshops on various natural history topics. Check out UNH Cooperative Extension Event Calendars at http://extension.unh.edu. You will find a comprehensive list of workshops by different organizations listed on its Forestry and Wildlife calendar. Several courses and training programs are also offered, including the Natural Resources Stewards, and Master Gardener volunteer programs, and the NH Coverts Project (wildlife).

However, there's no substitute for a knowledgeable friend, neighbor, teacher, or community volunteer who can help you understand what plant and animal communities share the spaces where you live, work, and play.

Inventory Worksheets

Turn to the Inventory Worksheets found in Appendix C. You may want to make photocopies of them so you can use the originals again in the future. The multiple questions will help build your awareness of the abundance of natural processes that you and "your" landscape and gardens are part of. By answering all the questions, you will integrate each of the 10 natural landscape principles, along with considerations for design, establishment, and care.

Try not to get discouraged by the number of questions. Just work through them one at a time. Make a list of the questions you can't answer yourself and set them aside for now. You may decide you need to consult a landscape professional or resource specialist later on. By completing this process with as much patience and enthusiasm as you can muster, you will have a thorough inventory and understanding of the property, making the next steps much easier.

Wild lupine, Lupinus perenis, an endangered plant in New Hampshire, is an indicator of a pine-barren community with sandy soils. Other plants associated with pine barrens include pitch pine and scrub oak. Many rare butterflies and moths are also associated with pine-barren communities including the Karner blue.

Once you have completed the inventory worksheet, look back over your answers to help determine which components will have a higher priority in the landscape design. You may want to highlight these to make sure you incorporate them in the design process. For instance, if you want to improve an existing landscape, your site may already have some components even though it lacks others.

Outside and Onsite: Taking Stock of What You Have

CHAPTER 4

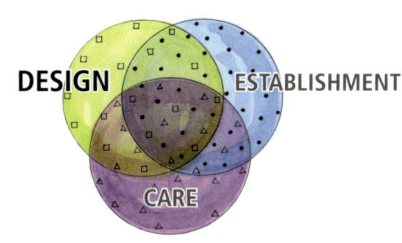

Designing Landscapes with Establishment and Care in Mind

In addition to classic design topics, integrated landscaping also considers the impacts of human needs on existing plants and animals, water and air quality, soils, and our sense of place. Good design practices consider and incorporate the best practices for establishment and care.

Creating the base plan: putting it on paper

With the 10 natural principles in mind, and your completed inventory worksheets in hand, it's time to begin the base plan for your design.

What you will need

This list may seem daunting, but each component helps take you through the process step by step. You'll need:

- A tax map.
- A topographic map.
- A USDA soil survey for the area (available at: http:websoilsurvey.nrcs.usda.gov).
- The soil information gathered on site and the soil test results.
- Building plans or site plan, which will also show buildings (check with town offices).
- State-approved septic plan (for proper location/placement), in New Hampshire available through the Subsurface Systems Division of the NH Department of Environmental Services (NHDES) at: www.des.state.nh.us/ssb.
- A directional compass.
- A 2-foot by 3-foot sheet of paper or vellum (purchase three as you'll need two additional pieces later on in the process).
- Drawing pencils, colored pencils or fine markers.
- A ruler or engineer scale.
- A roll of trace paper (large enough to cover the 2-ft. by 3-ft. sheet of paper).
- Your inventory worksheets.

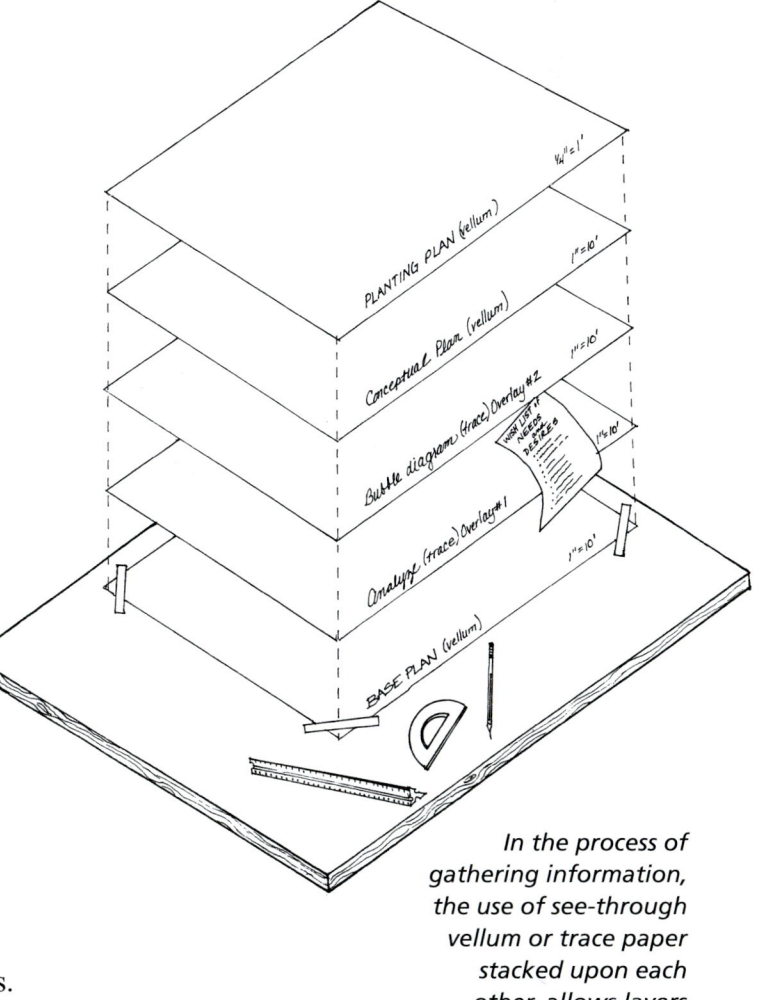

In the process of gathering information, the use of see-through vellum or trace paper stacked upon each other, allows layers of information to be considered without crowding the final conceptual plan.

Designing Landscapes with Establishment and Care in Mind

You don't have to be a professional mapmaker or an artist to create your own base plan. As you build layers of information on paper and overlays, we will walk you through the process step by step. Use the bullet points in each step below as a guide. There may be some bullets that don't apply and others not listed that you might want to add. Be patient and build your layers. The final outcome will be worth the time and effort.

Step 1. It's time to build the base plan, the foundation for your design.

Use a ruler to measure 1 inch = 8 feet, or an engineering scale to measure 1 inch = 10 feet. Begin with a large sheet of paper (2 feet x 3 feet), a drawing pencil, and your tax map or building plans. The first step on your base plan is to draw:

- Property lines.
- Roads and driveways.
- Compass points (transfer from your building plans or topographic map).
- Any easements, setbacks or rights-of-way.

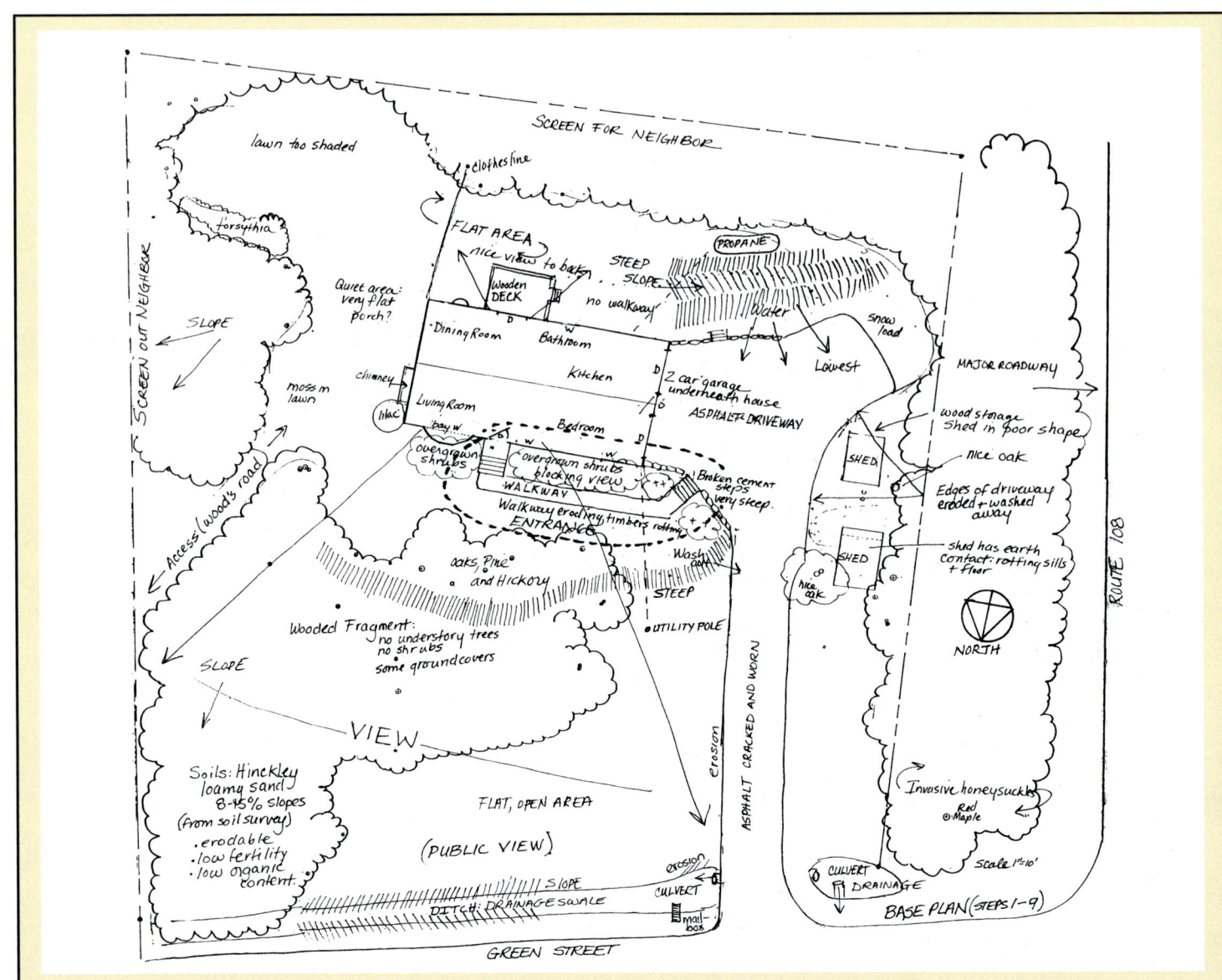

Base plan *showing property lines, roads and driveway, directional orientation, building footprint, and all utilities. Information regarding landforms (slopes, low areas, swales), soil information, weather patterns, and views are also noted on the base plan.*

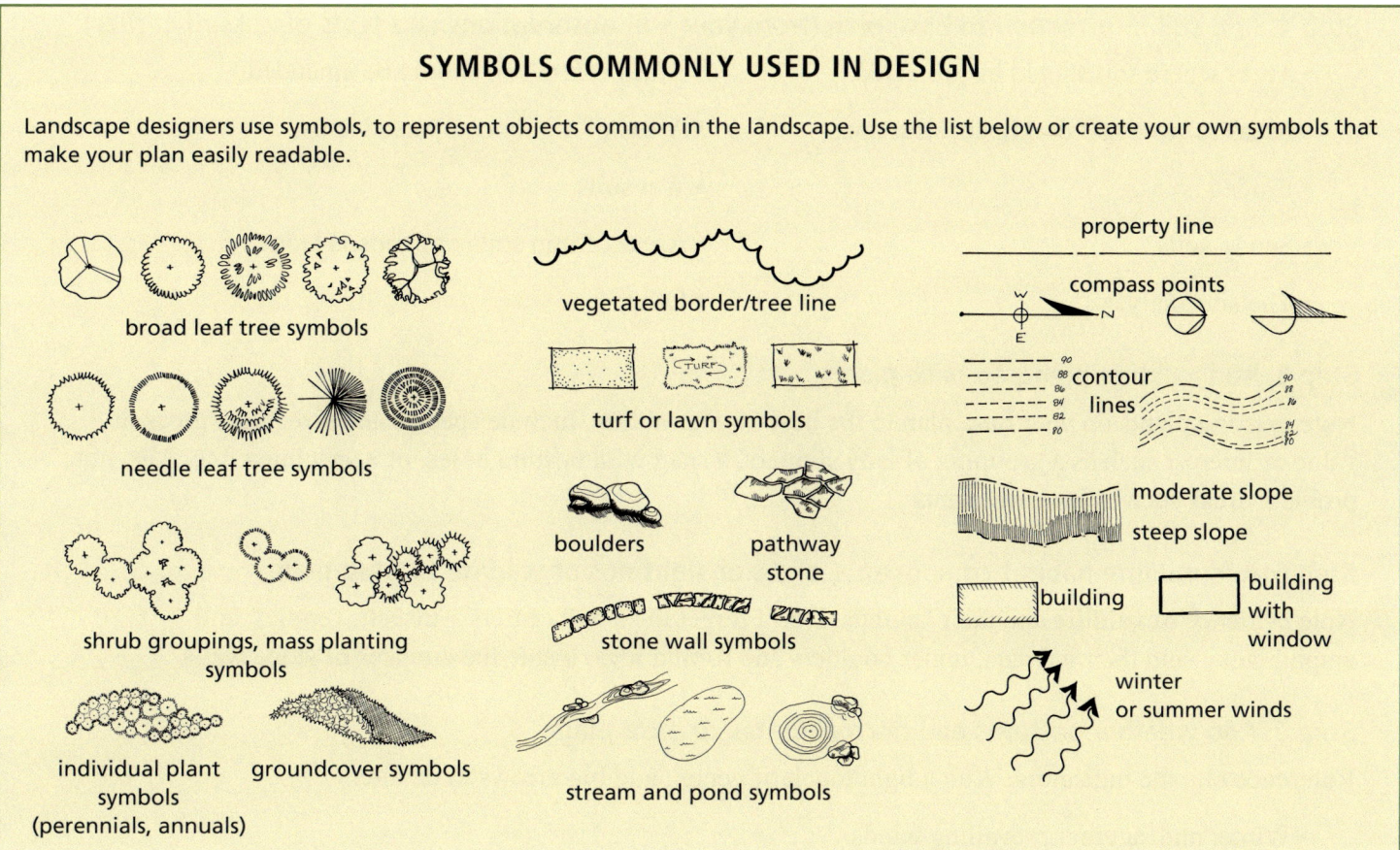

SYMBOLS COMMONLY USED IN DESIGN

Landscape designers use symbols, to represent objects common in the landscape. Use the list below or create your own symbols that make your plan easily readable.

Step 2. Add building footprints and utilities to the base plan.

The next component of the base plan will include the measurement and placement of buildings. Continue to use the same scale 1 inch = 8 feet if using a ruler, or 1 inch = 10 feet if using an engineering scale. For this step you can use building plans or take your own measurements. Include the following additions to the base plan:

- Footprint (dimensions) of your building.

- Size and placement of doors and windows, including heights of windows off the ground.

- Floor plan of interior layout.

- Locations of utilities, including electrical, water, gas, oil, and septic. (Your septic plan will give you its exact location, depth and typical components including septic tank, distribution box, leach field, and location of your well.)

- Outbuildings and permanent structures. (Once you've drawn the footprint of your home/building, locate the outbuildings accurately by taking measurements from the corners of your home.)

Step 3. Add physical features to base plan.

A topographic map can help you locate physical features including:

- Landforms, such as sloped areas, ridges, flat areas, wetlands, vernal pools, shoreline, and drainage swales. These features will show how water moves across your property. In almost all cases you will see that water travels down hill toward the body of water.

- Surface waters: vernal pools, streams, rivers, ponds, lakes, salt water bodies.

Designing Landscapes with Establishment and Care in Mind

Step 4. Add soil information to base plan (from your soil observations and tests discussed earlier).

- Areas where soil should be protected.
- Areas to store soil during construction.
- Eroded areas.
- Sandy soils.
- The site analysis.
- Areas where soil should be amended.
- Areas of highly compacted soils.
- Wet soils.
- Areas of thin soils or exposed ledge.
- Other.

Step 5. Add existing plants to base plan.

Note existing plants on your base plan to the best of your ability. Include species and size. Note areas of value or interest such as a grouping of lady slippers, a snag with nesting holes, or a specimen tree. Also note problem areas such as invasive plants.

Step 6. Add wildlife habitat components, signs or sightings of wildlife to base plan.

Note evidence of wildlife and their habitats. Don't forget the small critters—insects, reptiles, and amphibians—and their habitats: under boulders and rotting logs, inside the crevices of stone walls.

Step 7. Add weather patterns and microclimates to base plan.

Reference climate indicators. With a light touch of pencil, add big arrows to denote:

- Winter and summer prevailing winds.
- Angle of the sun throughout the day/seasons (use this information later to increase year-round comfort by proper placement of screens, windbreaks and openings).
- Shadiest to sunniest areas (use cross-hatching to indicate shade).
- Microclimates, areas where the temperature, humidity and exposure vary from the dominant conditions enough to increase or decrease human comfort or diversity of plantings.

Step 8. Add views to base plan.

From the building's interior windows, look out in all directions to help decide where to keep views open and where you may need plants for screening. Elevation views from building plans may help with this task, as they show first- and second-story windows. With a light touch of a pencil add these to the Base Plan. Later in the process you will refine, enhance, and preserve the views.

Step 9. Add inventory results.

With your inventory worksheets in hand, use a colored pencil to transcribe findings to the base plan. Note areas of erosion, lawn area needed for certain activities, buffers that can be increased, a neighbor's garage that needs screening, etc. At this point the relationship between your inventory and the base plan should begin communicating with each other.

32 Designing Landscapes with Establishment and Care in Mind

Adding layers to your base plan

Analyze your site: trace paper Overlay #1

Now that you've completed the base plan, it's time to add a layer of details that show how the property is currently used. Place a sheet of trace paper over your base plan. With a different colored pencil use broad strokes, shading, circles, etc., to add information that shows critical uses such as:

- Circulation paths—the way you move through your site; include pathways, stopping area, and seating areas.

- Service areas (functional areas that serve needs). For homes, include items such as clotheslines, utility sheds, and fuel delivery areas. For business or schools, you might include signage, loading docks, mechanical equipment areas, etc.

- Areas to be protected: vegetation undisturbed for 40 years or more, vernal pools, root zones of large trees, wetlands, pond or lake, etc.

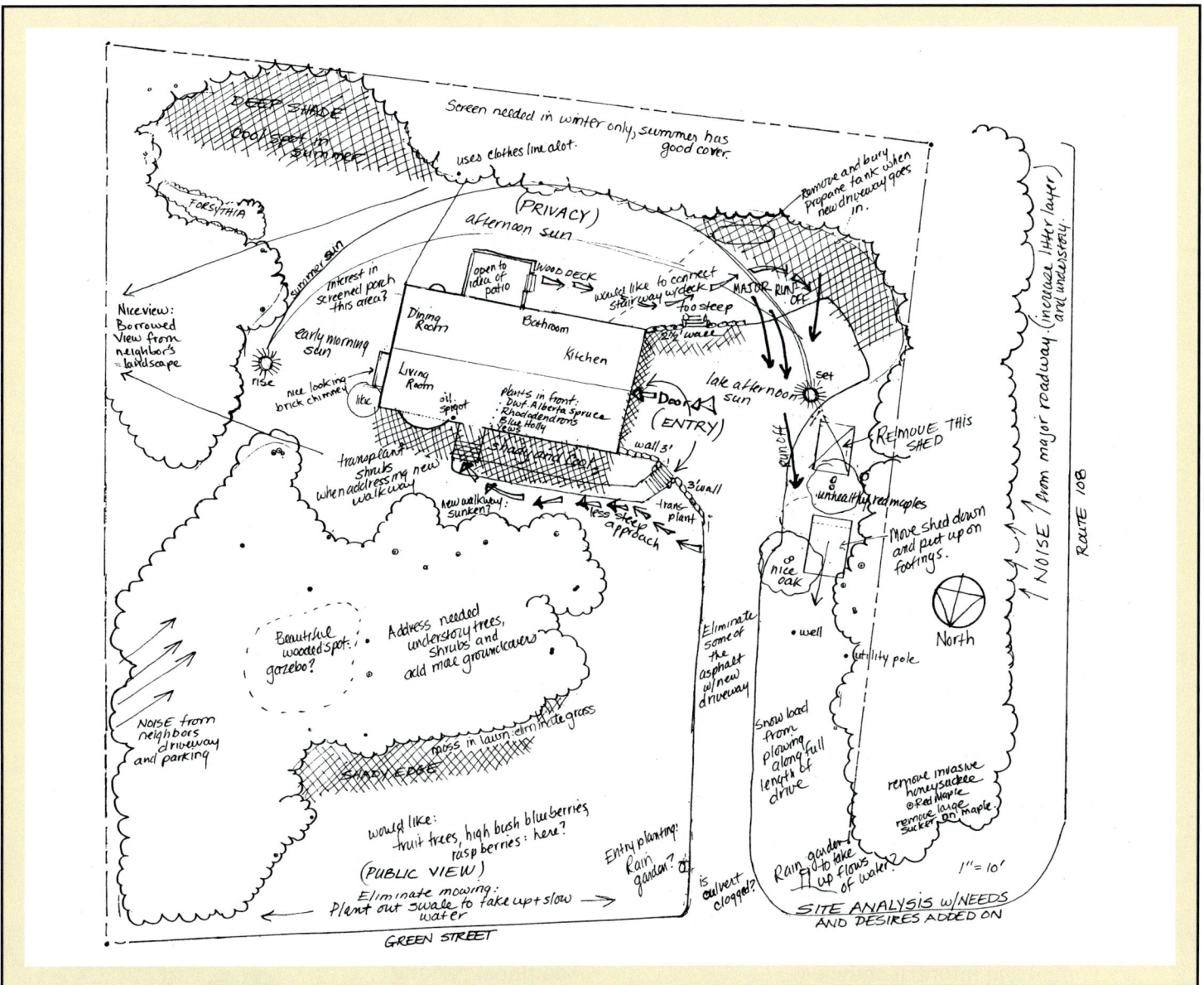

Site analysis is a thorough recording of information depicting current functions, circulation paths, uses of space, and the relationship between the interior and exterior functions. Needs and desires are noted, too. Capabilities, limitations, and interacting elements are recorded and highlighted as necessary.

Designing Landscapes with Establishment and Care in Mind

- Access to water: outdoor spigots, hoses, wells (anywhere from where you draw water).
- Areas used for storing chemicals such as deicers, fertilizers, pesticides, petroleum products.
- Lawn and open areas—indicate what activities take place.

- Parking and vehicular pathways
- Areas seen by the public
- Front yard and backyard
- Entertainment area(s)
- Sitting areas
- Quiet spaces
- Recreational or play areas
- Vegetable and flower gardens
- Other
- Compost bins

Also note areas that raise environmental concerns such as noise pollution, air quality problems, snow buildup, and storm-water runoff.

Develop a wish list of needs and desires

Needs and desires depict the property owners' current and intended uses of space, including essential needs, non-essential-but-desired features, and wish-list items. Create your wish list on a separate piece of paper. Jot down your needs and desires. They may include but aren't limited to:

For home/personal property:

- Relaxation areas such as gazebo, screen house, or deck
- Buffers to be increased such as areas near water bodies
- Various recreational or play areas (swings, slides, basketball backboard, badminton, or volleyball field)
- Views to be screened (for example, a neighbor's garage, a dumpster, etc.)

- Storage areas
- Pets and their needs
- Firewood storage
- Clothesline
- Swimming areas
- Patios and outdoor cooking area
- Vegetable and food gardens
- Flower gardens
- Compost bins
- Windbreaks, natural openings
- Habitat features to attract wildlife
- Water features
- Plant systems to mimic natural areas
- Other

For schools or municipalities:

- Outdoor classroom spaces
- Staff break or relaxation areas
- Walking paths
- Formal and informal entrances
- Playgrounds
- Passive recreation areas
- Additional parking
- Storage areas
- Snow storage
- Wildlife gardens
- Water features
- Compost bins
- Flower gardens
- Other

For commercial properties:

- Formal and informal entrances
- Additional parking
- Employee break or relaxation areas
- Sidewalks
- Storage areas
- Other

34 Designing Landscapes with Establishment and Care in Mind

With your wish list in hand, using a third colored pencil, locate your needs and desires on Overlay #1. This begins to fill in the details of how you will use your property. It helps determine how indoor and outdoor functions relate to each other. For example, you might locate herb gardens and entertainment areas such as outdoor dining close the kitchen, firewood storage close the fireplace or woodstove, and reflective spaces or natural areas close to the bedrooms.

For a school or business landscape you may want to create a pathway from the building to a break area located under an existing shade tree, or in an area that can be planted with shade trees. You might choose to screen views of the parking lot or roadway, or define a path and entryway that connects a building to a parking lot.

For the next step, you will need a second piece of trace paper to create a third layer.

Create a functional bubble diagram: trace paper Overlay #2

Take some time to absorb the information on the base plan and Overlay #1. Begin to think about grouping similar functions into units of space. For example, outside an office window, screen a row of dumpsters with a dense planting of shrubbery. This planting could also offer an interesting view, and serve as a convenient spot for a birdfeeder. At home, you might choose to group a vegetable garden, compost bins, access to a hose, and a tool shed together. Each group of functions can be mapped onto a second layer of trace paper with informal circles and other shapes (bubbles), like these examples below.

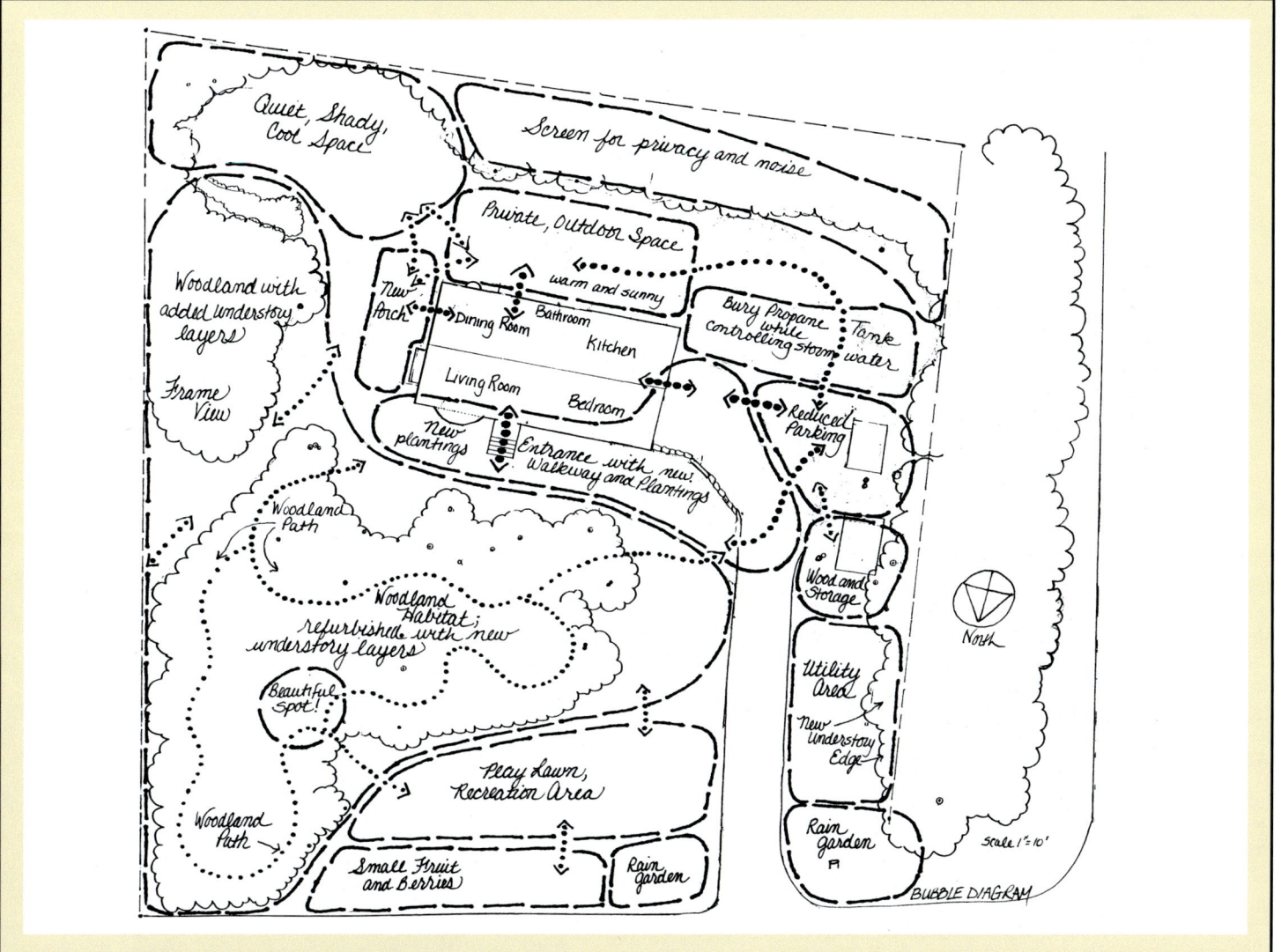

In helping the design to flow, **functional bubble diagrams** map out indoor functions, outdoor activities, and circulation patterns based on the capabilities and limitations of the site analysis.

Here are some other examples that group similar functions:

For Homes:

- Front lawn/public views/entryway to home
- Private/quiet areas/screens
- Kennel/outdoor play areas for pets
- Lawn/recreational spaces
- Entertainment/terrace/patio areas

For Schools:

- Outdoor storage areas/utility service areas
- Parking/public access
- Outdoor classrooms/picnic areas/recreational trails
- Recreational fields/sports areas/playgrounds

For Municipalities or commercial properties:

- Outdoor storage areas/ service areas
- Public views/ parking/public access/directional signage
- Break areas/recreation areas/trails

Functional bubble diagrams bring attention to the interrelationships of indoor and outdoor spaces and uses. At home your entire property can serve as valuable living space and an extension of your home's interior layout. Bridge together as many indoor-outdoor links as possible.

In adding this layer of information you may discover valuable spaces you never considered such as a small pocket of unused space outside your bedroom that could become a quiet sitting area. The bubble diagram also helps you see mapped functions that won't work together. For example, as you look through the bubble diagram at the different layers, you find underground utilities in the area outside your kitchen where you'd hoped to locate a patio for cooking. Instead, you decide to move the patio to the area outside the dining room where there is no conflict; in the space outside of the kitchen you could plant an herb garden, perennials and annuals, whose shallow roots won't interfere with the utilities.

Your conceptual plan (on paper or vellum)

After spending time with the three layers of information you've already collected, using paper or vellum, trace/transfer to your final design all the features you want to carry over to it.

Determine outdoor spaces you want to develop. You may want to think of them as "outdoor rooms." Begin to place "rooms" and carve out open spaces for recreation, quiet spaces, patios, paths, utilities, or other uses. Look at the interrelationships between and among all the rooms both indoors and out.

Integrated landscaping practice suggests keeping areas outside these "rooms" heavily vegetated. Trees, shrubs, flowers, and grasses, along with built structures, can help form the "walls" to your rooms. These heavily vegetated areas can also serve as wildlife habitat, help protect soils and filter air and water. Locate these walls or vegetated areas on your concept plan (fourth layer). Although you don't need to designate specific plants yet, you will want to record the amount of space available for them.

As part of this process you may want to try to imagine how your property looked before it was developed. Look for undisturbed patches of vegetation that still exist to help you visualize what your land might have been like and incorporate these into your outdoor walls or rooms. Existing vegetation will also provide clues to help you later determine which plants will grow well with minimum care on your site.

If you identified areas with views, think beyond the conventional wide-open expanses overlooking large lawn areas. For example, consider framing a view with vegetation. "Windows" through vegetated areas can attract the eye and add depth to a view. This also works in areas that lack pleasant views. Artful placement of plants creates a framing effect and can draw the eye to a more attractive spot such as a single tree. You can create views in heavily vegetated areas through selectively thinning trees or pruning branches. Cutting windows within the foliage, or thinning foliage to provide a filtered view of a land form, water body, outdoor sculpture or other interesting view allows you to keep these views without decreasing privacy.

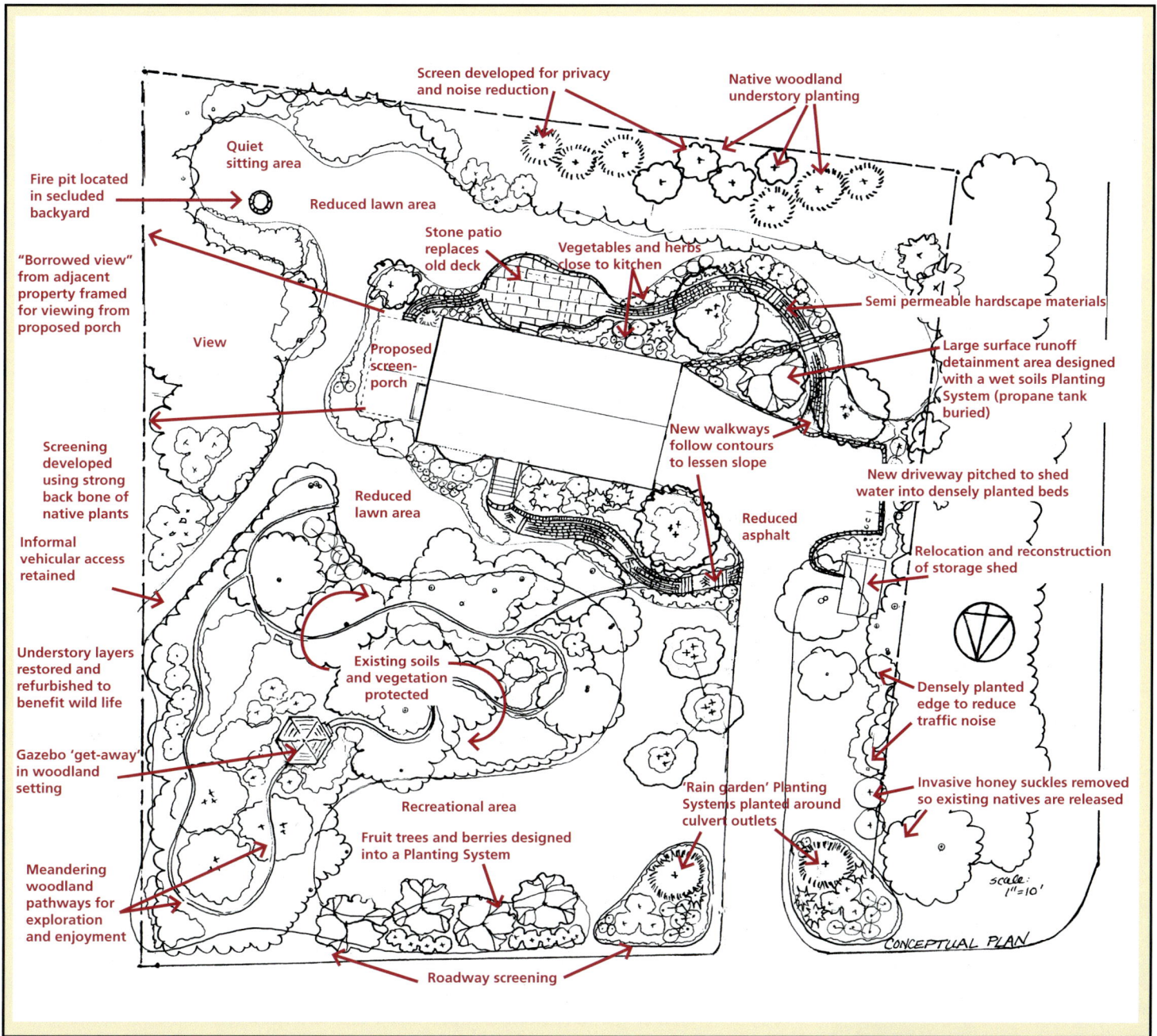

The **conceptual plan** provides a visual overview of all features, vegetation, and actions planned to establish an ecological landscape that increases infiltration and filtration of water, provides a diverse wildlife habitat, protects and builds soil over time, and is pleasing and functional for human use.

Designing Landscapes with Establishment and Care in Mind

Designing for wildlife

Whatever the characteristics or size of your landscape, you influence the local wildlife by what you do with that land. No matter how large or small, your site can support wildlife and you can influence the abundance and variety of the wildlife by providing habitat for a wide variety of species on your property, some that you'll get to enjoy up close—especially birds, butterflies, and other insects. Enhancing wildlife habitat also helps re-create some of the rapidly disappearing natural landscapes that define the traditional New Hampshire "character."

While that rich patch of original wilderness may be gone, re-creating aspects of it on your site can support an array of wildlife and help limit habitat loss, the most significant problem facing wildlife worldwide. (For more information on natural communities see Appendix D.)

As an area is transformed from rural forest to smaller, more fragmented suburban and urban landholdings, the wildlife that inhabit the area change.

No matter how large or small a site, vegetation attracts birds, butterflies, and insects to enjoy up close.

Which wildlife you will see on your land depends on several factors, which include the size of your property and adjoining lands, your location in the state, the site's characteristics and features, available habitat and its arrangement, and human activity on the site.

Urban, suburban and rural sites provide different habitats that attract different wildlife species. A typical suburban neighborhood will have more than 25 kinds of birds and mammals, including squirrels, songbirds, hawks, raccoons, and even foxes. Some wildlife are generalists that adapt to change and can live in human-built areas (consider the skunk, gray squirrel, or coyote), while the specialists have more specific habitat needs and are more sensitive to disturbance (such as the hermit thrush, spotted salamander, or bobcat).

Providing habitat

Providing a place for wildlife doesn't require digging up your entire site and starting fresh. You can make a few small changes to start; the key is to work with the type of site you have. (See inset on page 41 for ideas.) There is no one recipe for wildlife habitat. Different kinds of areas call for different strategies.

All animals—wild, domesticated, and human—need habitat: a suitable combination of cover (shelter), food, water, and adequate space within the area they call home.

The needs of a particular species are specific to that species. Space should be adequate for seeking a mate, breeding and rearing offspring.

Appropriate cover would provide protection from the elements and escape from predators, as well as a place to rest and raise young. With adequate

The native New England cottontail rabbit has become a species of concern because habitat loss has drastically reduced their population. They need early successional habitats such as abandoned farmlands, shrub thickets, and other regenerating plant communities. These habitat types, important breeding, feeding, and cover have largely disappeared from the New Hampshire landscape because of forest maturation and human development. In contrast, the introduced and more adaptable Eastern cottontail can thrive in suburban environments dominated by mowed lawns, shrub cover, and abandoned house lots.

year-round food resources, an animal can survive when energy demands are greatest, such as for reproduction in spring, warmth during winter, or for migration or hibernation. Water sources should be clean and accessible.

Consider three questions for wildlife habitat: What do I have? What do I want? How will I get it? Your inventory worksheets will have answered the first question. Now, what do you want? Knowing that a habitat can be many things to many creatures makes your job of designing a wildlife landscape easier. You can select habitat elements for your site that will attract and support particular groups of wildlife species at the same time it satisfies other landscape needs such as windbreak, color, or structure. In any case, provide the essentials for wildlife habitat: food, water, and cover, in an arrangement that allows animals easy access to access each.

Rocks provide hiding places for wildlife and add interest to the landscape.

How will you get it? Food + water + cover + space = wildlife habitat. The key is to provide diversity. Use what you have, then add a few layers of low-maintenance, locally available plants that have wildlife value. Set up a birdbath or pond. As you develop a landscape plan, take your cues from the surrounding plant communities. Choosing native plants from that palette will connect your yard to the broader landscape.

Look to see what plants are nearby. New Hampshire has many native plants that provide an excellent source of food for wildlife.

Applying the plant-system approach will also help you provide for wildlife (with the added value of bringing some species in close enough to observe), as the plants are arranged in vertical layers, from groundcovers, grasses and perennials, to shrubs and trees. This supports a diversity of wildlife, from insects on up. When insects are drawn into the garden from local, relatively natural areas, some of them will find a preferred food and will be induced to stay. Insects are a key component of food webs. Providing for them will invite the wildlife that feed on them (such as songbirds or spiders), and the wildlife that feed on birds and spiders (reptiles, raptors, and certain mammals), and so on. According to Douglas Tallamy's research, 96% of breeding birds depend on insects (Tallamy 2009).

Insects not only pollinate plants in our landscape, but also attract other wildlife, making them a key part of the food web.

Designing Landscapes with Establishment and Care in Mind

Potential wildlife conflicts

People occasionally have negative interactions with wildlife, typically with those species well-adapted to human habitation known as "generalists" (deer, skunks, woodchucks, beavers, mosquitoes). If you have problems with what you may consider nuisance wildlife, check out these resources, which will help you understand why the wildlife are where they are, what they are doing there, and how to adapt to their presence, deter them, or protect your property from possible damage. Contact the U.S. Department of Agriculture's office of Wildlife Services (Appendix D). A helpful book on this topic is *Living with Wildlife: How to Enjoy, Cope with, and Protect North America's Wild Creatures around Your Home and Theirs*, by Diana Landau and Shelley Stump.

FIELDS AND GRASSLANDS FOR NEW HAMPSHIRE WILDLIFE

Fields and grasslands provide another habitat option in a largely forested landscape. Timing mowing to work with wildlife needs provides recreational and aesthetic benefits as well.

Most New Hampshire fields and grasslands are remnants of earlier agricultural times. Native Americans and later European settlers cleared forestland for agriculture, timber and fuel wood. By the mid-1800's, about 80 percent of New England was cleared for agricultural production, including livestock. Cleared pasture and cropland left fallow to recover its fertility provided substantial early-successional habitat in the form of grassland and mixed-shrub land/grassland. Consequently, there was an increase in the wildlife that depend on these areas including grassland birds like bobolinks, meadowlarks, and grasshopper sparrows, and a diversity of insects, reptiles, and amphibians, as well as predatory hawks and mammals.

When vastly richer farmlands opened up in the Midwest in the mid- to late-19th century, many New England farmers abandoned their fields and migrated west. Over time, these fields returned to forests. Today, New Hampshire remains the second most-forested state. Much of the remaining land in New Hampshire not covered with trees has been developed, so those dwindling areas in fields and grassland are vital habitat for an array of wildlife, especially grassland birds.

If you have a field, consider these maintenance tips: To support bobolinks, the grassland bird with the lowest acreage requirements, a field should be at least 10 acres, alone or in conjunction with adjacent fields. Meadowlarks need at least 15 acres, and grasshopper sparrows require a minimum of 30 acres.

If you mow only once a year, just to keep the field open, wait until after August 1 (the later the better, to allow for young birds to fledge). Less-frequent mowing supports a greater diversity of wildlife, including insects, birds and mammals. It also yields a higher diversity of flowering plants, makes seedheads available for food and creates more thatch for cover.

By contrast, frequent mowing as for a hayfield produces important forage for fewer species such as deer and turkey. If you mow twice per year for a hayfield, consider waiting until August 1 for the first cut, to allow bobolinks to fledge their young. Also, use flushing bars on haying equipment, avoid mowing where birds are often seen, leave small patches such as edges or strips unmowed as nesting areas, and avoid or delay mowing in wetter areas.

SIMPLE ENHANCEMENTS FOR WILDLIFE

- To invite more diversity into the landscape, add water (even something as simple as a half-barrel with a few wetland plants in it).
- Include densely branched shrubs to shelter birds' nests from neighborhood cats and other predators.
- Use wildflowers to bring color to your landscape, provide summer nectar, and yield seeds for the wildlife in your yard.
- Where safe and feasible, leave snags (dead and decaying trees) standing, as they make great sites for birds to find insect food and nesting opportunities.
- Use structural components such as nest boxes to supplement plantings and replace missing habitat elements such as nesting trees, cavities, and perches.
- Reduce outdoor lighting to minimize impacts on nocturnal species.
- Note barriers to wildlife passage such as curbing, solid stone walls, terraces, fences, large open expanses of turf, and impervious surfaces, and allow access where possible.

Above: *Keep the traditional ornamental plantings close to the building, and plant the wild garden along the perimeter of the property, allowing the native plantings to link up with wild gardens in neighboring yards to maximize the size of continuous habitat.*

Water is an important component of wildlife habitat. Water features do not have to be large; even small depressions or bird baths support many forms of wildlife.

THE EVOLUTION OF AN ECOLOGICAL LANDSCAPE DESIGN

This steeply-sloped lot was originally cleared for a panoramic view of the water, but now lacks privacy. The sloped turf areas are dangerous and time-consuming to mow and have limited recreational use. Without a plant canopy, seasonal interest is diminished and lacks connections for wildlife movement. The direct pathway to the shoreline involves many stairs to climb, and channels runoff water directly to the shore, carrying with it soil, nutrients, pesticides, petroleum products, and other household substances. Portions of the exposed shoreline are lost to erosion each year.

Landscape improvement begins by planting a vegetative buffer area to protect the shoreline and by allowing much of the lawn to revert to a meadow-like condition. Reducing the expanse of lawn means less maintenance and more time to enjoy the property. Native plantings restore wildlife habitat, color and seasonal interest. The terraced, stone patio replaces a deck, eliminating one long stairway. Impervious surface is reduced by shrinking the asphalt driveway. Eliminating some of the docks reduces maintenance while still allowing a very usable lakeshore.

Designing for shorelines

Property along shorelines presents many opportunities for wildlife and people. For schools, shorelines provide outdoor classrooms. For homeowners, the shore offers a place to let go of day-to-day stress. For commercial and municipal properties, shorelines become gathering places that attract the public for social events and provide outdoor areas for shopping and restaurants. No matter the amount or type of shoreline, each property owner has the responsibility of protecting the soil, water, and wildlife that make these places special.

Each property is part of a larger watershed. Before making any landscape changes, read and understand your town, city, or state's regulations regarding shoreland protection, like those within New Hampshire's Comprehensive Shoreland Protection Act.

The first thing to consider in designing a plant system or any landscape along shorelines is protecting the valuable features already there, then move on to making improvements. To some degree, the existing vegetation on your property may already contain areas of aquatic, shoreline, lowland transition, and upland plant communities. All these areas work together to filter runoff from spring and fall rains, summer irrigation, and winter snowmelt, helping to protect the quality of the water body.

As aquatic and shoreline plants become established, the shore is protected against erosion. The larger lawn area is maintained for recreation, and the smaller one for relaxation. Meadows keep the view open while building diversity of habitat for wildlife. Native plantings connect the small fragmented woodlands, and pathways have been defined to create interesting strolls and maximize enjoyment of the property. The slopes are densely planted in layers to increase infiltration and protect soil from erosion. A meandering pathway follows the contour lines for a gentle approach to the water.

The addition of more plants maximizes the protection of slopes from erosion, the amount of water that is intercepted and infiltrates into the soil, and the diversity and interest of the landscape. Cover, food, and nesting sites are restored for wildlife, and a framed view of the lake creates privacy and easy access to the waterfront.

Heavily vegetated areas increase water infiltration to help stabilize soils, protect water quality, and provide habitat. Retain as much as possible of this existing vegetation. If some vegetation needs to be removed, selective thinning protects soil and water quality better than patch cutting. In New Hampshire refer to the Comprehensive Shoreland Protection Act for legal specifications before removing any plants in a shoreline property. Views need not be limited to wide-open expanses overlooking large lawn areas. Selective thinning can be used to create views by cutting "windows" within the foliage or thinning foliage to provide a filtered view of the water body, while still protecting privacy.

In addition to applying integrated landscaping principles, consider the following shoreland design guidelines before you put pencil to paper. These guidelines not only will help protect the water body and other natural resources, they will also help you create a beautiful, low-maintenance landscape that complements the natural world around you.

Design guidelines to help protect and improve shoreland properties

Always protect existing soil. Keep soils covered at all times using vegetation or mulches to reduce compaction and erosion. Shoreland properties benefit from slowing water flows across the landscape to help retain soil.

The design should consider reducing the steepness of slope to allow drainage to flow to vegetated areas where infiltration can take place. Intermittent boulders and ornamental rocks or granite can structurally stabilize slopes and look fairly natural. If grading is necessary, you can alter subsurface drainage to improve the speed of water infiltration, but remember that grading and heavy construction equipment can compact soil, reducing its absorption ability.

Maximize the amount of vegetative buffer along shorelines. A diverse, dense, and multi-layered planting will hold, protect, and stabilize the soils with thick mats of roots that penetrate the soil at different depths. To maximize the amount of buffer, combine your buffer with neighboring properties' buffers whenever possible. Refer to the Shoreline Plant Chart. (See Appendix E.)

Minimize areas of impermeable surface. Replacing existing asphalt or concrete driveways and walkways with water-penetrating materials (e.g., stone dust, brick, or semi-permeable pavers) helps increase water infiltration and can enhance the beauty of your landscape. For areas where erosion and runoff are problematic several techniques can help minimize and divert runoff, including rain gardens, berms, check dams, cut-ins, waterbars, infiltration trenches, swales, and vegetated buffers. For more information on these techniques and ecological landscaping for shoreline properties, see *Landscaping at the Water's Edge: An Ecological Approach.* (See Appendix D.)

Maximize the amount of vegetated buffers along shorelines, look for opportunities to continue vegetated buffers across property lines to increase benefits.

Rethink the size of lawns. Instead of grass, consider encouraging plant and wildlife diversity by using groundcovers and vertical layers of vegetation. These rougher surfaces also slow runoff and help filter water before it reaches the water body. Keep lawn areas nearly flat (2 percent grade or ¼-inch per foot) to retain water on site and reduce the need for irrigation.

When choosing plants, select "the right plant for the right place for the right function." This is especially critical for shoreline landscaping. Well-chosen, well-placed plants can reduce the severity of winds, modulating the immediate environment. By knowing a plant's mature size before putting it into the landscape, you can keep your views open without the need for pruning, while simultaneously framing a desirable view. For example, you may want to maintain a view to the water visible from facing windows. To achieve this you might choose 12 to 15 varied plants that stay under three feet tall, while other areas of the landscape where views aren't as important will allow for more vertical layers of plants that include understory and overstory trees. Refer to the Plant Lists in Appendix E which list plants by mature height.

Permeable asphalt allows water to penetrate rather than run off. A rain garden planted next to the permeable surface will catch any water that does run off.

This steeply sloped landscape has many layers, allowing more water to be retained on site rather than running into the lake.

Remember, all your actions on land directly affect the water body. Substances that go onto your land, no matter how far away from the shoreline, eventually end up in the water body. This also includes detergents used in car washing, including chemicals used in lawn treatments and herbicides applied to keep weeds from growing between paving stones, exhaust residues, gas and oil leaks from mowers and weed-whackers, seasonal products such as winter deicers, as well as open compost bins and pet waste. Reducing potentially harmful inputs such as pesticides, fertilizers, and deicers will reduce the potential for negative impacts on the water body. Practices that minimize the need for irrigation will reduce leaching and runoff into the water body.

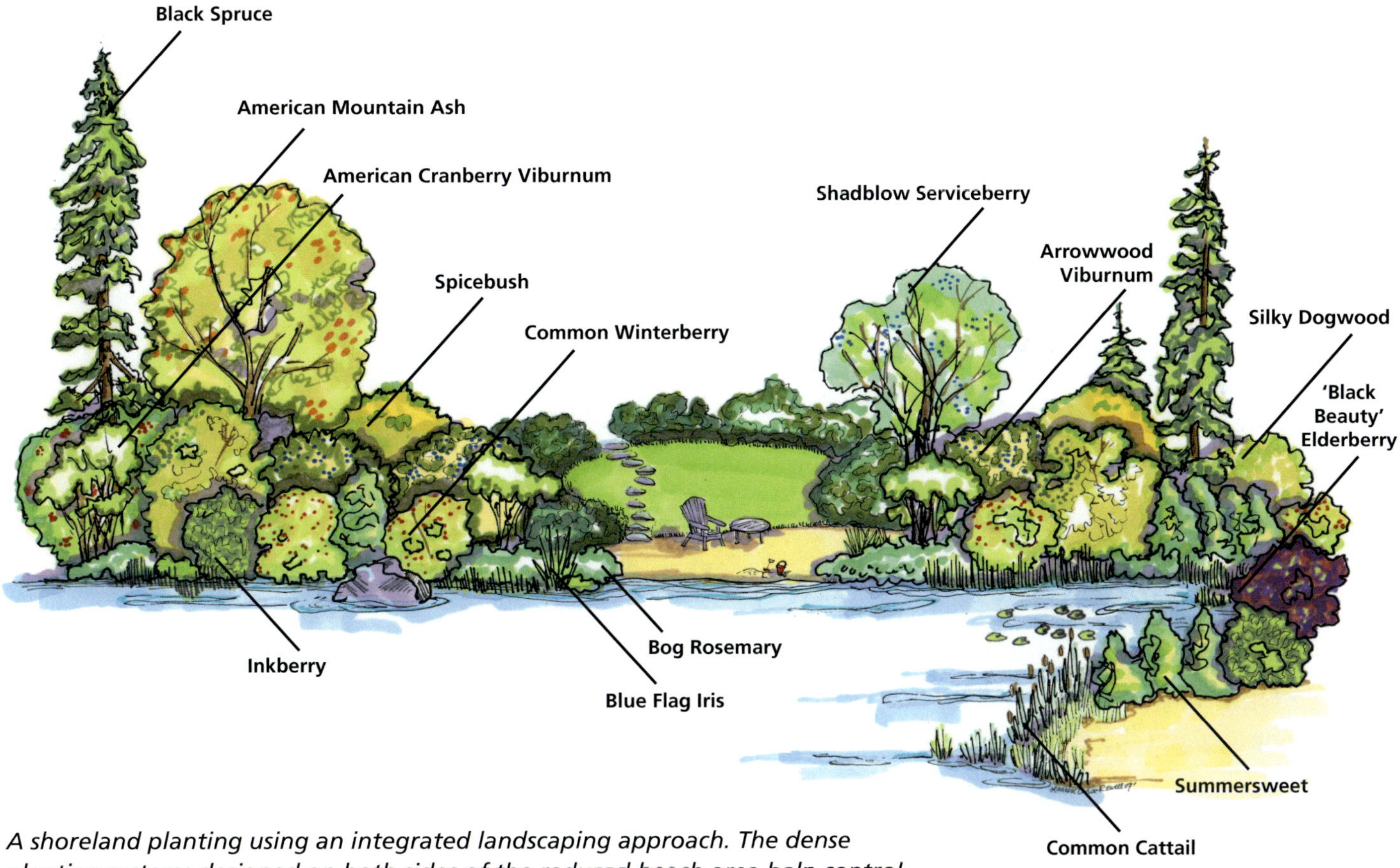

A shoreland planting using an integrated landscaping approach. The dense planting systems designed on both sides of the reduced beach area help control shoreline erosion, shade and cool shallow water for aquatic life, and provide abundant native species for wildlife.

Designing Landscapes with Establishment and Care in Mind

CHAPTER 5

The Plant Systems Approach

Locating and creating plant systems for the integrated landscape

Once you've formed the outdoor rooms on your trace map, it's time to locate plant systems on your conceptual plan and create them. As described earlier, a plant system is a collection of plants that imitate natural plant communities by adapting to the same growing conditions and growing in layers (some combination of groundcovers, grasses, perennials, vines, shrubs, understory, and overstory trees).

Why design with plant systems rather than simply adding a few of your favorite plants here and there? Because dense groupings of layered plants:

- Enhance wildlife habitat.
- Invite biodiversity and support local food webs.
- Increase root mass and soil stabilization.
- Enhance soil fertility.
- Conserve rainfall, reduce runoff, and protect water quality.
- Help prevent soil erosion.
- Recycle organic matter and nutrients.
- Resist pollution, drought, and environmental stress.

These biological and environmental benefits reflect the principles inherent in natural systems.

Plant systems also provide beauty and economic benefits. They:

- Allow you to include your favorite plants in the mix.
- Can provide shade in summer and windbreaks in winter.
- Reflect the character of the surrounding area.
- Offer year-round interest (through plant structure, fruit, bark, and flowers) and sequential bloom throughout the growing season.
- Minimize maintenance costs and labor.
- Channel snow away from walkways and driveways.
- Create an intentionally landscaped look using many native plants that support more species of wildlife than non-native plants.
- Shade parking areas
- Develop a sense of place.

Where to locate plant systems

To help you decide on where to locate plant systems, look back at your wish list of needs and desires and the bubble diagram. (See page 34.) Some obvious areas might be places where you want to create:

- Additional wildlife habitat.
- The "walls" of outdoor rooms.
- A protective buffer near any water bodies.
- A quiet sitting area.
- A softened edge along side of a building or fence.
- Focal points (e.g. within traffic islands).
- Biodiversity and human interest in place of unused lawn space or impervious surfaces.

Also, look for current functions on your site analysis, (see page 33), and see if there are any locations where plant systems can help:

- Decrease maintenance needs, which in turn decrease costs.
- Create attractive spaces in difficult areas such as a traffic island or steep slope.
- Replace invasive species with native species where possible. (See Appendix A.)
- Frame signage, an entrance, or the end of a walkway.
- Visually describe and organize an area for rest, recreation, or outdoor work.
- Provide interest at all times of the year.
- Filter water (in wet areas, on slopes).

Use your imagination to think of ways plant systems could enhance your existing landscape. For example, if you have a tree or shrub standing by itself in a lawn area, you may want to add plants around and beneath it to create a plant system.

It is also important to consider all the site factors when locating plant systems, including soil volume, especially in tight spaces within parking areas or along sidewalks. Large shade trees need much more soil volume than groundcovers, perennials, and shrubs.

The amount of water available is also a critical factor in locating plant systems. It makes sense to group plants together according to their water requirements. For dry, sandy areas, or areas you can't water regularly after planting, choosing drought-tolerant plants can help ensure their survival.

> **PLAN ENOUGH ROOTING SPACE FOR TREES**
>
> *Recommended root growth space is calculated using the maximum projected tree crown spread for each species expressed in feet. The figures for length and width are equal to 50% of the maximum projected tree crown spread; the depth dimension is uniformly three feet. For example, a sugar maple, Acer saccharum, with a maximum projected tree crown spread of 100 feet needs a recommended root growth space of approximately 50 feet x 50 feet x 3 feet for growth. If this amount of space isn't available on the property being considered, a sugar maple isn't the tree of choice for planting on that site; a smaller tree should be considered.*
>
> Source: Mary K. Reynolds and Raymond M. Boivin, *Selecting Trees for Urban Landscape Ecosystems: Hardy Species for Northern New England Communities*
>
>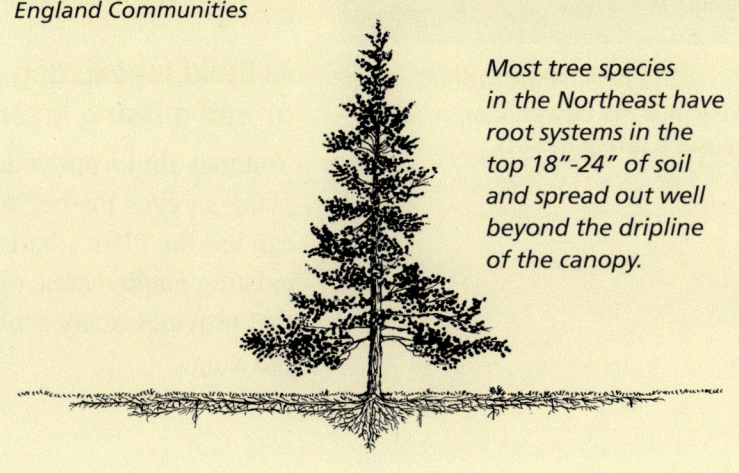
>
> *Most tree species in the Northeast have root systems in the top 18"-24" of soil and spread out well beyond the dripline of the canopy.*

Too big for the space, this tree interfered with the power lines. It was "topped," creating a path for disease and insects to invade. Always consider the mature size of the tree before planting.

This white pine, Pinus strobus, grew into the power lines, where it creates a safety hazard.

Add plant-system locations to your conceptual plan

Record areas on your conceptual plan where you could establish plant systems. Indicate the appropriate maximum height of mature layers in the system. Under windows, for example, you may need to choose plants that grow no taller than three feet at maturity, to prevent them from blocking windows. In areas where there are overhead utility wires, you may wish to include small trees to create an understory layer, but you would want to avoid taller, overstory trees that would need to be heavily pruned because of the interference with the wires. Hold off adding specific plants to the conceptual plan, as the next step will take you through the process of creating a plant system or systems to meet your needs.

Choosing plants for your system

There are several ways to go about creating a plant system for your property. Read over the options that follow and choose the one that makes the most sense for you.

Once you decide the best way to move forward, you will create a representation of that plant system on a planting plan. You may have many places where plant systems are appropriate or you may just have one small space. We suggest you choose one small area to start with and go from there. Once you have created one plant you may find it easier to create a second or to replicate the first system in other spaces.

To further help you, we have also developed 12 Plant-System Models. These models can help you visualize and apply the concept of layering and begin to understand how plants work together in both high-stress and low-stress settings.

Following the Plant-System Models, starting on page 90 you'll find an extensive Plant Chart. Each plant is listed with its mature size, hardiness zone, wildlife value, soil preferences, and sun exposure, along with additional comments.

Another helpful resource is the Plant Lists (Appendix B) that group plants by specific characteristics (e.g., purple-leafed plants, outstanding fall foliage, fruit-bearing, and flowering).

A. Build on existing plantings to develop a plant system or add missing layers.

You may find from your inventory that you already have many individual plants or even the beginnings of a plant system on the property. You can use the Plant Chart to select individual plants to incorporate into an existing planted area, creating your own multi-layered, bio-diverse system that provides many ecological services in addition to being aesthetically pleasing.

Case study:

Public Service of NH's Energy Park Integrated Landscaping Demonstration Site in Manchester is an example of this approach. The before picture shows a native pin oak by itself in the middle of a lawn area. A volunteer landscape committee enhanced the site by creating a plant system around the tree. The committee chose to add more trees, shrubs, perennials, and groundcovers, many that were native. The arrangement of this plant system encourages employees and visitors to stroll through the landscape or find a quiet area to sit among the plants. (To visit this demonstration site, see Acknowledgments, page vi.)

Left: This outdoor space at Public Service of New Hampshire's (PSNH) Energy Park in Manchester didn't attract many people or wildlife until they added a plant system and transformed the park into an integrated landscaping demonstration site. Middle and Right: PSNH with new integrated landscape. Below: Proposal for plant systems approach at PSNH Energy Park.

The Plant Systems Approach

B. Adopt a Plant-System Model.

We designed each of the 12 models starting on page 56 to fit a variety of site conditions and space needs. Choose a model plant system that best fits your property, site conditions, and conceptual plan. You can adjust the model to fit your space needs/desires (e.g., if your area is larger, you'll need more plants). You may want to duplicate the system with additional plants of the same species. You may also arrange the plants in a different configuration, such as along a building. Refer to the drawings of plant layouts starting on page 66 for ideas and guidance.

C. Adapt a model.

Because of the variability in site conditions and personal preferences, different sites call for different strategies. You can begin with these 12 models and customize them to your site. The Plant Chart starting on page 90 can help you find plants that provide a variety of characteristics. You may substitute certain plants from a model using the plants from this chart. Don't forget to design for a variety of uses. (Note: Some plants may be more available than others in garden centers or nurseries.)

> **Case study:**
> At the Grafton County Complex in North Haverhill, NH, UNH Cooperative Extension Master Gardeners created an Integrated Landscaping demonstration site in the middle of a large lawn area. They looked to the nearby river for inspiration, choosing river birches and using them as the focal point of their plant system. They included some of their favorite plants to add layers and included species especially valuable for wildlife. (To visit the Grafton County Site, see Acknowledgments, page vi.)
>
>
>
> *This lawn area at the Grafton County Complex in North Haverhill, NH, was transformed into an integrated landscaping demonstration site.*

D. Create your own plant systems by imitating nature's design.

If you are starting from scratch to plant an open area, you may want to use a good field guide to identify the key species in the plant communities nearby. You can then select plants that suit the local conditions and build on the native plant community, arranging the plants in layers and providing wildlife habitat.

The Plant Chart contains a column that specifies certain plants associated with their natural plant communities (although this is limited due the huge amount of plant associates). It may help you to mimic a chosen plant community. You may be interested in using all native plants to help retain a sense of place, or create a haven for wildlife by using layers of plants that all have high wildlife value. With site conditions in mind, you can mix and match plants from the different lists to create your own plant system. Just remember to incorporate as many vertical layers as possible and consider the plants' mature size, growth habit, and exposure needs. Plant systems can be very creative. Have fun!

> **Case study:**
> The natural landscape surrounding the NH Fish and Game headquarters in Concord, NH, is a pine-barrens community with an overstory layer that includes pitch pine, white pine, gray birch, and red maple; a shrub layer of serviceberry, huckleberry, and low-bush blueberry; a ground layer of teaberry and Canada mayflower; and a meadow edge with asters and goldenrod. To help the landscape connect to the surrounding plant community, and to demonstrate a schoolyard habitat project, the plant system design includes an overstory of paper birch with masses of grey dogwood, New Jersey tea, silky dogwood and bayberry as an understory, and sweep of sweetfern combined with the same three naturally-occuring groundcovers (lowbush blueberry, mayflower, and teaberry). Several clumps of little bluestem grasses 'The Blues' were planted through the ground plane. At the center, a two-tier pond provides water for wildlife and is planted with a combination of blue flag iris, and other submergent vegetation. A stonewall with lichens makes a good addition to this schoolyard demonstration plant system.
>
> The only enhancement made to the existing plant community is a selective thinning that leaves healthy plants characteristic of that community with enough space to flourish. Possible challenges such as dogwood sawfly can serve as educational investigations in the outdoor classroom for all grade levels.

When creating a plant system isn't appropriate

Existing natural ecosystems such as pockets of woodlands, swamps, bogs, and vernal pools already have functioning natural plant systems. Relatively undisturbed natural ecosystems will always function, regenerate, and filter better than those created by humans. In creating plant systems, we are trying to mimic the natural systems around us, so removing or altering healthy natural systems goes against the integrated landscaping practices we are trying to establish in our landscapes.

Relatively undisturbed natural ecosystems will always function, regenerate and filter better than those created by humans.

Dealing with invasive species

When an area has been disturbed or degraded significantly by human influences, one common effect is the invasion of oriental bittersweet, glossy buckthorn, autumn olive, Asian honeysuckles, multiflora rose, Norway maple, or other invasive species. In such cases you'll want to identify the invasive plants, make a plan for their removal and use the plant-system approach to help restore the area, ideally mimicking native plant communities that exist on or nearby the property. To learn more about eradicating invasive species, see Appendix D for a list of helpful resources.

Areas where invasives are removed need continuous monitoring. When plants are removed, sunlight is able to reach the newly exposed

In the fall these oriental bittersweet berries turn yellow and orange, a favorite for decorations. However, bittersweet is so invasive that it is even illegal to cut and use the berries for decoration or crafts. The pretty berries are viable plants, and when a centerpiece or wreath is thrown out, the seeds are eaten by birds to spread through their droppings, or sprout where they lie, climbing up and choking out other vegetation.

The Plant Systems Approach

Japanese knotweed, another highly invasive plant found along roadsides where mowing has occurred, can reproduce from just one small piece of stem. Mowing or cutting this plant can increase its spread.

pockets of soil, encouraging germination of the invasive plants' seeds. Once you've removed invasive plants, quickly establish a soil covering for those areas, including a mulch layer and groundcovers.

Not only do invasive plants out-compete native plant species, but they may not provide as nutritious a food source for native wildlife. If you remove an area of invasive plants that bear abundant fruit upon which wildlife—especially migrant birds—have come to depend, be sure to replace those invasive plants with native, fruit-bearing trees, shrubs, and vines. In this way, you will sustain the "bread basket" for those wild creatures.

Capturing desirable characteristics in your landscape

Invasive plants not only move into disturbed areas by various natural means of propagation, but humans (including the authors of this manual) have brought them into their landscapes as specimens prized for characteristics such as interesting foliage, fruit, form, size, and the ability to survive in a wide variety of conditions and settings with little maintenance.

Although such beautiful plants as burning bush, Japanese barberry, and Norway maple have been banned from sale in New Hampshire and Massachusetts, landscapers don't have to do without the many characteristics we all find desirable in these and other banned invasives.

In developing each of the 12 Plant-System Models that follow, we intentionally introduced many of these desirable characteristics, but in the collective form that a plant system can provide, rather than offering a plant-for-plant approach. With all their layers, shapes, textures, colors, fruits, forms, and ecological benefits, plant systems are far superior to those individuals and blocks of invasive plants that still inhabit many landscapes and quietly invade natural systems.

Case study:

At the Hislop Park Demonstration Site in Portsmouth, NH, the Atlantic Heights Garden Club created a plant system after removing a patch of Norway maple that had colonized the site. They looked into the site's history when it was known as "The Pines" and began to capture that concept in their newly established plant system, which includes native plants associated with a pine and oak forest. (To visit the Hislop Park site, see Acknowledgments, page vi.)

Left: *This "before" photo taken of Hislop Park in Portsmouth shows an almost pure stand of Norway maple with little to no regeneration of any plants below.*
Right: *A section of this Norway maple stand was cleared, and the Atlantic Heights Garden Club of Portsmouth replaced it with a plant system of mostly native species. The improved site design provides visual interest and wildlife habitat, and serves as a model for further removal and replacement of additional Norway maple throughout the park.*

ABOUT NATIVE VERSUS NON-NATIVE PLANTS

Native plants, as defined here, grow as part of natural ecosystems that have co-evolved within the same planting zone. In the Plant-System Models that follow we have included many plants native to the Northeastern U.S., as they tend to be more adaptable to site conditions found throughout New Hampshire. Natives meet critical habitat requirements for native wildlife, such as providing pollen, fruits, and seeds. They also help us better mimic natural ecosystems in landscapes and avoid introducing species that may become invasive.

In addition to native plants, we include some of our favorite "well-behaved" non-native/exotic plants that originated outside of the eastern U.S., but that provide high-value food for wildlife, reduce the need for maintenance, or possess desired aesthetic qualities. However, we deliberately don't list non-native *invasive* plants, as well as those documented as potentially invasive.

Many native and non-native plants listed in the Plant-System Models are available locally, and propagated by professional plant growers. Buy from reputable local dealers who propagate the plants they sell or who can tell you who did. Ask to make certain they weren't collected from the wild. Besides breaking laws, wild collecting disrupts plant communities and can cause their demise. (See Appendix A for best native plants for butterflies and moths.)

This native plant butterfly weed Asclepias tuberosa *attracts many species of butterflies and tolerates droughty conditions.*

For those of you who don't have invasive species on your site, but still yearn for that bright-red fall foliage that the now-illegal burning bush provides, look at the *Qualities* row in the Plant-Systems Models for those systems that provide great fall color, as well as other qualities such as fruit for wildlife. Another resource that provides some of these characteristics is the Plant Lists in Appendix B.

Plant systems for wildlife

While many people often think of structures such as bird feeders and nest boxes as the way to enhance wildlife habitat in general, layered plant systems with at least 80 percent native species will meet most wildlife needs. Besides providing food in the forms of flowers, seeds, fruits, and nuts, cover within trunks, branches and foliage, and even water from stems and leaves, plants also add aesthetic value to the landscape such as rich colors, sequence of bloom, and interesting forms.

Plants grow in association with other plants that require similar conditions of climate, light, soil, and moisture. Plants have evolved to adapt to certain conditions. The more you can mimic or encourage natural plant associations, the better your chances of creating ecologically complex, functional wildlife habitat.

The structure and type of vegetation also contribute to wildlife use of an area. The density, height, and shape of plants provide varying levels of cover and foraging opportunities for wildlife. The ground-level plants, the shrub layer, the middle-level trees and shrubs, and the upper canopy trees form the foundation of the forest ecosystem and wildlife habitat. Horizontal structure such as a field adjoining a forest is also important; encourage a gradual progression of plants from the edge of the field to the forest.

Layered plants around a fallen log add an artistic flair and critical habitat.

Other factors for functional wildlife habitat include structure (heights, shapes, and age classes of plants), patchiness (sun and shade, vertical and horizontal shapes), edge (zones of transition), size, special features (water, cavities, perches), and other organisms (competition and prey).

The ultimate aim is species-rich, environmentally diverse habitats. A monoculture of grass offers little in the way of wildlife habitat. Gradually reduce the size of lawn areas and replace them with more species-diverse meadows or fields or a full plant system.

All 12 Plant-System Models beginning on page 56 include wildlife food and cover plants. If you want to increase the abundance of good wildlife plants, refer to the descriptions that accompanies the system models, the plant charts, plant lists, and other plant resources in Appendix D.

To help you create a wildlife-friendly landscape when creating your own plant system, we suggest adding the following:

- A combination of evergreen and deciduous trees and shrubs with vines, groundcovers, and perennials, for a variety of layers and age classes of plants.

- As many native plants as possible (at least 80 percent). See Appendices A and B.

- Fruit or nut bearing plants, and plants that produce flowers or seeds at different times of the year (you may also supplement with bird feeders).

- Flowering ornamentals (cherries, plums, crabapples), which usually blossom during the time when many insect-eating migrants are passing through and will attract pollinating insects.

- Densely branched shrubs and evergreen cover to shelter birds from neighborhood cats and other predators.

This natural ecosystem includes many of the characteristics we try to mimic in integrated landscaping plant systems to provide diverse wildlife habitat: horizontal structure, a gradual progression of plants from the edge of the field to the forest, patchiness, perches, and water.

This plant system began by planting two crabapples; over time shrubs and perennials were added beneath, creating layers, enhancing habitat and aesthetics, and reducing lawn size.

This perennial plant, purple coneflower Echinacea purpurea, self seeds and has a long flowering period providing nectar for many types of pollinators.

- Perennials and wildflowers that add color to your garden, and summer nectar and fall seeds for wildlife in your yard.

- Coniferous evergreens such as spruce, fir, and hemlock to protect over-wintering animals from snow, ice, rain, and wind. These provide important cover for migrant birds and key nesting places for birds in spring.

- Stone walls to provide escape for small mammals such as squirrels, hares, and chipmunks.

- A water source such as a small pond or birdbath set on the ground, shallow running water or wet gravel or pebbles which will benefit a variety of wildlife from birds to butterflies to amphibians. (Clean a birdbath regularly or install a circulating pump in a pond to discourage mosquitoes from laying eggs.)

- Diverse litter layers to protect and conserve a diversity of microorganisms. Use on-site resources for mulch and compost.

- Snags (dead or dying trees) with cavities to provide nesting sites for birds and small mammals. Woodpeckers will excavate a hole in the snag to find insects. Other cavity nesters such as tree swallows will adopt the hole for nesting. (To avoid accidents, keep a dead or dying tree away from the house and other areas of ongoing human use.)

- Where cavities aren't available, build a nest box designed for the species you want to support.

The recommended practices for low maintenance on page 118 will benefit wildlife as well, enabling the site to support an array of wildlife and help recover some of the rapidly disappearing natural landscapes that define the character of New Hampshire.

In these ways, you create a garden plant community that mimics a natural plant community, while providing different options for wildlife at different times of the year. See Appendix D for further readings on planting for wildlife.

Include evergreens in plant systems. Even evergreen shrubs such as this mugo pine, Pinus mugo, *provide winter protection and nesting opportunities.*

"Let sleeping logs lie." Follow nature's lead and add fallen logs to your plant systems. Amphibians such as salamanders and toads need the cool, damp shelter of leaf litter and rotting logs. As the logs decompose, they will also add organic matter to the soil.

ATTRACTING WILDLIFE MAY ALSO ATTRACT INVASIVE PLANTS

Let's assume you've chosen to attract wildlife by planting native species and some fruit-bearing non-natives such as crabapple. Two years later, you find your landscape has produced a healthy crop of invasive plant seedlings. What's happening? Chances are invasive plants are still thriving in surrounding yards, lots and woodlands. By attracting birds and other wildlife to your property, you inadvertently end up bringing in invasive plants, as wildlife eat the rose hips of the multiflora rose down the road and then travel to your landscape to eat crabapples and defecate the seeds. Rather than discouraging wildlife, understand that this will happen and plan for it. Keep soil covered as much as possible to stop germination of invasives. Learn to recognize the seedlings of invasive plants so you can remove them while they're still young. Remember that wildlife also feed off native plants and help disperse their seeds as well.

Invasive seedlings like this multiflora rose can get a foothold even in mature plant systems. Keep your eye out for invasive seedlings and remove when small.

WILDLIFE GARDENING BASICS

Think of your site as a mini-ecosystem.

- Food + water + cover + space = Habitat
- Mimic natural communities.
- Increase diversity by increasing variety and layers of vegetation.
- Work with existing conditions.
- Leave logs, rocks, leaves and snags in place.
- Reduce lawn.
- Cooperate with neighbors to create corridors and unfragmented patches.
- Because the landscape is constantly changing, allow yours to remain a work in progress.

The Plant-System models

After choosing the best option for your needs, look over the 12 Plant-System models descriptions starting on page 58. These models can help you apply the concepts of layering and visualize how plants work together in both high-stress and low-stress settings. The models were originally designed to provide alternatives to three popular but invasive species—Norway maple, burning bush, and Japanese barberry—in a variety of site conditions:

- Droughty areas such as medians, sandy, or shallow soil.

- Wet areas or rain gardens. (See sidebar below.)

- Tight spaces that virtually act as "glorified containers" (e.g., islands within parking lots or the planting space between a road and sidewalk).

- Low-stress settings such as a backyard.

In some locations, you might not be able to include all layers in a plant system. For example, because of their eventual size, shade trees probably wouldn't work in a tight space against a building. As an alternative you might choose to increase the diversity of plants within the layers the site will accommodate.

Each of the 12 models combines the characteristics that made these three invasive species so popular, including their ability to adapt to high-stress sites. The models and the plant lists capture the desirable characteristics, including color, form, size, wildlife habitat, and survivability that you may want to bring into your plant system.

We've presented the 12 models, a set of descriptions, and a matrix. Eight of these 12 are illustrated. To supplement this information, we also provide you with a Plant Chart and Plant Lists. These last two items will allow you to create your own systems by selecting plants with specific characteristics.

Matrix and Descriptions

We've organized the Matrix by *settings* and *qualities*. The settings include three high-stress conditions—drought, wet/rain garden, and containerized—and a single low-stress condition—a residential yard. Plant qualities mimic those provided by the invasives we intend to replace.

To select a model from the Matrix (see page 57) that meets the needs of your site, look across the top for the column heading "Settings." Then look down the left side for the row of "Qualities" you may wish to include. Where this setting column and quality row intersect is a plant system model that will fit your site.

> **RAIN GARDENS**
>
> Rain gardens are an innovative approach to capturing significant amounts of stormwater runoff through natural processes. Rain gardens are shallow depressions usually four to eight inches deep and planted with water-tolerant species. Their shallow depth allows water to infiltrate the soil quickly rather than "ponding" on the surface. Rain gardens are typically sited in areas that rainwater drains to—the edge of a parking lot, near down spouts or areas of roof runoff, areas down slope from buildings and other impervious surfaces—to filter pollutants before they can enter streams, ponds, lakes or other water bodies. Along with the plants listed in Plant-System Models #4 - #6, many of the shoreline plants listed in the Shoreline Plant Chart in Appendix E would make great choices for rain gardens. For more information on creating rain gardens see Appendix D.
>
> *In 2006 the city of Nashua, NH, created this rain garden on the edge of the Public Works Facility parking lot. Both the rain garden and the permeable pavement of the parking lot catch runoff. Such methods help reduce pollutants such as fertilizers, pesticides, petroleum products, industrial chemicals, sediments, salts, and animal wastes from entering and contaminating the nearby Nashua River.*

The Plant Systems Approach

Next, go to the Plant-System Model Descriptions (see page 58). The 12 models in the Matrix are laid out sequentially from 1-12. Find the number you selected, and you will get a complete description of that model. For instance, Plant-System Model #3 could tolerate a full-sun, drought setting and would include the desirable characteristics of a Japanese barberry. It includes New Jersey tea for a low shrub; weigela for red-colored leaves; winterberry holly or sweetspire for wildlife fruits; chokecherry for red color and fruits; and mountain lover, sweetfern and little bluestem grass to fill the groundcover layer. Adding Colorado blue spruce can provide a tall conifer for the canopy layer. (*Note: Most models include a shade tree. You may leave these out in situations where a large tree is not appropriate.*)

Illustrations

The illustrations provide four views that can help you create an accurate, well-proportioned planting plan.

- First, the color-concept illustration gives you a sense of the finished product. It brings texture, depth, color, and realistic attributes to the planting plan. These artist's renderings focus on the primary plants in each system (trees, shrubs, vines, groundcovers), and do not necessarily include all the suggested perennials or grasses.

- Second, the **conceptual elevation** identifies the species. The realistic habits and forms of landscape elements get sketched inside the boxes.

- The third illustration, a **scale diagram**, shows you the relative sizes of the plants at maturity. This box-elevation schematic originates from the same horizontal base and is drawn to the same scale as the plan view. Squares and rectangles are drawn to encompass not only the full width but also the height of all plants at maturity. The box-elevation helps you visualize all the layers, including groundcovers, and notes the line of the ground plane. Proposed berms or swales show as an uneven baseline.

- Fourth, the **plan view** shows how to lay the plants out in a planting bed. This illustration places circles depicting plants on your plan where needed. The circle represents the mature width of the plant and enough space to accommodate its future growth. Symbols used show the quantity and placement of different species, as well as the placement of evergreen and deciduous materials. (A rule of thumb says that about one-third of all plants may be evergreen to promote winter interest and mimic natural patterns of New Hampshire's evergreen/deciduous ratio.) Circles are positioned so they line up in staggered sweeps, curves and random patterns, suggesting a more informal natural planting. The plan view is a great layout tool, but it doesn't show heights.

Using all four of these illustrations will give you a clearer understanding of the eventual outcome of your planting plan.

Matrix of Plant System Models

Qualities	Settings			
Invasive Plants	Drought	Wet	"Container"	Low Stress
similar to Crimson King Norway Maple	Model 1	Model 4	Model 7	Model 10
similar to Burning Bush	Model 2	Model 5	Model 8	Model 11
similar to Japanese Barberry	Model 3	Model 6	Model 9	Model 12

Plant-System Model Descriptions

Model 1

Setting: drought

Conditions: salt, heat, wind, drought, sun, sand (Examples: traffic circle, median, playground, sunny border, parking lot, along street)

Qualities: red/maroon foliage, salt tolerance, street trees, such as found in Crimson King Norway Maple *Acer platanoides 'Crimson King'*

Plant List

Trees:
Schubert Flowering Cherry *Prunus virginiana 'Schubert'*
Eastern Red Cedar *Juniperus virginiana*

Shrubs/Vines:
Virginia Creeper *Parthenocissus quinquefolia*
Gray Dogwood *Cornus racemosa*
Diablo Common Ninebark *Physocarpus opulifolius 'Diablo'*
Lowbush Blueberry *Vaccinium angustifolium*

Groundcovers/Grasses:
Pennsylvania Sedge *Carex pensylvanica*
Effusa Common Juniper *Juniperus communis 'Effusa'*
Black Crowberry *Empetrum nigrum*
Candytuft *Iberis sempervirens*

Perennials:
Beard-tongue or Penstemon *Penstemon spp.*
Blue-eyed Grass *Sisyrinchium spp.*
Golden Alexander *Zizia aptera*
Butterfly Weed *Asclepias tuberosa*

Model 2

Setting: drought

Conditions: salt, heat, wind, drought, sun, sand (Examples: traffic circle, median, playground, sunny border, parking lot, along street)

Qualities: red to pink fall foliage, salt tolerance, neat form, red-yellow-orange fruit, interesting twigs, such as found in Burning Bush *Euonymous alatus*

Plant List

Trees:
Shadblow, Serviceberry *Amelanchier canadensis*

Shrubs/Vines:
Gray Dogwood *Cornus racemosa*
Mountain Laurel *Kalmia latifolia*

The Plant Systems Approach

Compact American Cranberry Viburnum *Viburnum trilobum 'Compactum'*
Lowbush Blueberry *Vaccinium angustifolium*

Groundcovers/grasses:
Pennsylvania Sedge *Carex pensylvanica*

Perennials:
Big Leaf Aster *Aster macrophylla*
Stonecrop *Sedum spectabile*
Barren Strawberry *Waldstenia fragarioides*
Big Root Geranium *Geranium macrorrhizum*

Model 3

Setting: drought

Conditions: salt, heat, wind, drought, sun, sand
(Examples: traffic circle, median, playground, sunny border, parking lot, along street)

Qualities: red fall foliage, low growing, neat form, fruit, as seen in Japanese Barberry *Berberis thunbergii*

Plant List

Trees:
None listed

Shrubs/Vines:
New Jersey Tea *Ceanothus americanus*
Java Red Weigela *Weigela florida 'Java Red'*
Colorado Blue Spruce *Picea pungens 'Montgomery'*
Virginia Sweetspire *Itea virginica 'Henry's Garnet'*
Chokecherry *Prunus virginiana*
Sweetfern *Comptonia peregrina*

Groundcovers/Grasses:
Little Bluestem *Schizachyrium scoparium*
Cliff Green, Oregon Boxwood, Mountain Lover *Paxistima canbyi*

Perennials:
Blue False Indigo *Baptisia australis*
Blazing Star *Liatris spicata*
Oxeye Sunflower *Heliopsis helianthoides*

Model 4

Setting: wet, rain garden

Conditions: wet to intermittent, pollutants, compacted soils
(Examples: stormwater area, backyard rain garden, swale, infiltration bed, naturally wet area)

Qualities: red/maroon foliage, salt tolerance, street trees, such as found in Crimson King Norway Maple *Acer platanoides 'Crimson King'*

Plant List

Trees:
Black Gum *Nyssa sylvatica*
Or
Red Maple *Acer rubrum*
Black Spruce *Picea mariana*

Shrubs/Vines:
Sweet Gale *Myrica gale*
Speckled Alder *Alnus incana subsp. rugosa*
Meadowsweet *Spirea alba var. latifolia*
Or
Steeplebush *Spirea tomentosa*
Spicebush *Lindera benzoin*

Groundcovers/Grasses:
Creeping Phlox *Phlox stolonifera*

Perennials:
Blue Flag Iris *Iris versicolor*
Cardinal Flower *Lobelia cardinalis*
Joe Pye Weed *Eupatorium maculatum*
Swamp Milkweed *Asclepias incarnata*

Model 5

Setting: wet, rain garden

Conditions: wet to intermittent, pollutants, compacted soils
(Examples: stormwater area, backyard rain garden, swale, infiltration bed, naturally wet area)

Qualities: red to pink fall foliage, salt tolerance, neat form, red-yellow-orange fruit, interesting twigs, such as found in Burning Bush *Euonymous alatus*

Plant List

Trees:
River Birch *Betula nigra*

Shrubs/vines:
Silky Dogwood *Cornus amomum*
Winterberry Holly (male) *Ilex verticillata*
Black Chokeberry *Aronia melanocarpa*
Or
Red Chokeberry *Aronia arbutifolia*
Red Sprite Winterberry Holly *Ilex verticillata* 'Red Sprite'

Groundcovers/grasses:
Bunchberry *Cornus canadensis*
Sheep Laurel *Kalmia angustifolia*

Perennials:
Bluebead Lily *Clintonia borealis*
Jack-in-the-pulpit *Arisaema triphyllum*
Whorled Aster *Aster acuminatus*

Model 6

Setting: wet, rain garden

Conditions: wet to intermittent, pollutants, compacted soils
(Examples: stormwater area, backyard rain garden, swale, infiltration bed, naturally wet area)

Qualities: red fall foliage, low growing, neat form, fruit, as seen in Japanese Barberry *Berberis thunbergii*

Plant List

Trees:
Shadblow, Serviceberry *Amelanchier canadensis*
Or
Pagoda Dogwood *Cornus alternifolia* as a transition tree, will tolerate wet feet

Shrubs/vines:
Diablo Common Ninebark *Physocarpus opulifolius 'Diablo'*
Or
Pinkshell Azalea *Rhododendron vaseyi*
Winterberry Holly (male) *Ilex verticillata*
Swamp Rose *Rosa palustris*
Red Osier Dogwood *Cornus sericea (stolonifera)*
Winterberry Holly *Ilex verticillata 'Red Sprite'*
Inkberry *Ilex glabra*

Groundcovers/grasses:
Bunchberry Dogwood *Cornus canadensis*
False Hellebore *Veratrum viride*

Perennials:
Marsh Marigold *Caltha palustris*
Turtlehead *Cheloni lyonii*
Bottle Gentian *Gentiana clausa*
Blazing Star, Gayfeather *Liatris spicata*
New York Ironweed *Veronia noveboracensis*

Model 7

Setting: "glorified container"

Conditions: small contained spaces, droughty, compacted soils
(Examples: traffic island, median, traffic circle, sidewalk cut)

Qualities: red/maroon foliage, salt tolerance, street trees, such as found in Crimson King Norway Maple *Acer platanoides 'Crimson King'*

Plant List

Trees:
Japanese Pagoda Tree *Styphnolobium japonicum (Sophora japonica)*

Shrubs/vines:
Slender Deutzia *Duetzia gracilis*
Common Ninebark *Physocarpus opulifolius 'Nugget'*
Summersweet Clethra *Clethra alnifolia 'Ruby Spice'*
Nelly Moser Clematis *Clematis 'Nelly Moser'*

Groundcovers/grasses:
Blue Fescue *Festuca ovina var. 'Glauca'*
Scotch Heather *Calluna vulgaris 'Martha Herman'*
Calluna vulgaris 'Gold Haze'
Calluna vulgaris 'Springtorch'
Calluna vulgaris 'County Wicklow'

Perennials:
Coral Bells *Heuchera micrantha 'Palace Purple'*
Fringed Bleeding Heart *Dicentra eximia*

Model 8

Setting: "glorified container"

Conditions: small contained spaces, droughty, compacted soils
(Examples: traffic island, median, traffic circle, sidewalk cut)

Qualities: red to pink fall foliage, salt tolerance, neat form, red-yellow-orange fruit, interesting twigs, such as found in Burning Bush *Euonymous alatus*

Plant List

Trees:
Jack Pine *Pinus banksiana*

Shrubs/vines:
Pasture Rose *Rosa carolina*
Fragrant Sumac *Rhus aromatica*
Common Juniper *Juniperus communis*

Groundcovers/grasses:
Bearberry *Arctostaphylos uva-ursi*
Creeping Thyme *Thymus praecox (serphyllum)*

Perennials:
Asters *Aster spp.*
Purple Coneflower *Echinacea purpurea*
Siberian Barren Strawberry *Waldstenia ternata*
Goldenrods *Solidago spp.*

Model 9

Setting: "glorified container"

Conditions: small contained spaces, droughty, compacted soils
(Examples: traffic island, median, traffic circle, sidewalk cut)

Qualities: red fall foliage, low growing, neat form, fruit, as seen in
Japanese Barberry *Berberis thunbergii*

Plant List

Trees:
Black Hills (White) Spruce *Picea glauca 'Densata'*

Shrubs/Vines:
Shadblow, Serviceberry *Amelanchier canadensis*
Red Chokeberry *Aronia arbutifolia 'Brilliantissima'*
Beach Plum *Prunus maritima*
Bayberry *Myrica pensylvanica*
Lowbush blueberry *Vaccinium angustifolium*

Groundcovers/Grasses:
Bearberry *Arctostaphylos uva-ursi*
Common Juniper *Juniperus communis 'Repanda'*
Blue Grama Grass *Bouteloua gracilis*
Or
Crinkled Hair Grass *Deschampsia flexuosa*
Switch Grass *Panicum virgatum 'Hanse Herms'*

Perennials:
Asters *Aster spp.*

Model 10

Setting: low stress

Conditions: decent soil, sun and shade exposure, low compaction, protected from salt
(Examples: residential yard, very large planting bed)

Qualities: red/maroon foliage, salt tolerance, street trees, such as found in Crimson King
Norway Maple *Acer platanoides 'Crimson King'*

Plant List

Trees:
River's Purple Beech *Fagus sylvatica 'Riversii'*

Shrubs/vines:
American Cranberry Viburnum *Viburnum trilobum*
Common Ninebark *Physocarpus opulifolius 'Dart's Gold'*
Pinxter Azalea *Rhododendron periclymenoides (nudiflorum)*
Mountain Laurel *Kalmia latifolia* (w)
Colorado Blue Spruce *Picea pungens 'Montgomery'*

The Plant Systems Approach

Groundcovers/grasses:
Junipers *Juniperus communis 'Effusa'* or 'Green Carpet'
Dwarf Japanese Garden Juniper *Juniperus procumbens 'Nana'*

Perennials:
Running Tapestry Foamflower *Tiarella cordifolia 'Running Tapestry'*
Blue-eyed Mary *Omphalodes verna*

Model 11

Setting: low stress

Conditions: decent soil, sun and shade exposure, low compaction, protected from salt (Example: residential yard, very large planting bed)

Qualities: red to pink fall foliage, salt tolerance, neat form, red-yellow-orange fruit, interesting twigs, such as found in Burning Bush *Euonymous alatus*

Plant List

Trees:
Persian Parrotia or Persian Ironwood *Parrotia persica*

Shrubs/vines:
Redvein Enkianthus *Enkianthus campanulatus*
Coast Leucothoe *Leucothoe axillaris*
Dwarf Fothergilla *Fothergilla gardenii*

Groundcovers/grasses:
Bird's Nest Spruce *Picea abies 'Nidiformis'*
Or
Dwarf Pine *Pinus strobus 'Soft Touch'*
Evergreen Candytuft *Iberis sempervirens*
Sweet Woodruff *Galium odoratum*

Perennials:
Wild Ginger *Asarum canadensis*
Foamflower *Tiarella cordifolia*
Ostrich Fern *Matteuccia struthiopteris*
Christmas Fern *Polystichum acrostichoides*

Model 12

Setting: low stress

Conditions: decent soil, sun and shade exposure, low compaction, protected from salt (Example: residential yard, very large planting bed)

Qualities: red fall foliage, low growing, neat form, fruit, as seen in Japanese Barberry *Berberis thunbergii*

Plant List

Trees:
None listed

Shrubs/vines:
Golden Elder Elderberry *Sambucus canadensis* 'Aurea'
Or
Black Beauty Elder *Sambucus nigra* 'Black Beauty'
Kalm's St. Johnswort *Hypericum kalmianum*
Blue Mist Spirea *Caryopteris x clandonensis*
Winter Gem Boxwood *Buxus microphylla* 'Wintergem'

Groundcovers/grasses:
Running Tapestry Foamflower *Tiarella cordifolia* 'Running Tapestry'

Perennials:
Chocolate Chip Bugleweed *Ajuga x* 'Chocolate Chip'
Brunette Bugbane or Baneberry *Actea racemosa* 'Brunette'
Brit-Marie Crawford Ligularia *Ligularia dentata* 'Brit-Marie Crawford'
Chocolate Joe Pye Weed *Eupatorium rugosum* 'Chocolate'

(Note: The following Plant Model illustrations are artist renditions by Marilyn Wyzga.)

The Plant Systems Approach

Model 1

Conceptual Elevation View

Scale Diagram or Box Elevation View

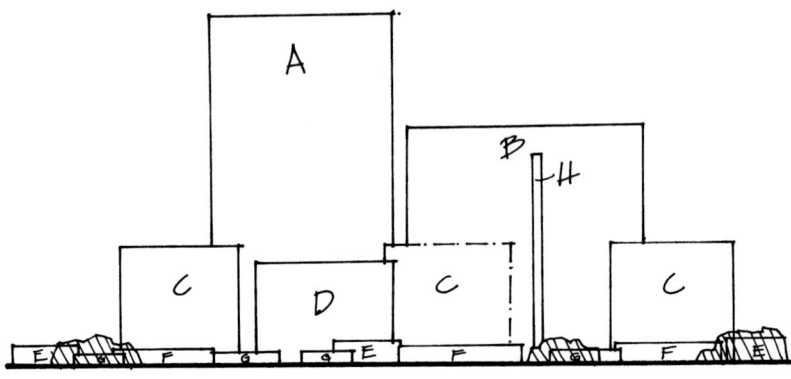

Planting Plan View

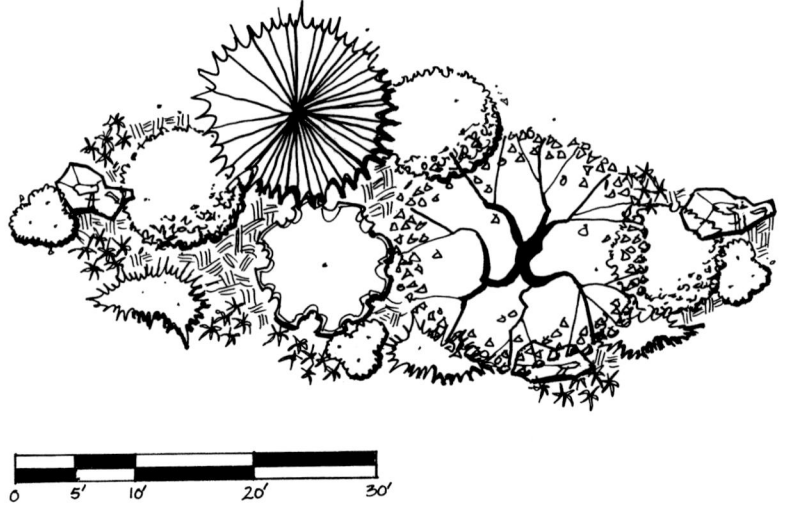

A Eastern Red Cedar *Juniperus virginiana* (1)

B 'Schubert' Flowering Cherry *Prunus virginiana 'Schubert'* (1)

C Gray Dogwood *Cornus racemosa* (3)

D Diablo Common Ninebark *Physocarpus opulifolius 'Diablo'* (1)

E Lowbush Blueberry *Vaccinium angustifolium* (9)

F Effusa Common Juniper *Juniperus communis 'Effusa'* (3)

G Pennsylvania Sedge *Carex pensylvanica* (30)

H Virginia Creeper *Parthenocissus quinquefolia* (1)

I Butterfly Weed *Asclepia tuberosa* (3)

Model 1
Shown in spring

- A Eastern Red Cedar
- B 'Schubert' Flowering Cherry
- C Gray Dogwood
- D Diablo Common Ninebark
- E Lowbush Blueberry
- F Effusa Common Juniper
- G Pennsylvania Sedge
- H Virginia Creeper
- I Butterfly Weed

Model 2

Conceptual Elevation View

Scale Diagram or Box Elevation View

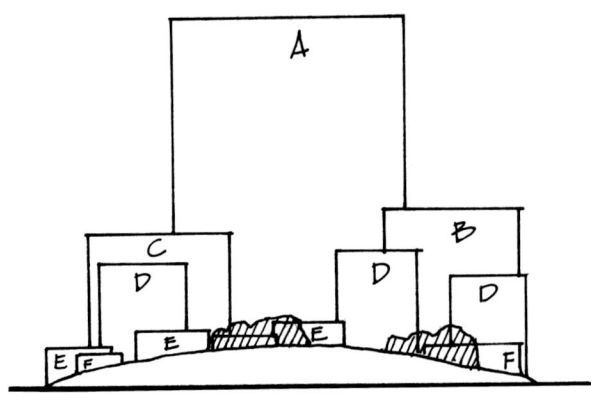

Planting Plan View

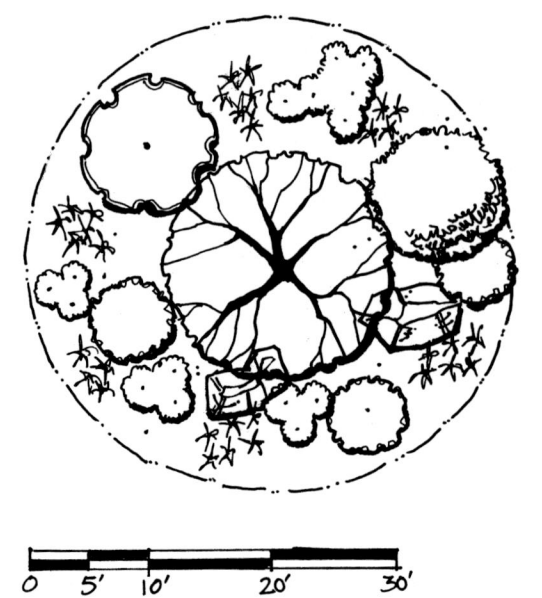

0 5' 10' 20' 30'

A Shadblow, Serviceberry *Amelanchier canadensis (1)*

B Gray Dogwood *Cornus racemosa (1)*

C American Cranberry Viburnum *Viburnum trilobum (1)*

D Mountain Laurel *Kalmia latifolia (3)*

E Lowbush Blueberry *Vaccinium angustifolium (15)*

F Pennsylvania Sedge *Carex pensylvanica (30)*

Model 2
Shown in summer

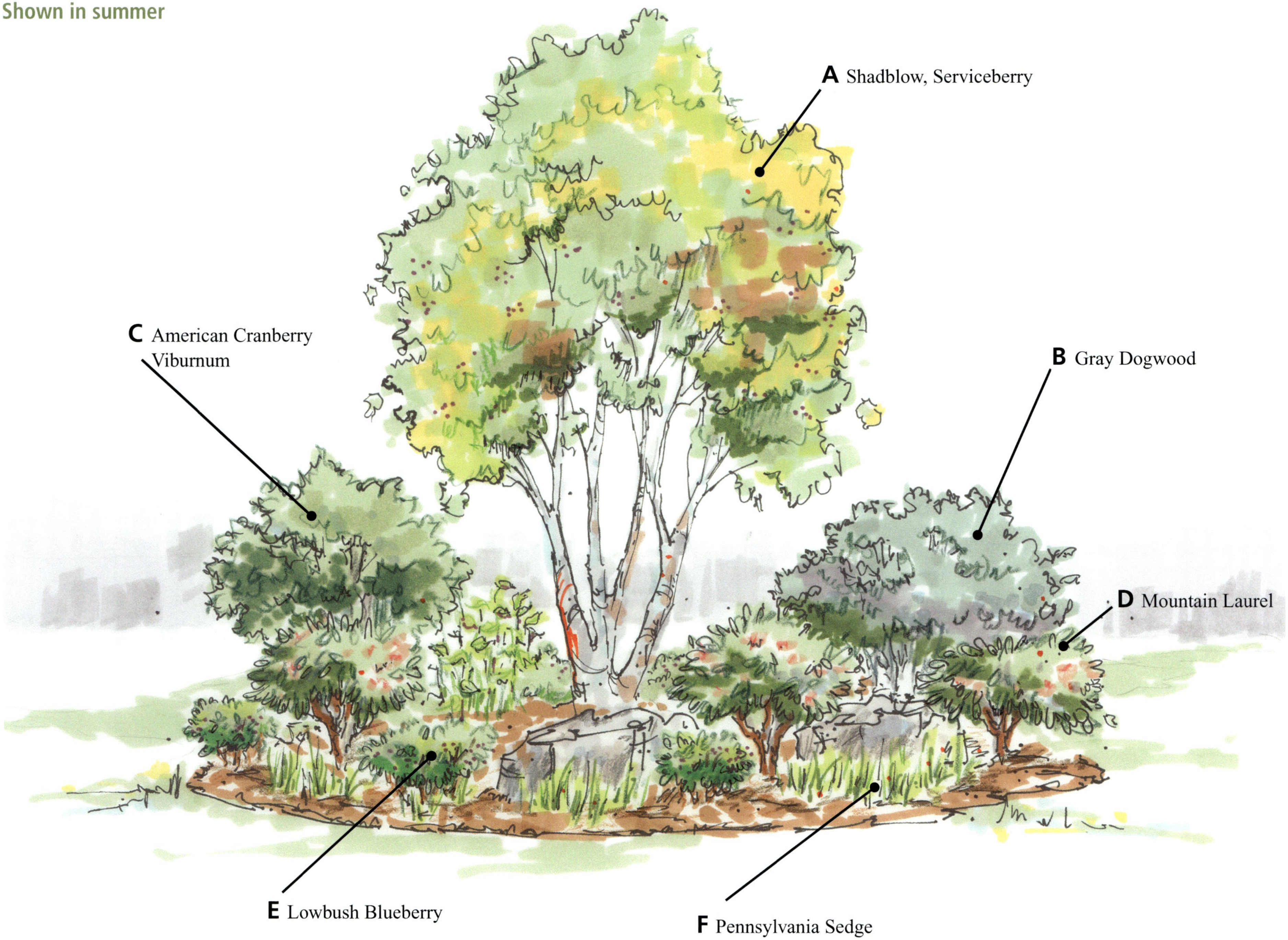

A Shadblow, Serviceberry
B Gray Dogwood
C American Cranberry Viburnum
D Mountain Laurel
E Lowbush Blueberry
F Pennsylvania Sedge

Model 3

Conceptual Elevation View

Scale Diagram or Box Elevation View

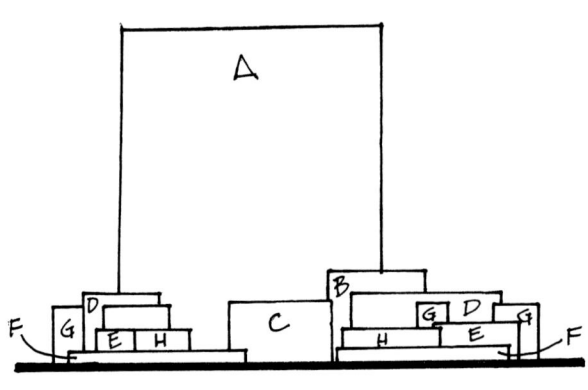

Planting Plan View

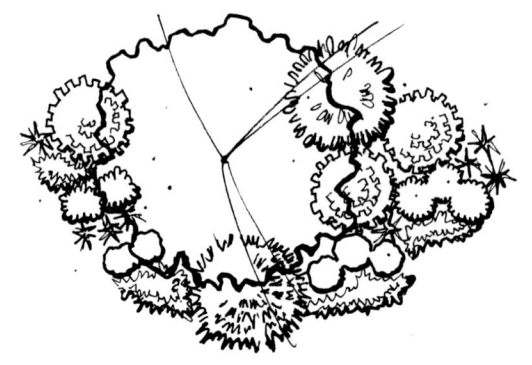

A Chokecherry *Prunus virginiana* (1)

B Java Red Weigela *Weigela florida* 'Java Red' (1)

C Colorado Blue Spruce *Picea punguns* 'Montgomery' (1)

D Virginia Sweetspire *Itea virginica* 'Henry's Garnet' (3)

E New Jersey Tea *Ceanothus americanus* (5)

F Cliff Green *Paxistima canbyi* (18)

G Little Bluestem *Schizachyrium scoparium* (8)

H Sweetfern *Comptonia peregrina* (5)

Model 3
Shown in fall

Model 4

Conceptual Elevation View

Scale Diagram or Box Elevation View

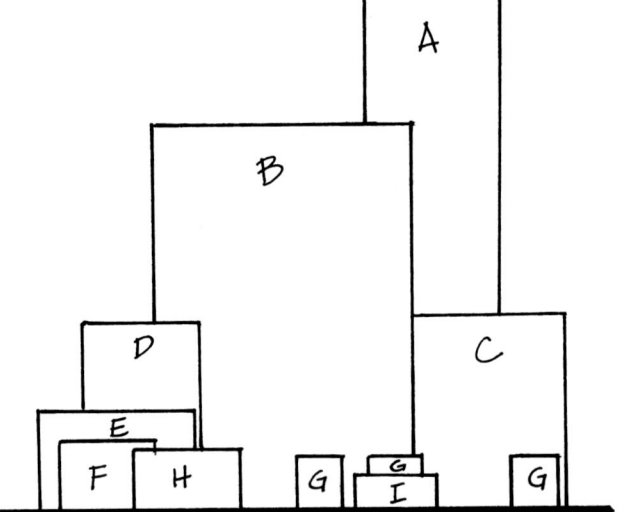

Planting Plan View

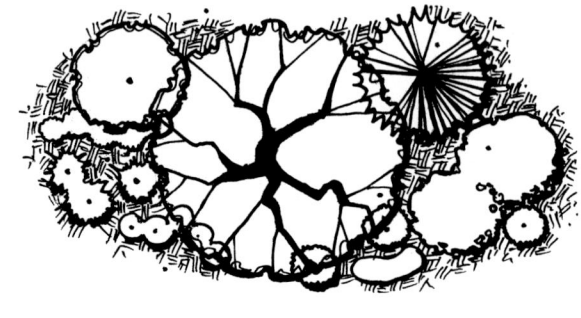

A Black Spruce *Picea mariana (1)*

B Black Gum *Nyssa sylvatica (1)*

C Spicebush *Lindera benzoin (2) (male & female)*

D Speckled Alder *Alnus incana subsp. rugosa (1)*

E Joe Pye Weed *Eupatorium maculatum (5)*

F Sweet Gale *Myrica gale (2)*

G Meadowsweet *Spirea alba var. latifolia (3)*

H Swamp Milkweed *Asclepias incarnata (5)*

I Cardinal Flower *Lobelia cardinalis (4)*

Model 4

Shown in early fall

- **A** Black Spruce
- **B** Black Gum
- **C** Spicebush
- **D** Speckled Alder
- **E** Joe Pye Weed
- **F** Sweet Gale
- **G** Meadowsweet
- **H** Swamp Milkweed

Model 5

Conceptual Elevation View

Scale Diagram or Box Elevation View

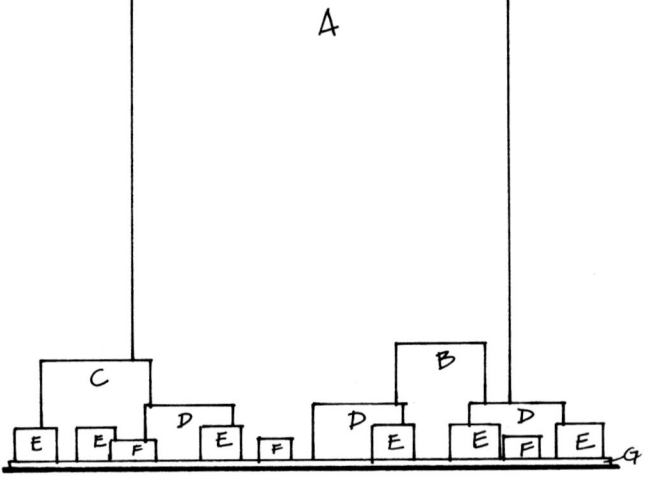

Planting Plan View

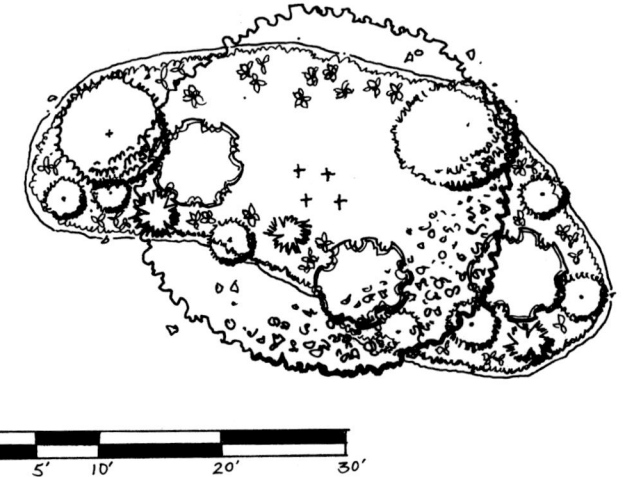

A River Birch *Betula nigra (1)*

B Silky Dogwood *Cornus amomum (1)*

C Winterberry Holly *Ilex verticillata, (male) (1)*

D Black Chokeberry *Aronia melanocarpa (3)*

E Red Sprite Winterberry Holly *Ilex verticillata 'Red Sprite' (7)*

F Sheep Laurel *Kalmia angustifolia (3)*

G Bunchberry *Cornus canadensis (24)*

Model 5
Shown in fall

Model 6

Conceptual Elevation View

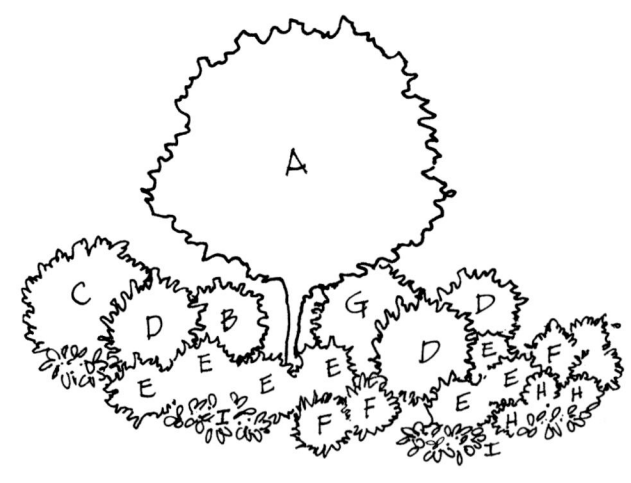

Scale Diagram or Box Elevation View

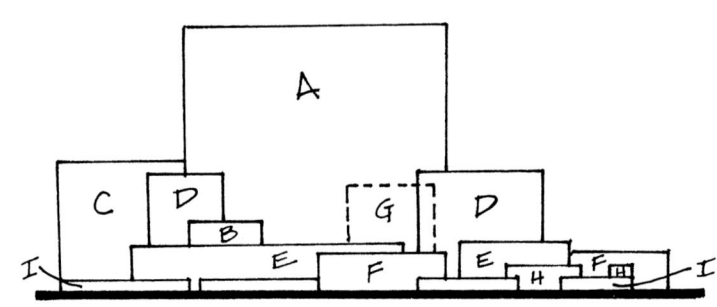

Planting Plan View

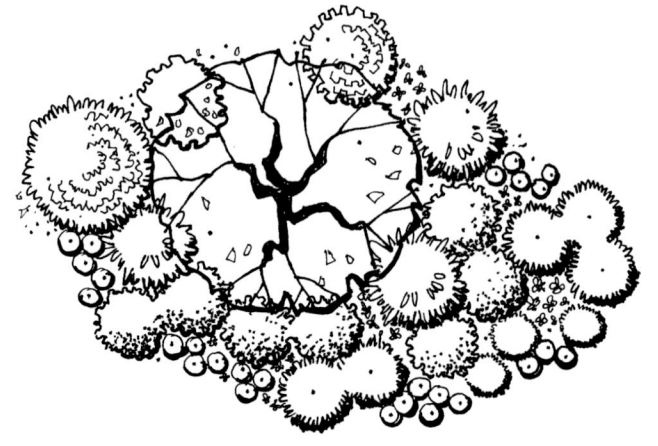

A Pagoda Dogwood *Cornus alternifolia (1)*

B Pinkshell Azalea *Rhododendron vaseyi (1)*

C Winterberry Holly *Ilex verticillata (male) (1)*

D Red Osier Dogwood *Cornus sericea (stolonifera) (3)*

E Swamp Rose *Rosa palustris (7)*

F Winterberry Holly *Ilex verticillata 'Red Sprite' (5)*

G Inkberry *Ilex glabra (1)*

H Sheep Laurel *Kalmia angustifolia (3)*

I Bunchberry *Cornus canadensis (27)*

Model 6
Shown in late fall

A Pagoda Dogwood
B Pinkshell Azalea
C Winterberry Holly
D Red Osier Dogwood
E Swamp Rose
F Red Sprite Winterberry Holly
G Inkberry
H Sheep Laurel
I Bunchberry

Model 7

Conceptual Elevation View

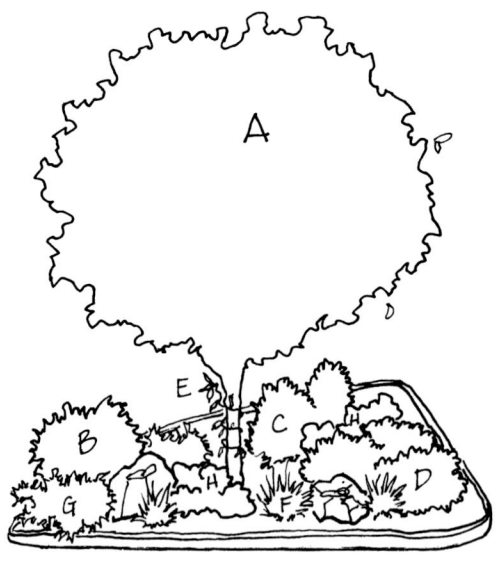

Scale Diagram or Box Elevation View

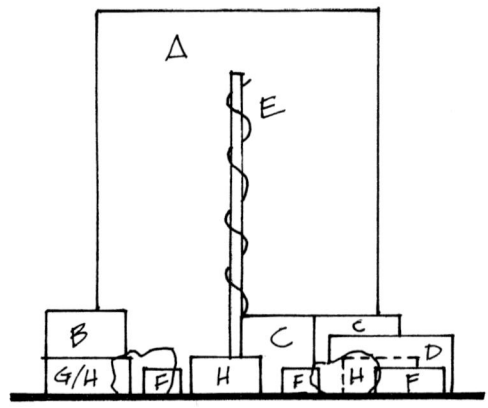

Planting Plan View

A Japanese Pagoda Tree *Styphnolobium japonicum* (1)

B Common Ninebark *Physocarpus opulifolius* 'Nugget' (1)

C Summersweet Clethra *Clethra alnifolia* 'Ruby Spice' (2)

D Slender Deutzia *Deutzia gracilis* (3)

E Nelly Moser Clematis *Clematis paniculata* 'Nelly Moser' (1)

F Blue Fescue *Fescue ovina var.* 'Glauca' (6)

G Scotch Heather *Calluna vulgaris* varieties, (11)

H Coral Bells *Heuchera micrantha* 'Palace Purple' (9)

Model 7
Shown in spring

Model 8

Conceptual Elevation View

Scale Diagram or Box Elevation View

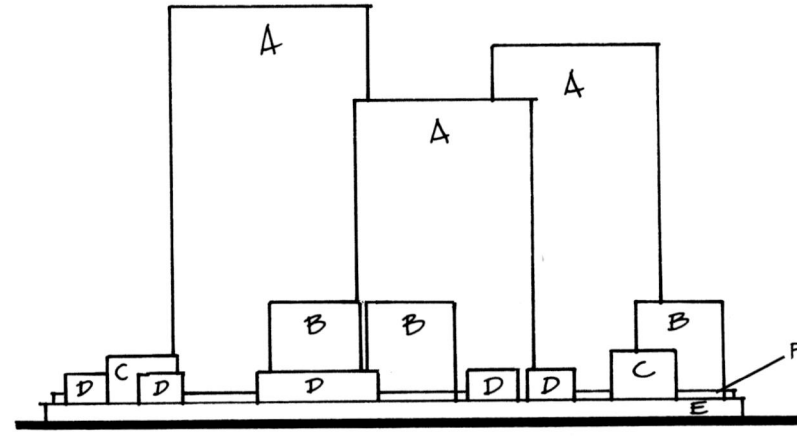

Planting Plan View

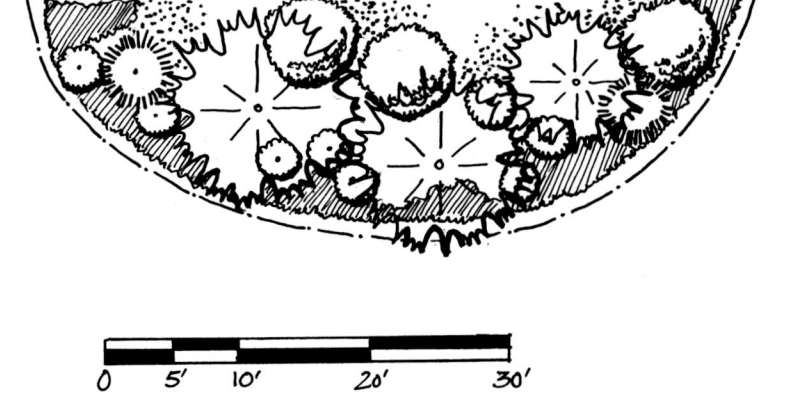

A Jack Pine *Pinus banksiana* (3)

B Fragrant Sumac *Rhus aromatica* (3)

C Common Juniper *Juniperus communis* (2)

D Pasture Rose *Rosa carolina* (8)

E Bearberry *Arctostaphylos uva-ursi* (12)

F Siberian Barren Strawberry *Waldstenia ternata* (6-12)

Model 8
Shown in early summer

Model 9

Conceptual Elevation View

Scale Diagram or Box Elevation View

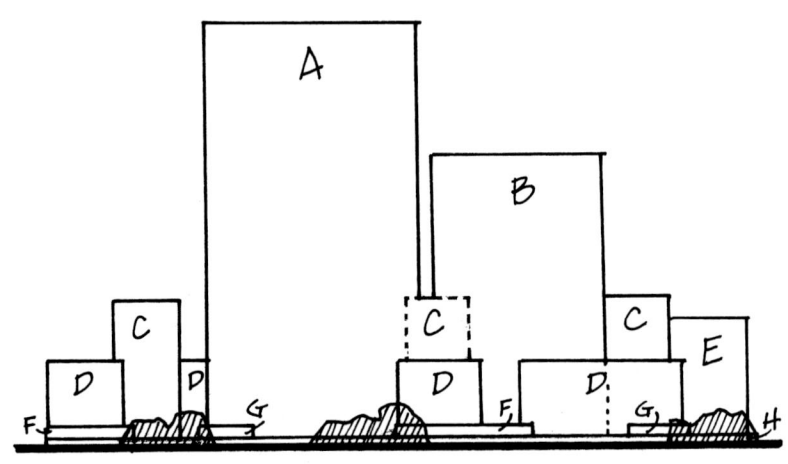

Planting Plan View

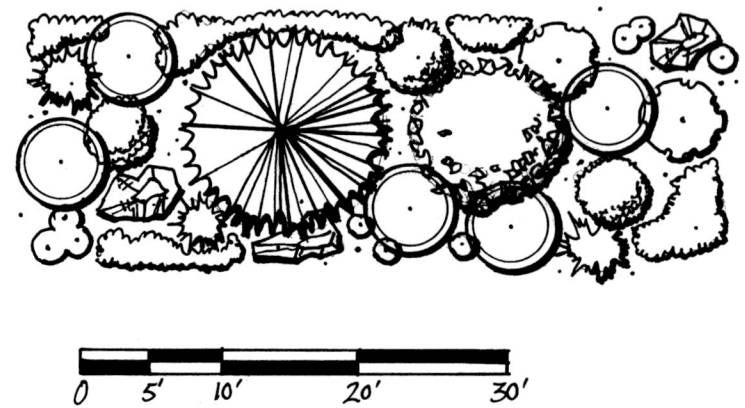

    A Black Hills Spruce *Picea glauca 'Densata' (1)*
    B Shadblow, Serviceberry *Amelanchier canadensis (1)*
    C Red Chokeberry *Aronia arbutifolia 'Brillantissima' (3)*
    D Beach Plum *Prunus maritima (2)*
    E Bayberry *Myrica pensylvanica (5)*
    F Lowbush Blueberry *Vaccinium angustifolium (9)*
    G Common Juniper *Juniperus communis 'Repanda' (3)*
    H Bearberry *Arctostaphylos uva-ursi (12)*
    I Switch Grass *Panicum virgatum 'Hanse Herms' (9)*

Model 9
Shown in winter

- A Black Hills Spruce
- B Shadblow, Serviceberry
- C Red Chokeberry
- D Beach Plum
- E Bayberry
- F Lowbush Blueberry
- G Common Juniper
- H Bearberry
- I Switch Grass

Model 10

Conceptual Elevation View

Scale Diagram or Box Elevation View

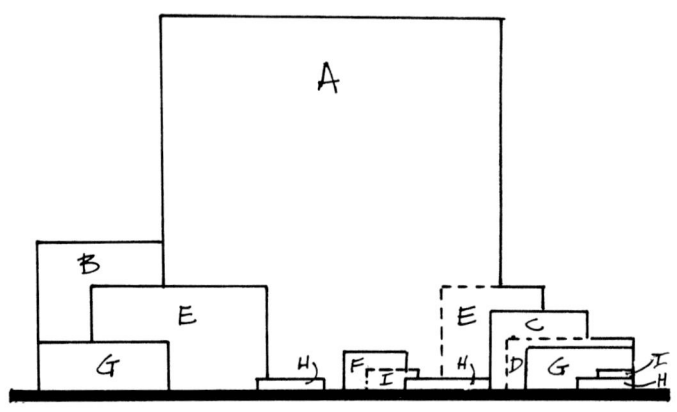

Planting Plan View

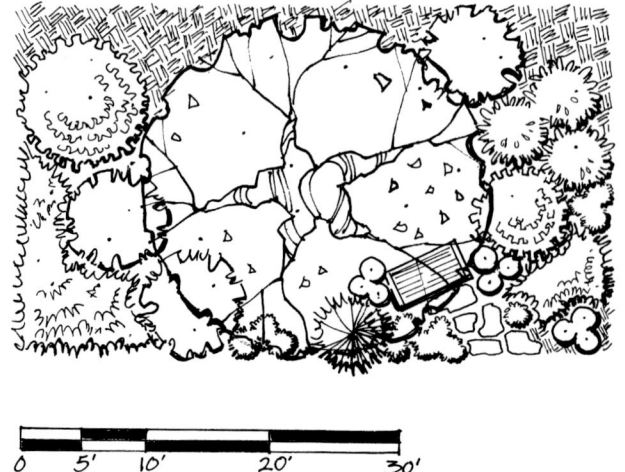

A River's Purple Beech *Fagus sylvatica 'Riversii'* (1)

B American Cranberry Viburnum *Viburnum trilobum* (1)

C Common Ninebark *Physocarpus opulifolius 'Dart's Gold'* (1)

D Pinxter Azalea *Rhododendron periclymenoides (nudiflorum)* (3)

E Mountain Laurel *Kalmia latifolia* (w) (3)

F Colorado Blue Spruce *Picea pungens 'Montgomery'* (1)

G Junipers *Juniperus communis 'Effusa'* (3)

H Blue-eyed Mary *Omphalodes verna* (12)

I Running Tapestry Foamflower *Tiarella cordifolia 'Running Tapestry'* (9)

Model 10
Shown in early spring

Model 11

Conceptual Elevation View

Scale Diagram or Box Elevation View

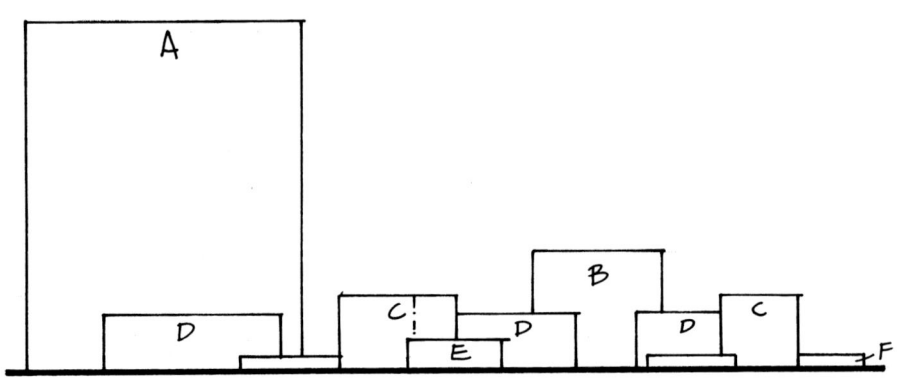

Planting Plan View

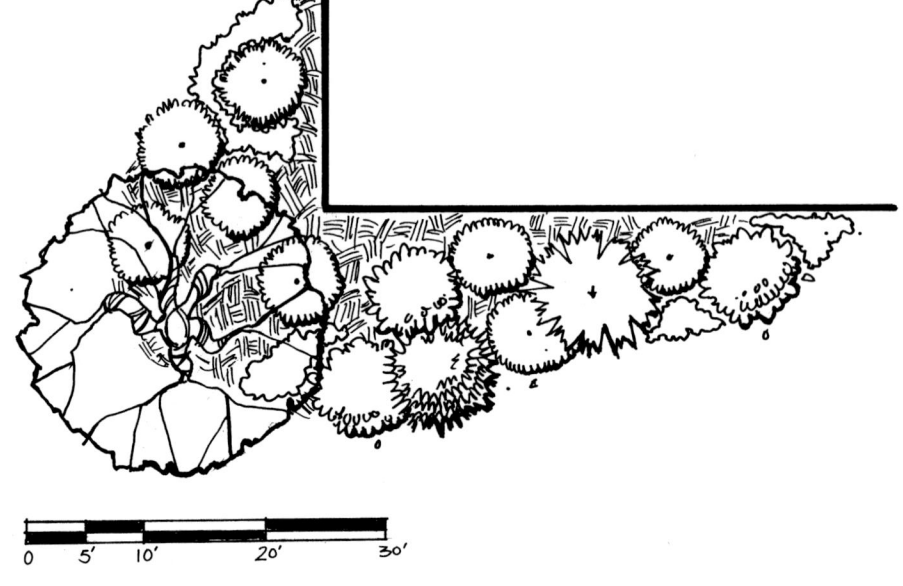

A Persian Parrotia or Persian Ironwood *Parrotia persica (1)*

B Redvein Enkianthus *Enkianthus campanulatus (1)*

C Dwarf Fothergilla *Fothergilla gardenii (3)*

D Coast Leucothoe *Leucothoe axillaris (8)*

E Bird's Nest Spruce *Picea abies Nidiformis (1)*

F Wild Ginger *Asarum canadensis (28)*

Model 11
Shown in fall

A Persian Parrotia or Persian Ironwood
B Redvein Enkianthus
C Dwarf Fothergilla
D Coast Leucothoe
E Bird's Nest Spruce
F Wild Ginger

Model 12

Conceptual Elevation View

Scale Diagram or Box Elevation View

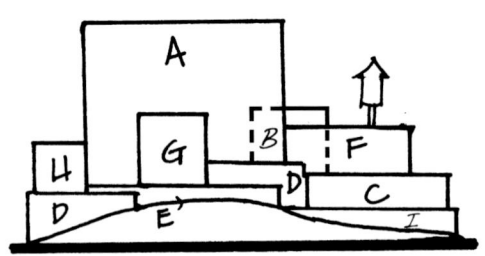

Planting Plan View

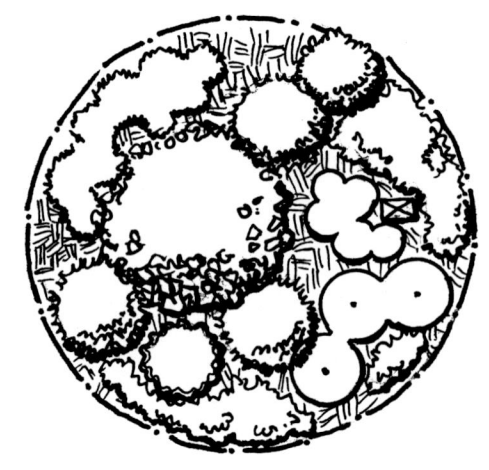

A Golden Elder Elderberry *Sambucus canadensis 'Aurea'* (1)

B Kalm's St. Johnswort *Hypericum kalmianum* (1)

C Blue Mist Spirea *Caryopteris x. clandonensis* (3)

D Winter Gem Boxwood *Buxus microphylla 'Wintergem'* (3)

E Chocolate Chip Bugleweed *Ajuga x 'Chocolate Chip'* (3-6)

F Brunette Bugbane or Baneberry *Actea racemosa 'Brunette'* (5)

G Brit-Marie Crawford Ligularia *Ligularia dentata 'Brit-Marie Crawford'* (1)

H Chocolate Joe Pye Weed *Eupatorium rugosum 'Chocolate'* (5-8)

I Running Tapestry Foamflower *Tiarella cordifolia 'Running Tapestry'* (3-5)

Model 12
Shown in late summer

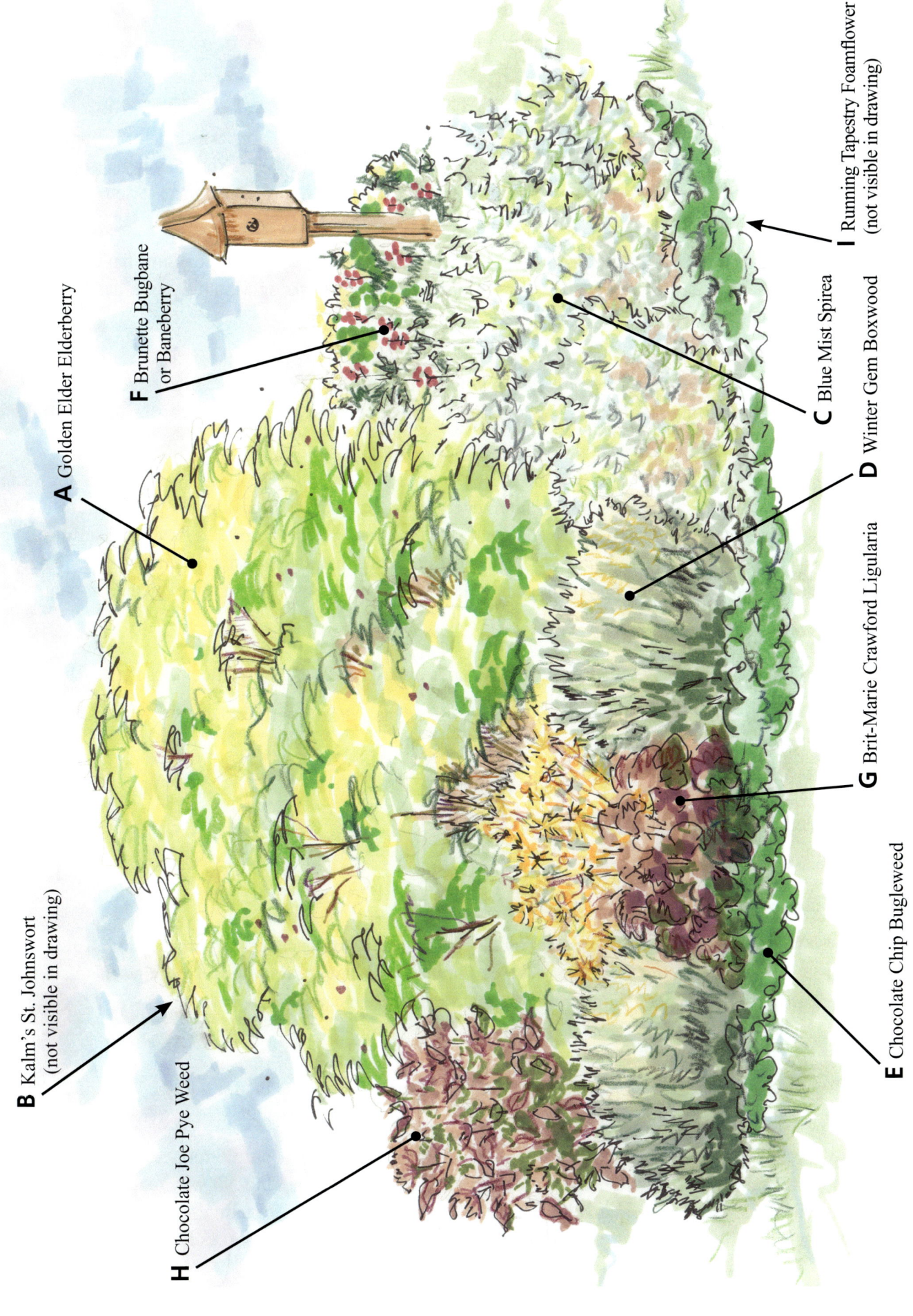

A Golden Elder Elderberry
B Kalm's St. Johnswort (not visible in drawing)
C Blue Mist Spirea
D Winter Gem Boxwood
E Chocolate Chip Bugleweed
F Brunette Bugbane or Baneberry
G Brit-Marie Crawford Ligularia
H Chocolate Joe Pye Weed
I Running Tapestry Foamflower (not visible in drawing)

Using the Plant Chart to create your own plant systems

You can develop your own plant system, using the models and the plant chart. As you do, consider these factors:

Sun exposure

Your plant systems will change over time as they grow, with the taller plants creating shade for the lower plants. We have chosen many plants adaptable to sunny to shady conditions. You may need to check conventional references for other plant selections if you have very sunny or deep-shade settings.

Salt tolerance

If you're looking for salt-tolerant plants, look toward seacoast ecosystems where plants have adapted to salt conditions. Also, each of the high stress settings within the Matrix and Plant System descriptions incorporates salt-tolerant plants.

Color and bloom

You may wish to create more color balance in your landscape. You may also be interested in successive bloom, plants of specific bloom colors, heights, etc. Consult conventional references for this information.

Wildlife use

Choose early flowers to attract insects and draw them into the food web. Include early flowers for nectar, deciduous leaves and shedding twigs for litter, evergreens for bird cover, and layers for structure. Add logs, rocks, birdbaths, and benches to create cool spots for toads and microorganisms. Arrange plantings in groups of three to five plants so animals that use them can find them. Include persistent winter fruit. Balance the variables, customizing the plant system using your inventory and considering the exposure on your site.

Plant Chart

Following is an extensive Plant Chart which includes a variety of plants that meet these criteria:

- Similar characteristics to the invasive species they were meant to replace, including being adaptable to a variety of conditions.
- Mostly native.
- Tolerant and adaptable to tough conditions.
- Available in the nursery trade.
- Fit into the models in the Matrix.

The plants in the Plant Chart are grouped by layers (overstory trees, understory trees, shrubs, etc). Some plants are specified as being associated with certain natural plant communities. Note that this list is limited as there are many more plant communities and associates than can be included.

Other plant lists

The Shoreline Plant List in Appendix E includes an extensive list of plants for aquatic, shoreline, lowland transition, and upland plant communities.

The plant lists in Appendix B group plants by specific characteristics—purple foliage, brilliant red fall foliage, prolific fruit—that will help you find alternatives to Crimson King Norway maple, burning bush, and Japanese barberry. Appendix A lists Douglas Tallamy's Best Bets for native woody and herbaceous plants for butterflies and moths, which are pollinators and serve as food sources for birds and other wildlife.

PLANT CHART KEY

This collection of plants includes those in Plant System Models 1 - 12 and alternatives to plants within those systems. There are many other plants outside of this chart that could also be used to create plant systems, but as this list could be a book in itself, we chose many on the basis of their reliability and tolerance to tough conditions, other plants are some of our favorites. Please note that the comments are perspectives and opinions of the authors and reviewers and may differ from others.

Exposure

S = full sun   **PS** = part sun   **Sh** = shade   **PSh** = part shade

Native To Northeastern U.S. (loosely defined, as some plants may be a bit outside of that range)

Y = Yes   **Y*** = Derived from a native   **U.S.** = Native to the U.S.

Foliage

- Outstanding Fall Foliage - red to orange and pink (replaces Burning Bush and Japanese Barberries)
- Purple Foliage - replaces purple-leaved Japanese Barberries and Norway Maple 'Crimson King'
- = Prolific Fruit - replaces Burning Bush and Japanese Barberries

Plant System Models

1 - 12.
If blank, can be used as alternative to plant in system

Comments

🍁 = may be easier to find in native nurseries

*Natural Plant Communities   Color Key

Spruce - Fir Forest	(lavender)
Northern Hardwood - Conifer Forest	(yellow)
Oak Pine - Hickory Forest	(green)
Beech - Maple Forest	(maroon)
Mixed Pine - Red Oak Woodland	(blue)
Seaside Association	(orange)
Wetland and Riparian plant list	APPENDIX E

*A natural plant community or association is defined here as a recurring assemblage of species found in particular physical environments. Climate, topography, geology and soil, disturbance and biotic interactions (including human influence) determine the structure and physical conditions in which the community prevails.

Note on "Wildlife Value": while all plants provide the physical structure of habitat, and therefore benefit wildlife, we selectively indicated certain plants in this chart as having wildlife value.
A woody plant is marked "Y" if it provides food and/or cover and is cited in at least two of the following: Alexander C. Martin, Herbert S. Zim and Arnold L. Nelson's *American Wildlife Plants: A Guide to Wildlife Food Habits*; William Cullina's *Native Trees, Shrubs and Vines*; and Carrol L. Henderson's *Landscaping for Wildlife*. An herbaceous plant is checked "Y" if cited in either William Cullina's *Growing and Propagating Wildflowers of the US and Canada*, or Carrol L. Henderson's *Landscaping for Wildlife*. (See Appendix D for full references.)

The Plant Systems Approach

Common Name	Scientific Name	Mature Height	Cold Hardiness Zone	Exposure
Tree Layer Over 45'				
Balsam Fir	Abies balsamea	45 - 75'	3	S, PSh
Red Maple	Acer rubrum	60 - 75'	4	S, PSh
Silver Maple	Acer saccharinum	60 - 80'	4	S, PSh
Sugar Maple	Acer saccharum	50 - 60'	4	S
Yellow Buckeye	Aesculus flava 'octandra'	60 - 75'	4	S
Yellow Birch	Betula alleghaniensis	50 - 60'	3	S, PSh
Black Birch	Betula lenta	50 - 65'	4	S, PSh
River Birch	Betula nigra	50 - 70'	4	S
Paper Birch	Betula papyrifera	50 - 70'	2	S
Pignut Hickory	Carya glabra	75 - 100'	5a	S
Shagbark Hickory	Carya ovata	75 - 100'	4	S
Northern Catalpa	Catalpa speciosa	50 - 60'	4	S
Atlantic White Cedar	Chamaecyparis thyoides	up to 50'	4	S, PSh
Yellowwood	Cladastris kentukea (lutea)	30 - 50'	4	S
Beech	Fagus grandifolia	50 - 70'	3	S, PSh
Copper Beech	Fagus sylvatica 'Purpurea'	50'	4	S, PSh
River's Purple European Beech	Fagus sylvatica 'Riversii'	50 - 60'	4	S, PSh
Spaeth Purple Beech	Fagus sylvatica 'Spaethiana'	50'	4	S
Black Ash	Fraxinus nigra	50 - 70'	2	S,PSh
Green Ash	Fraxinus pensylvanica	50 - 70'	2	S, PSh
Gingko	Gingko biloba	50 - 60'	4	S
Kentucky Coffee Tree	Gymnocladus dioicus	60 - 75'	3	S
American Larch	Larix laricina	40 - 80'	2	S
American Sweet Gum	Liquidambar styraciflua	75 - 100'	5	S
Tulip Poplar	Liriodendron tulipifera	70 - 90'	4	S
Dawn Redwood	Metasequoia glyptostroboides	45' and up	5	S
Black Gum, Tupelo	Nyssa sylvatica	40 - 60'	4	S, PSh
White Spruce	Picea glauca	40 - 60'	3	S
Hoops Blue Spruce	Picea pungens 'Hoopsii'	50'	3	S
Jack Pine	Pinus banksiana	55 - 65'	3	S
Red Pine	Pinus resinosa	75'	3	S
Pitch Pine	Pinus ridgida	40 - 50'	4	S, PSh

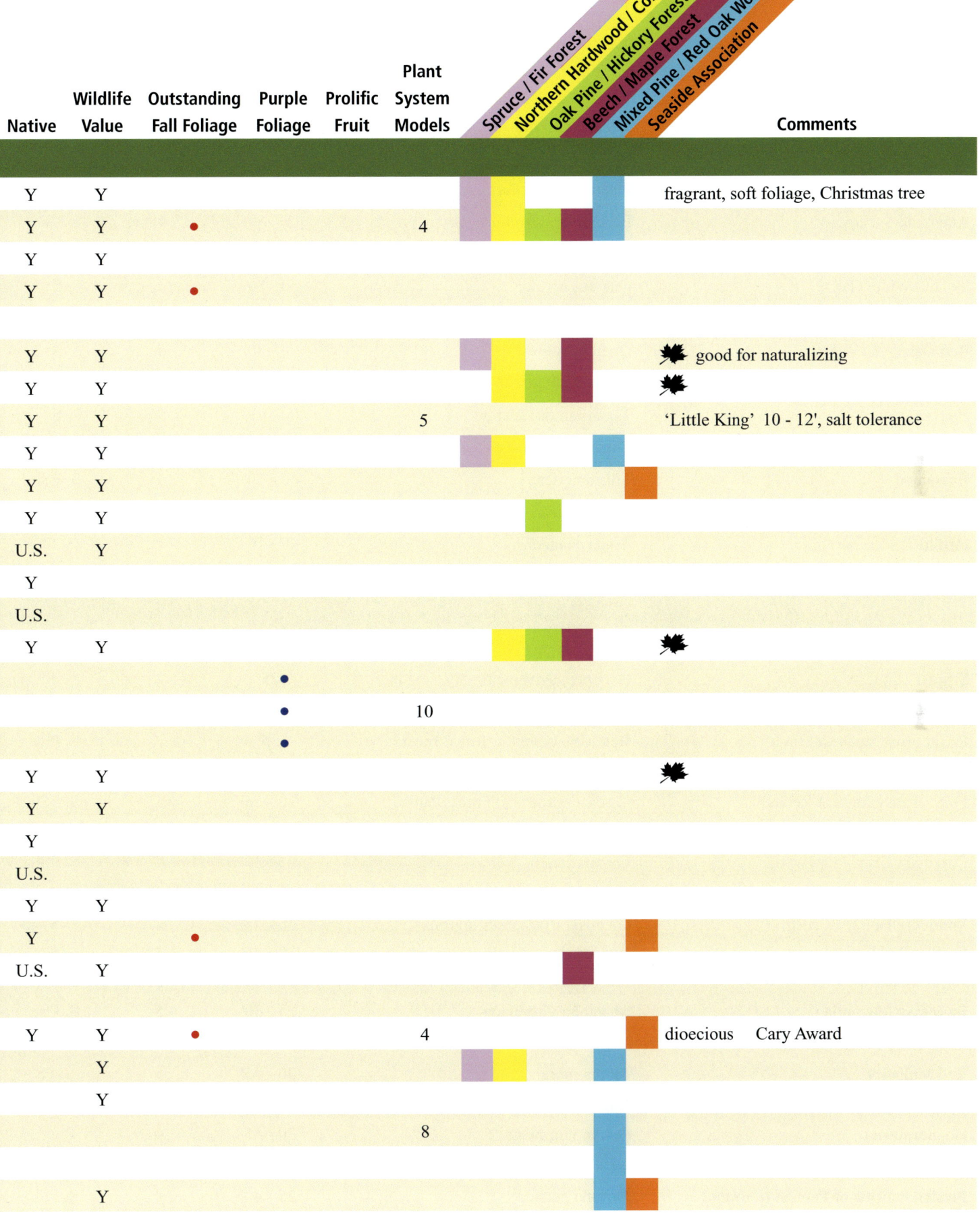

Common Name	Scientific Name	Mature Height	Cold Hardiness Zone	Exposure
Tree Layer Over 45'				
London Plane Tree	Platanus acerifolia	70 - 90'	4	S
American Sycamore	Platanus occidentalis	75 - 100'	4	
Quaking Aspen	Populus tremuloides	75 - 100'	3	S
Swamp White Oak	Quercus bicolor	50 - 80'	3	S
Pin Oak	Quercus palustris	60 - 70'	4	S
Red Oak	Quercus rubra	70 - 80'	4	S
Shumard Oak	Quercus shumardii	60 - 70'	4	S
Bald Cypress	Taxodium distichum	75 - 100'	5	S
Eastern Arborvitae	Thuja occidentalis	50 - 75'	2	S, PSh
Basswood	Tilia americana	60 - 70'	3	S, PSh
Littleleaf Linden	Tilia cordata	50 - 60'	3	S
Hemlock	Tsuga canadensis	40 - 70'	4	S, Sh
Japanese Zelkova	Zelkova serrata	50 - 65'	4	S
Tree Layer 25' - 45'				
Paperbark Maple	Acer griseum	20 - 30'	4	Sh
Striped Maple	Acer pennsylvanica	25'	2	S, Sh
Crimson Frost Japanese Birch	Betula platyphylla 'Crimson Frost'	35'	3	S
Royal Frost Japanese Birch	Betula platyphylla 'Royal Frost'	35'	3	S, PSh
American Hornbeam	Carpinus caroliniana	25 - 35'	3	S, PSh
Forest Pansy Eastern Redbud	Cercis canadensis 'Forest Pansy'	20 - 30'	5	S, PSh
Kousa Dogwood, Japanese Flowering Dogwood	Cornus kousa	25'	5	S, PSh
Cornelian Cherry Dogwood	Cornus mas	25 - 30'	4	S, PSh
Rohani Purple Beech	Fagus sylvatica 'Rohanii'	40 - 50'	5	S
Thornless Honey Locust	Gleditsia triancathos inermis	35 - 45'	4	S
Eastern Red Cedar	Juniperus virginiana	30 - 45'	3	S
Amur Maackia	Maackia amurensis	20 - 30'	3	S
Sweetbay Magnolia	Magnolia virginiana	25 - 30'	5	S, PSh
Wada's Memory Magnolia	Magnolia x. 'Wada's Memory'	30'	5	S, PSh
Red Mulberry	Morus rubra	30 - 45'	5	S, PS
Wildfire Tupelo	Nyssa sylvatica 'Wildfire'	30 - 40'	4	S, PSh
Hophornbeam	Ostrya virginiana	30 - 45'	4	
Sourwood	Oxydendrum arboreum	25 - 30'	4	S
Persian Parrotia or Persian Ironwood	Parrotia persica	25 - 40'	4	S, PSh

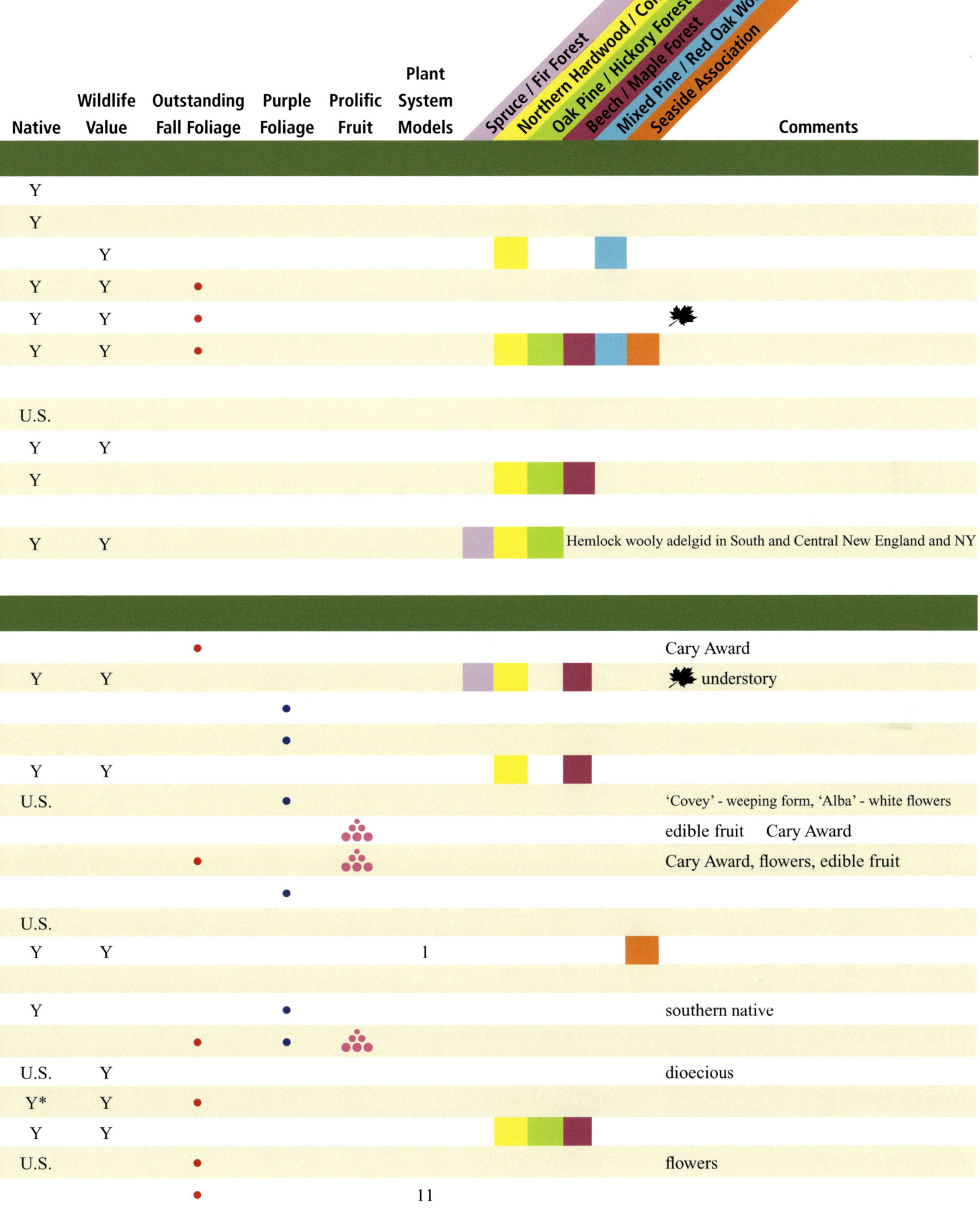

Common Name	Scientific Name	Mature Height	Cold Hardiness Zone	Exposure
Tree Layer 25' - 45'				
Amur Cork Tree	Phellodendron amurense	35 - 40'	4	S
Black Hill Spruce	Picea glauca 'Densata'	25'	3	S
Black Spruce	Picea mariana	30 - 40'	2	S, PSh
Red-leaf Plums	Prunus spp.	30 - 40'	4	S
Pin or Fire Cherry	Prunus pensylvanica	20 - 35'	2	S
Chokecherry	Prunus virginiana	25 - 45'	2	S
Canada Red Chokecherry	Prunus virginiana 'Schubert'	20 - 25'	2	S
Callery Pear	Pyrus calleryana	30 - 45'	4	S
Black Willow	Salix nigra	25 - 45'	3	S
Sassafras	Sassafras albidum	30 - 40'	4	S
Japanese Pagodatree	Sophora japonica (Styphnolobium)	30 - 45'	4	S
Korean Mountain Ash	Sorbus alnifolia	30 - 45'	3	S
American Mountain Ash	Sorbus americana	20 - 30'	2	S
Showy Mountain Ash	Sorbus decor	20 - 35'	2	S
Fragrant Snowbell	Styrax obassia	20 - 30'	5	S, PSh
Tree Layer 16' - 25'				
Amur Maple	Acer ginnala	15 - 18'	3	S, PSh
Japanese Maple	Acer palmatum	15 - 25'	5 - 8	PSh
Speckled Alder	Alnus incana subsp. Rugosa	20'	4	S, PSh
Smooth Alder	Alnus serrulata	up to 20'	2	S
Downy Serviceberry	Amelanchier arborea	16 - 25'	3	S, PSh
Shadblow, Serviceberry	Amelanchier canadensis	up to 25'	3	S, PSh
Allegheny Serviceberry	Amelanchier laevis	20 - 25'	3	S, PSh
Serviceberry	Amelanchier x. grandiflora	25'	4	S, PSh
Cole Serviceberry	Amelanchier x. grandiflora 'Cole'	25'	4	S, PSh
Japanese Summersweet	Clethra barbinervis	up to 20'	5	PSh, Sh
Pagoda Dogwood	Cornus alternifolia	15 - 25'	3	S, PSh
Eastern Flowering Dogwood	Cornus florida	25'	5	S, PSh
Grace Smoke Bush	Cotinus coggygria 'Grace'	15 - 25"	5	S
Purple Fountain Beech	Fagus sylvatica 'Purple Fountain'	20'	4	S, PSh
Common Witchhazel	Hamamelis virginiana	20 - 25'	3	S, PSh
Cardinal Tea Crabapple	Malus hupehensis 'Cardinal'	15 - 18'	4	S
Pink Spires Crabapple	Malus 'Pink Spires'	20'	2	S
Prairiefire Crabapple	Malus 'Prairiefire'	20'	4	S

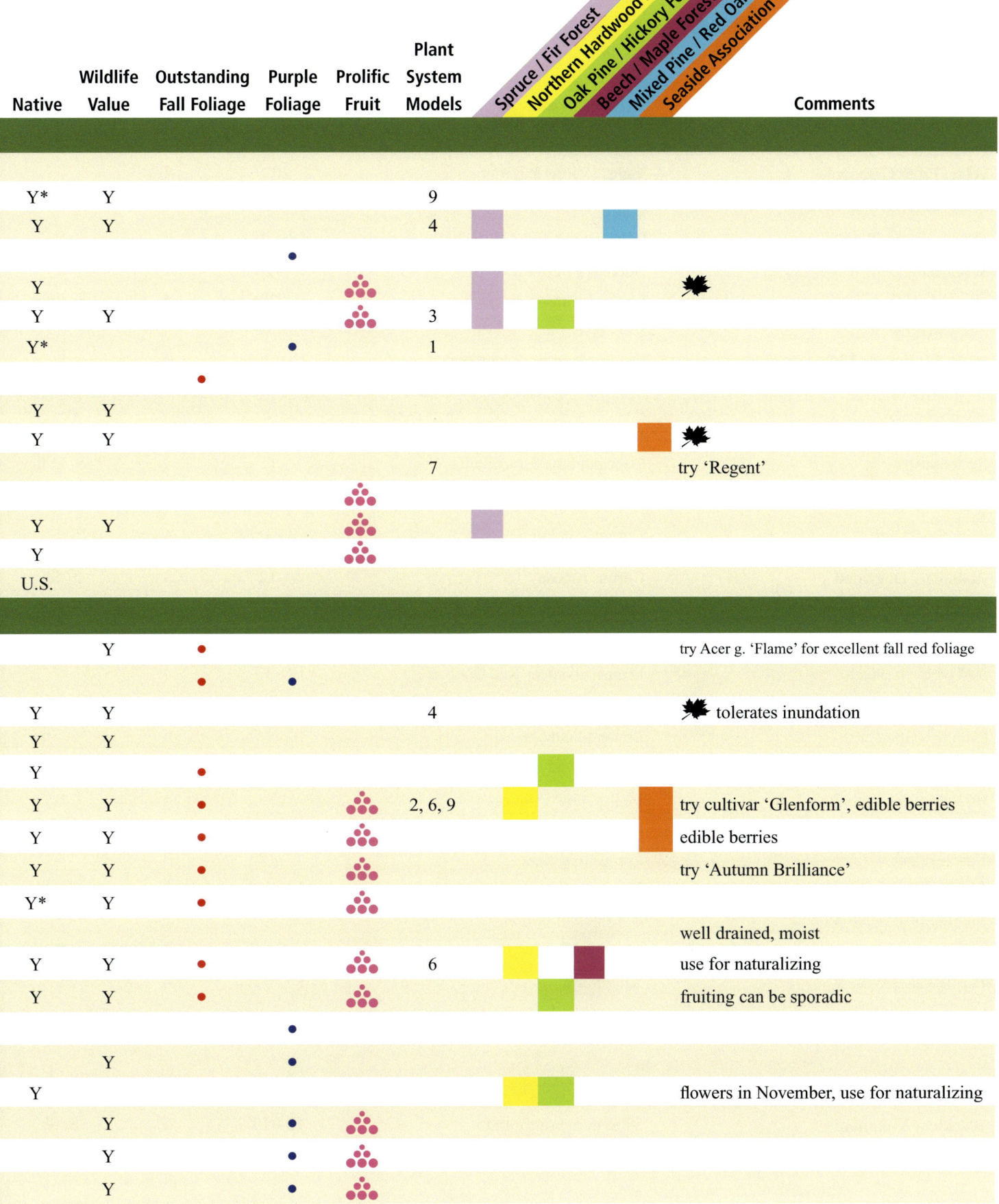

The Plant Systems Approach

Common Name	Scientific Name	Mature Height	Cold Hardiness Zone	Exposure
Tree Layer 16' - 25'				
Velvet Pillar Crabapple	Malus 'Velvet Pillar'	20'	4	S
Newport Flowering Plum	Prunus cerasifera 'Newport'	15 - 20'	4	S
Thundercloud Plum	Prunus cerasifera 'Thundercloud'	18 - 20'	4	S
Scrub Oak	Quercus illicifolia	12 - 20'	5	S
Sweet Azalea	Rhododendron arborescens	8 - 20'	4	S, PSh
Pussy Willow	Salix discolor	16 - 20'	3	S
Cutleaf European Elder	Sambucus nigra 'Laciniata'	10 - 20'	4	S
Shrub Layer 10'-15'				
Purple Fruit Chokeberry	Aronia prunifolia	6 - 12'	4	S, PSh
Buttonbush	Cephalanthus occidentalis	8 - 15'	4	S, PSh
Sweet Pepperbush	Clethra alnifolia	10 - 14'	4	S, Sh
Gray Dogwood	Cornus racemosa	10 - 15'	4	S, Sh
Roundleaf Dogwood	Cornus rugosa	6 - 12'	3	S, Sh
Royal Purple Smokebush	Cotinus coggygria 'Royal Purple'	15'	5	S
Weeping Purple Beech	Fagus sylvatica 'Purpurea Pendula'	12'	4	S, PSh
Red Obelisk Beech	Fagus sylvatica 'Red Obelisk'	10 - 12'	4	S
Pallida Chinese Witchhazel	Hamamelis mollis 'Pallida'	12 - 15'	5	S, PSh
Common Spicebush	Lindera benzoin	10 - 15'	4	S, Sh
Candymint Crabapple	Malus 'Candymint'	10'	4	S
Pink Princess Crabapple	Malus 'Pink Princess'	15'	4	S
Mountain Holly	Nemopanthus mucronata	8 -12'	4	S
Beach Plum	Prunus maritima	6 - 12'	3	S
Rosebay Rhododendron	Rhododendron maximum	10 - 12'	3	PSh, Sh
Shining or Winged Sumac	Rhus copallina	8 - 12'	5	S
Staghorn Sumac	Rhus typhina	10'	3	S
Purple-Osier Willow	Salix purpurea	10 - 12'	4	S
Highbush Blueberry	Vaccinium corymbosum	8 - 12'	3	S, PSh
Nannyberry Viburnum	Viburnum lentago	12 - 18'	2	S, Sh
Blackhaw Viburnum	Viburnum prunifolium	12 - 15'	3	S, Sh
American Cranberry Viburnum	Viburnum trilobum	8 - 12'	2	S, PSh

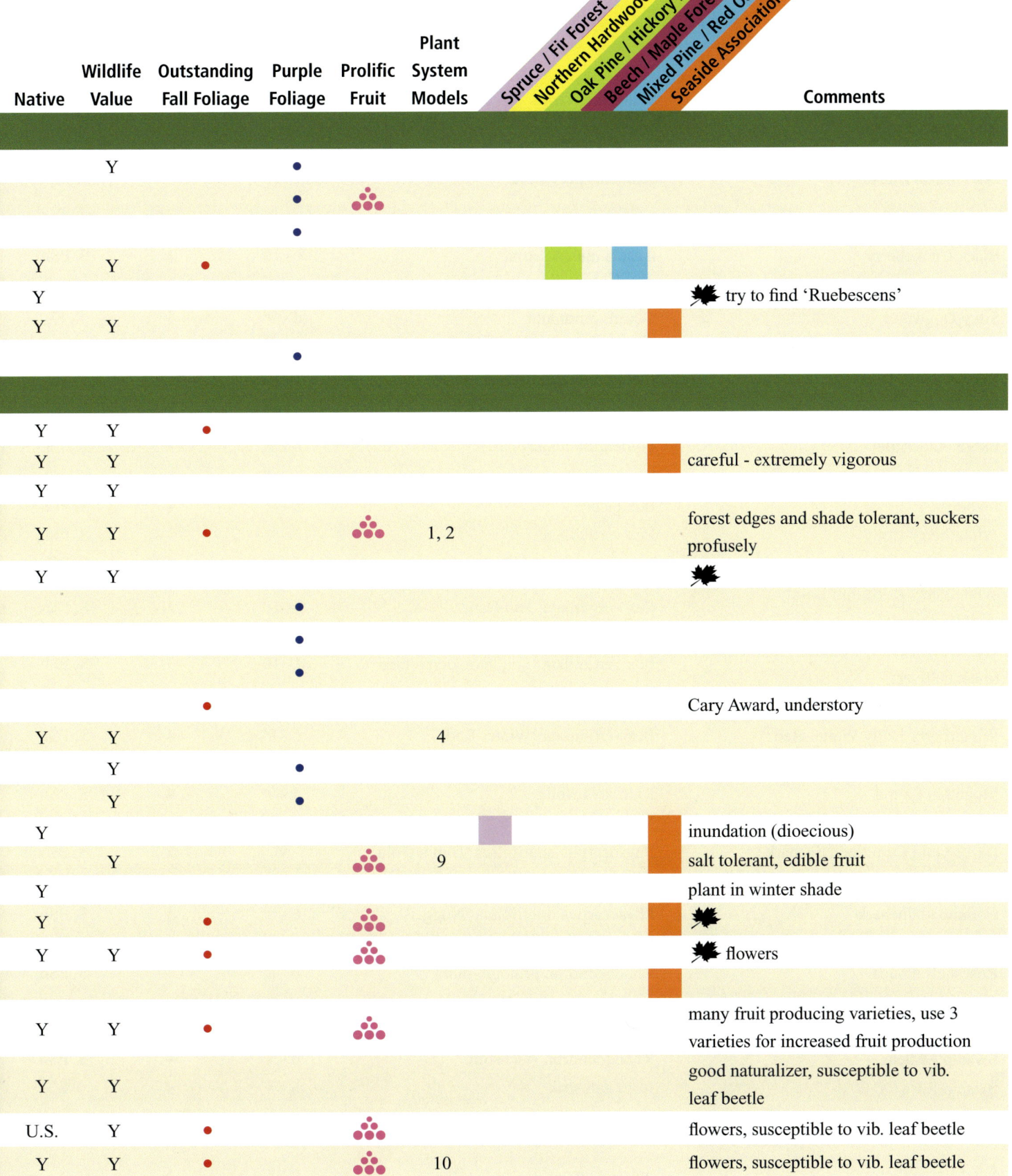

Common Name	Scientific Name	Mature Height	Cold Hardiness Zone	Exposure
Shrub Layer 6'-9'				
Bottlebrush Buckeye	Aesculus parviflora	8 - 10'	4	S, PSh
Red Chokeberry	Aronia arbutifolia 'Brilliantissima'	9'	4	S, PSh
Black Chokeberry	Aronia melanocarpa	8 - 10'	3	S, PSh
Sweetshrub	Calycanthus floridus	6 - 9'	4	S, PSh
Silky Dogwood	Cornus amomum	6 - 9'	4	S, Sh
Red-Osier Dogwood	Cornus sericea (stolonifera)	6 - 9'	3	S, PSh
Heart-Leaved Disanthus	Disanthus cercidifolius	6 - 10'	5	PSh
Redvein Enkianthus	Enkianthus campanulatus	6 - 9'	4	S, Sh
Large Fothergilla	Fothergilla major	6 - 9'	4	S, PS
Vernal Witchhazel	Hamamelis vernalis	6 - 9'	5	S, PSh
Inkberry	Ilex glabra	5 - 9'	4	S, PSh
Winterberry Holly	Ilex verticillata	6 - 9'	3 - 4	S, PSh
Winterberry Holly Afterglow	Ilex verticillata 'Afterglow'	6 - 9'	4	S, PSh
Winterberry Holly Jim Dandy (male cultivar)	Ilex verticillata 'Jim Dandy'	8 - 10'	3	S, PSh
Winterberry Holly Southern Gentlemen (male cultivar)	Ilex verticillata 'Southern Gentlemen'	8 - 10'	3	S, PSh
Winterberry Holly Sparkleberry	Ilex verticillata 'Sparkleberry'	8 - 10'	3	S, PSh
Winterberry Holly Winter Red	Ilex verticillata 'Winter Red'	6 - 9'	4	S, PSh
Common Juniper	Juniperus communis	6 - 9'	3	S
Mountain Laurel	Kalmia latifolia	4 - 9'	4	S, PSh
Northern Bayberry	Myrica pensylvanica	6 - 9'	2	S, PSh
Dart's Gold Common Ninebark	Physocarpus opulifolius 'Dart's Gold'	9'	2	S, PSh
Diablo Ninebark	Physocarpus opulifolius 'Diablo'	9'	2	S, PSh
Common Ninebark	Physocarpus opulifolius 'Nugget'	6 - 8'	3	S, PSh
Colorado Blue Spruce	Picea pungens 'Montgomery'	6 - 8'	4	S
Roseshell Azalea	Rhododendron prinophyllum	6 - 8'	3	S, PSh
Pinkshell Azalea	Rhododendron vaseyi	5 - 9'	4	S, PSh
Swamp Azalea	Rhododendron viscosum	6 - 9'	4	S, PSh
Swamp Rose	Rosa palustris	6 - 8'	4	S
Fragrant Sumac	Rhus aromatica	4 - 6'	3	S
Sand Bar Willow	Salix exigua	6 - 8'	4	S
Dwarf Blue Arctic Willow	Salix purpurea Nana	5 - 7'	3	S

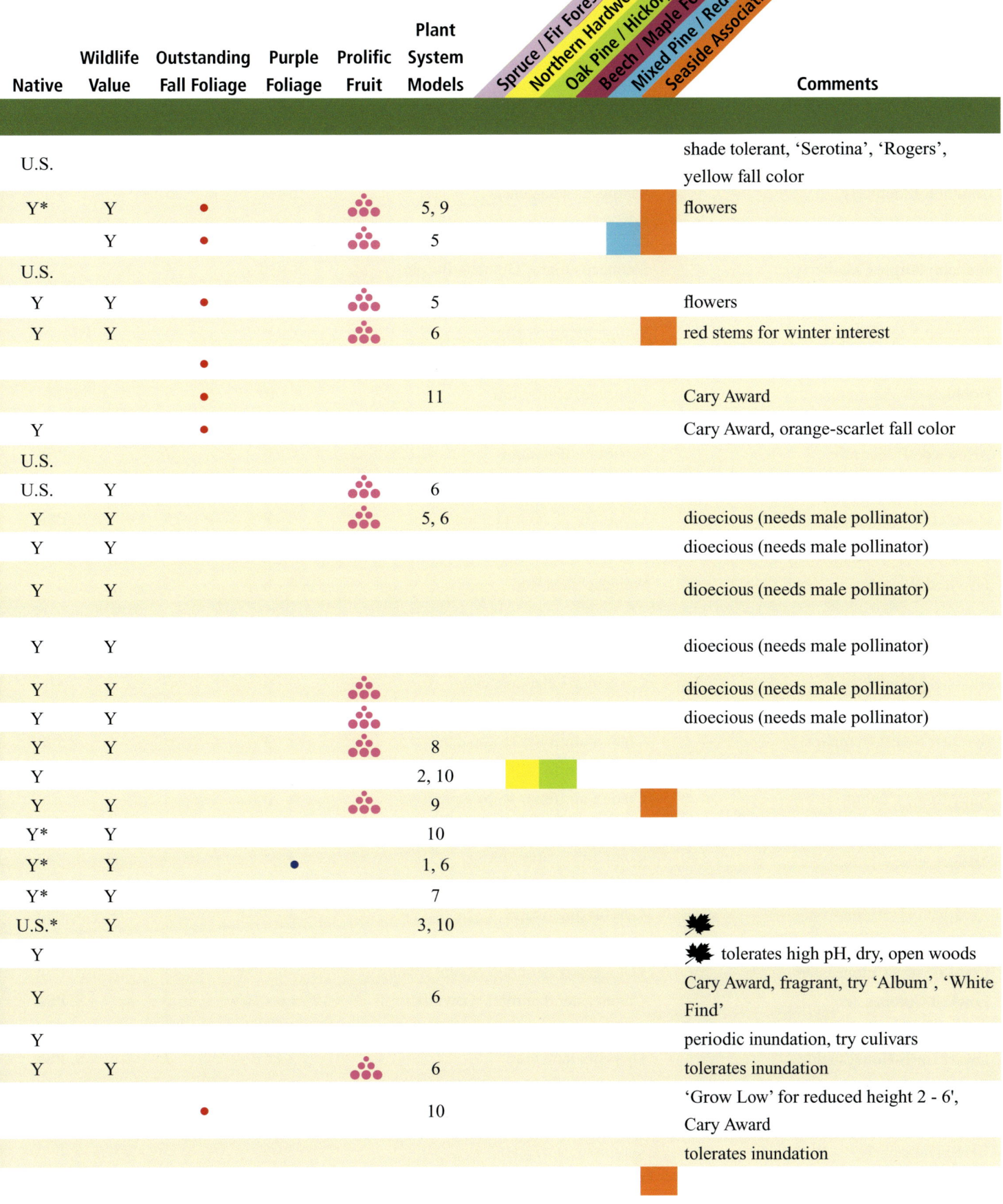

Common Name	Scientific Name	Mature Height	Cold Hardiness Zone	Exposure
Shrub Layer 6'-9'				
Bankers Dwarf Willow	Salix x cotteti	5 - 7'	4	S
Common Elderberry	Sambucus canadensis	6 - 9'	3	S
Black Beauty Elderberry	Sambucus nigra 'Black Beauty'	8 - 10'	4	S
Guincho Purple Elderberry	Sambucus nigra 'Guincho Purple'	8 - 10'	4	S
Red Berried Elderberry	Sambucus pubens	6 - 9'	3	S
Common Snowberry	Symphoricarpos albus	6 - 8'	3	PSh, Sh
Mapleleaf Viburnum	Viburnum acerifolium	5 - 8'	3	S, Sh
Hobblebush Viburnum	Viburnum alnifolium	6 - 10'	3	S, Sh
Wild Raisin, Witherod Viburnum	Viburnum cassinoides	6 - 10'	3	S, PSh
Arrowwood Viburnum	Viburnum dentatum	6 - 9'	2	S, PSh
Linden Viburnum	Viburnum dilatatum	6 - 10'	4	S, PSh
Doublefile Viburnum	Viburnum plicatum tomentosum	5 - 8'	5	S, PSh
Compact American Cranberry Viburnum	Viburnum trilobum 'Compacta'	5 - 6'	2	S, PSh
Java Red Weigela	Weigela 'Java Red'	6 - 8'	5	S
Shrub Layer 3'-6'				
Regent Serviceberry	Amelanchier alnifolia 'Regent'	4 - 6'	3	S, PSh
Blue Mist Spirea	Caryopteris clandonensis	3 - 4'	5	S
Summer Sweet Anne Bidwel	Clethra alnifolia 'Anne Bidwel'	4 - 6'	3	S, Sh
Summer Sweet Compacta	Clethra alnifolia 'Compacta'	3 - 4'	3	S, Sh
Summer Sweet Hummingbird	Clethra alnifolia 'Hummingbird'	3 - 4'	3	S, Sh
Ruby Spice Clethra	Clethra alnifolia 'Ruby Spice'	4 - 5'	3	S, Sh
Summer Sweet Sixteen Candles	Clethra alnifolia 'Sixteen Candles'	4'	3	S, Sh
Sweet Fern	Comptonia peregrina	3 - 5'	2	S, PSh
Spike Winterhazel	Corylopsis spicata	4 - 8'	5	S, PSh
American Hazelnut	Corylus americana	3 - 9'	4	S, PSh
Cranberry Cotoneaster	Cotoneaster apiculata	3' x 4 - 6'w	5	S, PSh
Coral Beauty Cotoneaster	Cotoneaster dammeri 'Coral Beauty'	2' x 6 - 9'w	5	S, PSh
Lowfast Cotoneaster	Cotoneaster dammeri 'Lowfast'	12" x 6 - 10'w	5	S, PSh
Slender Deutzia	Deutzia gracilis	2 - 4'	4	S
Dwarf Bush-Honeysuckle	Diervilla lonicera	3 - 5'	3	S, PSh
Atlantic Leatherwood	Dirca palustris	3 - 6'	3	S
Dwarf Fothergilla	Fothergilla gardenii	3 - 4'	5	S, PSh
Black Huckleberry	Gaylussacia baccata	3 - 5'	3	S
Smooth Hydrangea	Hydrangea arborescens	3 - 5'	3	S, Sh

Common Name	Scientific Name	Mature Height	Cold Hardiness Zone	Exposure
Shrub Layer 3'-6'				
Annabelle Hydrangea	Hydrangea arborescens 'Annabelle'	3 - 5'	3	S, Sh
Hills of Snow Hydrangea	Hydrangea arborescens 'Grandiflora'			S, Sh
White Dome Hydrangea	Hydrangea arborescens 'White Dome'	4 - 6'	3	S, Sh
Oakleaf Hydrangea	Hydrangea quercifolia	3 - 6'	5	S, PS
Kalm St. Johnswort	Hypericum kalmianum	3 - 5'	5	S, PSh
Inkberry	Ilex glabra	3 - 5'	4	S, PSh
Dwarf Inkberry	Ilex glabra 'Compacta'	4 - 6'	4	S, PSh
Black Inkberry	Ilex glabra 'Nigra'	3 - 4'	4 - 5	S, PSh
Viridis Inkberry	Ilex glabra 'Viridis'	3 - 4'	4 - 5	S, PSh
Red Sprite Winterberry Holly	Ilex verticillata 'Red Sprite'	3 - 4'	4	S, PSh
Shortcake Winterberry Holly	Ilex verticillata 'Shortcake'	3 - 5'	4	S, PSh
Henry's Garnet Virginia Sweetspire	Itea virginica 'Henry's Garnet'	3 - 4'	5	S, PSh
Sweetgale	Myrica gale	3 - 5'	1	S
Dwarf Ninebark	Physocarpus opulifolius 'Nanus'	4 - 6'	2	S, Sh
Summer Wine Ninebark	Physocarpus opulifolius 'Summer Wine'	4 - 6'	3	S, PSh
Rhodora	Rhododendron canadense	3 - 4'	2	S, PSh
Pinxterbloom Azalea	Rhododendron periclyminoides (nudiflorum)	4 - 6'	3	S, PSh
Low Grow Fragrant Sumac	Rhus aromatica 'Low Grow'	2 - 3'	3	S
Pasture Rose	Rosa carolina	3 - 5'	4	S
Rugosa Rose	Rosa rugosa	4 - 6'	4	S
Virginia Rose	Rosa virginiana	3 - 5'	4	S
Meadowsweet	Spirea alba var. latifolia	3 - 5'	3	S
Steeplebush Spirea	Spirea tomentosum	3 - 5'	3	S
Indian Currant Coralberry	Symphoricarpos orbiculatus	3 - 4'	2	S, PSh
Dwarf Korean Lilac	Syringa meyeri	4 - 6'	3	S
Tinkerbelle Lilac	Syringa 'Tinkerbelle'	5 - 6'	3	S
Wine and Roses Weigela	Weigela florida 'Wine and Roses'	4 - 5'	4	S
Vines Layer heights vary				
Nelly Moser Clematis	Clematis spp. 'Nelly Moser'	6 - 8'	4	S, PSh
Sweet Autumn Clematis	Clematis paniculata	15'	4	S, PSh
Virgin's Bower	Clematis virginiana	15'	4	S, PSh
Virginia Creeper	Parthenocissus quinquefolia	30 - 50'	3	S, PSh

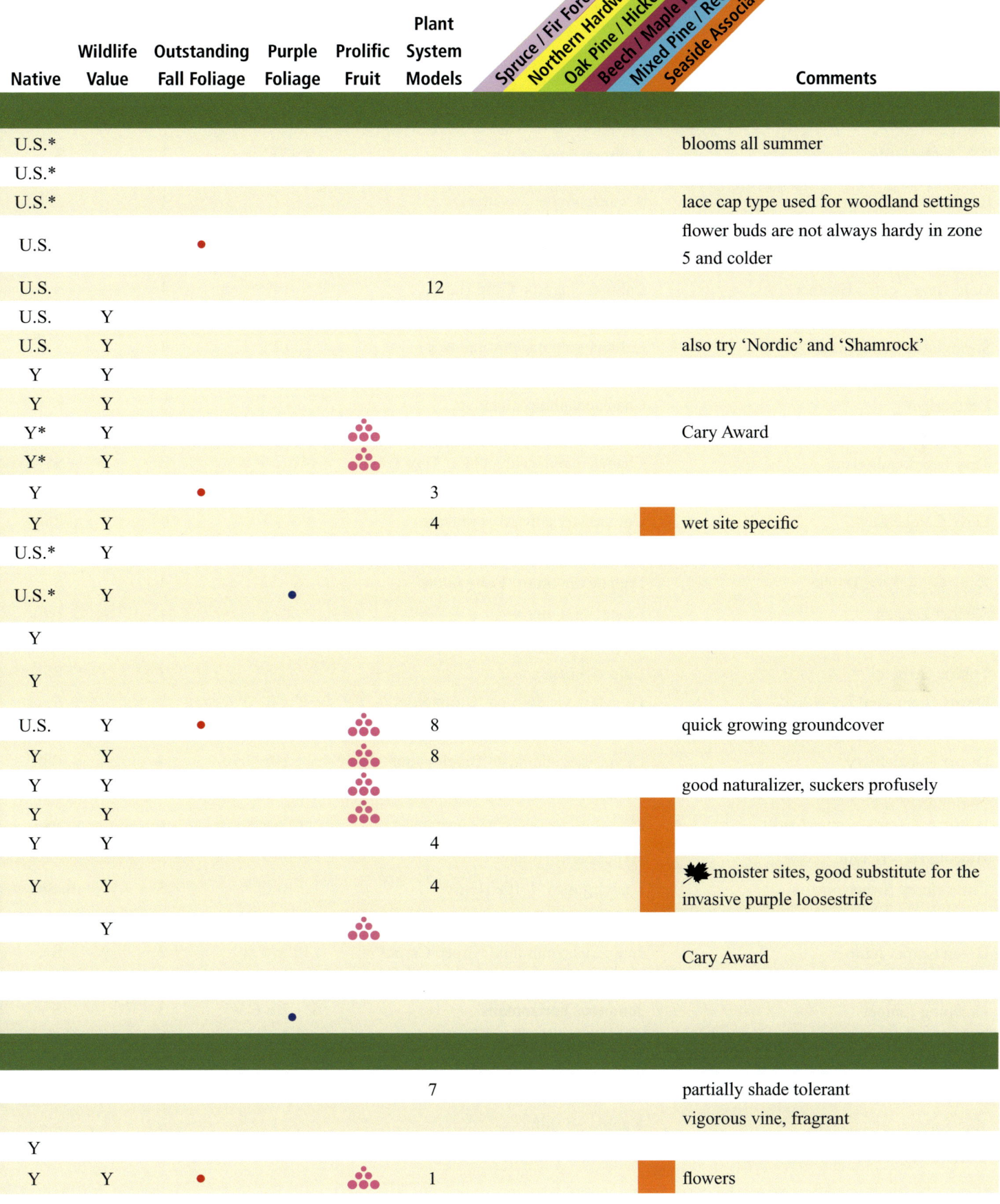

The Plant Systems Approach   105

Common Name	Scientific Name	Mature Height	Cold Hardiness Zone	Exposure
Woody Groundcovers & Shrub Layer up to 3′				
Bog Andromeda	Andromeda polifolia	8 x 18" w	2	S
Bearberry	Arctostaphylos uva-ursi	12"	4	S, PSh
Boxwood	Buxus macrophylla 'Wintergem'	2 x 4' - 5' w	4	S, PSh
County Wicklow Scotch Heather	Calluna vulgaris 'County Wicklow'	12"	4	S
Gold Haze Scotch Heather	Calluna vulgaris 'Gold Haze'	14"	4	S
Martha Herman Scotch Heather	Calluna vulgaris 'Martha Herman'	6"	4	S
Springtorch Scotch Heather	Calluna vulgaris 'Springtorch'	12"	4	S
New Jersey Tea	Ceanothus americanus	3'	5	S
Leatherleaf	Chamaedaphne calyculata	up to 3'	2	S
Cascade Leatherleaf	Chamaedaphne calyculata 'Cascade'	2 x 2' w	2	S
Tiny Tiny Leatherleaf	Chamaedaphne calyculata 'Tiny Tiny'	14 x 14" w	2	S
Bunchberry Dogwood	Cornus canadensis	6"	2	PSh, Sh
Early Cotoneaster	Cotoneaster adpressus praecox	2 - 3'	4	S, PSh
Rockspray Cotoneaster	Cotoneaster horizontalis	3'	4	S, PSh
Ruby Glow Rose Daphe	Daphne oneorum 'Ruby Glow'	6 - 12"	4	S
Slender Deutzia	Deutzia gracilis	2'- 3'	4	S, PSh
Black Crowberry	Empetrum nigrum	6 - 8"	3	S, PSh
Trailing Arbutus	Epigea repens	4 - 6"	3	S, PSh
Dwarf Greenstem Forsythia	Forsythia viridissima 'Bronxensis'	1 - 2' x 2 - 3' w	5	S
Wintergreen	Gaultheria procumbens	4 - 6"	3	PSh
Dwarf Huckleberry	Gaylussacia dumosa 'Bigeloviana'	18"	4	S, PSh
Expresso Spotted Cranesbill	Geranium maculatum 'Expresso'	10 - 16"	4	S, PSh
Hocus Pocus Hardy Cranesbill	Geranium pratense 'Hocus Pocus'	12 - 18"	4	S, PSh
Hidcote Hypericum	Hypericum 'Hidcote'	1 - 3'	5	S
Little Henry Sweetspire	Itea virginica 'Little Henry'	1 - 2'	5	S, Sh
Effusa Juniper	Juniperus communis 'Effusa'	12" x 4' w	2	S
Green Carpet Juniper	Juniperus communis 'Green Carpet'	12"x 4' w	2	S
Repanda Juniper	Juniperus communis 'Repanda'	15" x 6' w	2	S
Creeping Juniper	Juniperus horizontalis	6" - 2 x 6' w	3	S
Dwarf Japanese Garden Juniper	Juniper procumbens 'Nana'	1'x 10' w	4	S
Sheep Laurel	Kalmia angustifolia	2 - 3'	2	S, PSh
Bog Kalmia	Kalmia polifolia	3'	2	S
Coast Leucothoe	Leucothoe axillaris	3'	4	Sh

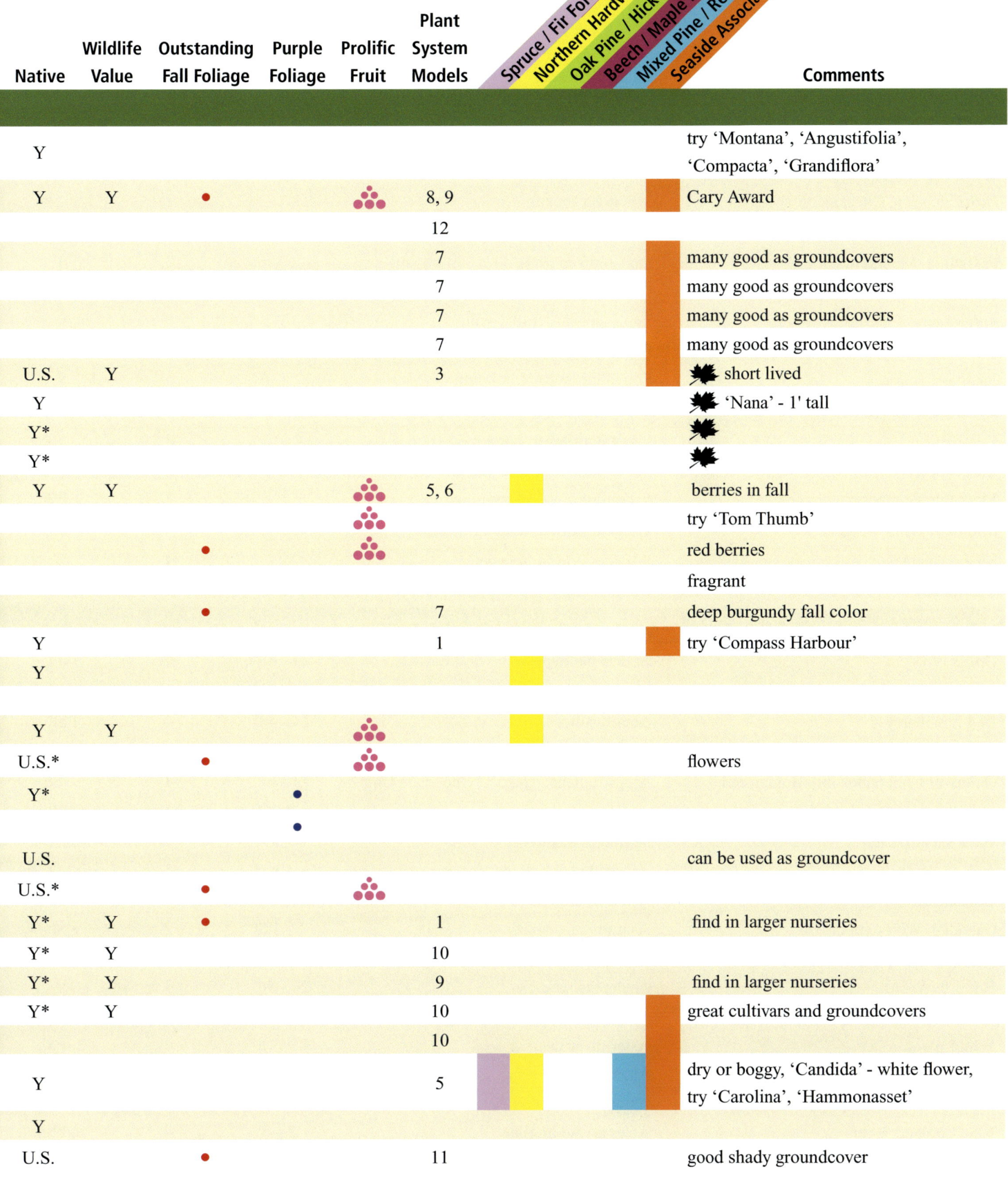

Common Name	Scientific Name	Mature Height	Cold Hardiness Zone	Exposure
Woody Groundcovers & Shrub Layer up to 3′				
Green Sprite Leucothoe	Leucothoe catesbaei	3 x 2′ w	5	PSh, Sh
Dwarf Mahonia	Mahonia repens	12"		PSh, Sh
Partridgeberry, Checker Berry	Mitchella repens	2"	3	PSh, Sh
Rosenkuppel Oregano	Origanum laevigatum 'Rosenkuppel'	15 - 18"	5	S
Paxistima, Mountain Lover	Paxistima canbyi	1 x 3′ w	3	S
Bird's Nest Spruce	Picea abies 'Nidiformis'	3 x 7′ w	2	S
Soft Touch White Pine	Pinus strobus 'Soft Touch'	3′	3	S
Sand Cherry	Prunus depressa	2 - 3′	4	S
Japanese Spirea	Spirea japonica 'Mertyann'	12 - 15"	3	S
Lowbush Blueberry	Vaccinium angustifolium	12"	2	S, PSh
Cranberry	Vaccinium macrocarpon	4 - 6"	3	S, PSh
Lingonberry	Vaccinium vitis idea majus	6"	2	S, PSh
Mountain Cranberry	Vaccinium vitis idea minus	2"	2	S, PSh
Midnight Wine Weigela	Weigela florida 'Midnight Wine'	3′	4	S
Minuet Weigela	Weigela florida 'Minuet'	2 - 3′	4	S
Yellowroot	Xanthorhiza simplicissima	3′	5	S, PSh
Herbaceous (Perennials & Grasses) Layer				
Doll's Eyes	Actaea pachypoda	24 - 48"	4	PSh
Brunette or Hillside Black Bugbane	Actaea racemosa	48 - 72"	3	S, Sh
Red Baneberry	Actaea rubra	24 - 48"	4	PSh
Maidenhair Fern	Adiantum pedatum	12 - 24"	3	PSh, Sh
Gaiety or Chocolate Chip Bugleweed	Ajuga reptans, Ajuga x 'Chocolate Chip'	2 - 6"	4	S, Sh
New England Columbine	Aquilegia canadensis	24"	2	S, PSh
Wild Sarsasparilla	Aralia nudicaulis	8 - 15"	3	PSh, Sh
Jack-in-the-pulpit	Arisaema triphyllum	6 - 12"	5	S, Sh, PSh
Goatsbeard	Aruncus dioicus	4 - 5"	3	PSh
Canadian Wild Ginger	Asarum canadense	6 - 12"	2	PSh
Purple (Swamp) Milkweed	Asclepias incarnata	36 - 48"	3	S
Butterfly Weed	Asclepias tuberosa	24 - 36"	3	S
Whorled Aster	Aster acuminatus	8 - 15"	3	S, PSh
White Wood Aster	Aster divaricatus	12 - 18"	4	S, PSh
Smooth Aster	Aster laevis	48"	4	S, PSh
Large-leaved Aster	Aster macrophylla	24 - 48"	4	S, PSh
New England Aster	Aster novae-angliae	3 - 6′	4	S, PSh
Astilbe	Astilbe, chinesis 'Pumila'	12"	4	PSh, Sh

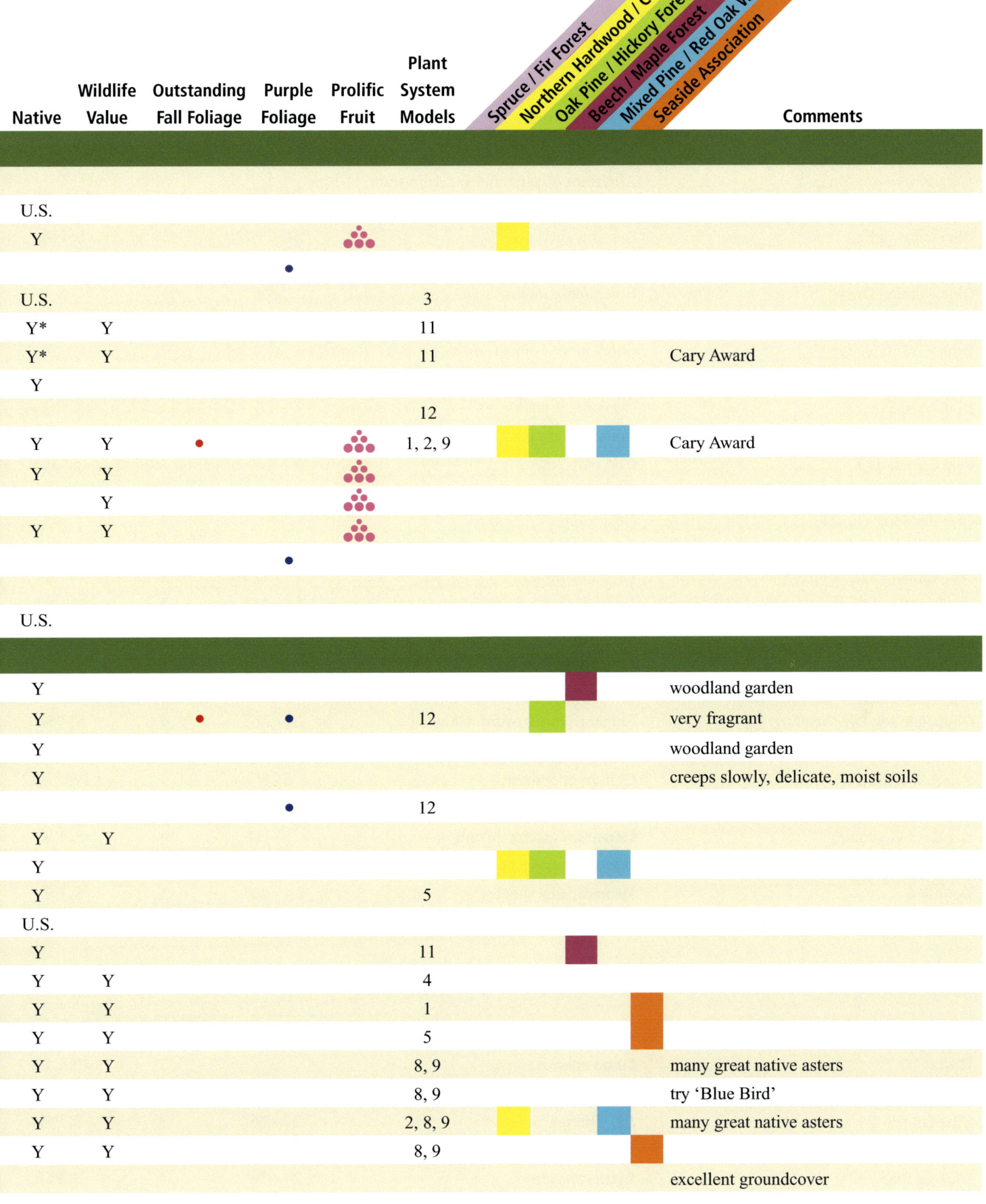

The Plant Systems Approach

Common Name	Scientific Name	Mature Height	Cold Hardiness Zone	Exposure
Herbaceous (Perennials & Grasses) Layer				
Northern Lady Fern, Lady in Red	Athyrium filix-femina var. angustum 'Lady in Red'	20 - 30"	4	PSh, Sh
Blue False Indigo	Baptisia australis	24 - 36"	3	S, PSh
Pigsqueak	Bergenia cordifolia	12 - 18"	3	S, Sh
Blue Gamma Grass	Bouteloua gracilis	12 - 16"	3	S
Marsh Marigold	Caltha palustris	12 - 18"	3	S, PSh
Pennsylvania Sedge	Carex pensylvanica	8"	4	S, Sh
Pink Turtlehead	Chelone lyonii	24 - 36"	3	S, PSh
Blue-bead Lily	Clintonia borealis	6 - 12"	3	Sh
Tall Tickseed	Coreopsis tripteris	48 - 72"	3	S, PSh
Pale Corydalis	Corydalis lutea	8 - 15"	5	S, Sh
Hayscented Fern	Dennstaedtia punctiloba	18 - 24"	4	S, PSh
Crinkled Hair Grass	Deschampsia flexuosa	30"	3	S
Fringed Bleeding Heart	Dicentra eximia	18"	4	S, Sh
Woodland (Yellow) Foxglove	Digitalis grandiflora	10 - 12"	3	PSh
Leather Wood Fern	Dryopteris marginalis	15 - 24"	4	PSh, Sh
Purple Coneflower	Echinacea purpurea	30"	3	S
Barrenwort	Epimedium rubrum	12"	4	PSh, Sh
Joe Pye Weed	Eupatorium maculatum	48 - 84"	3	S
Chocolate Joe Pye Weed	Eupatorium rugosum 'Chocolate'	24 - 36"	4	S, PSh
Blue Fescue	Festuca glauca	8 - 10"	4	S
Sweet Woodruff	Galium odoratum	6 - 8"	4	PSh, Sh
Praire Bottle Gentian	Gentiana andrewsii	12 - 24"	4	S, PSh
Big Root Geranium	Geranium macrorrhizum	15 -18"	4	S, PSh
Oxeye Sunflower	Heliopsis	36 - 48"	3	S, PSh
Daylilies	Hemerocallis species	14 - 40"	3	S, PSh
Round-lobed Hepatica	Hepatica americana	4 - 6"	3	PSh, Sh
Coral Bells	Heuchera species	4 - 24"	4	PSh
Palace Purple Coral Bells	Heuchera micrantha 'Palace Purple'	12 - 24"	4	PSh
Hosta	Hosta species	3'	3	PSh, Sh
Candy Tuft	Iberis sempervirens	8 - 10"	3	S, PSh
Siberian Iris	Iris siberica	24 - 36"	3	S, PSh
Blue Flag Iris	Iris versicolor	24"	4	S, PSh
Blazing Star	Liatris spicata	24 - 36"	4	S, PSh

Native	Wildlife Value	Outstanding Fall Foliage	Purple Foliage	Prolific Fruit	Plant System Models	Spruce / Fir Forest	Northern Hardwood / Conifer Forest	Oak Pine / Hickory Forest	Beech / Maple Forest	Mixed Pine / Red Oak Woodland	Seaside Association	Comments
Y*												
U.S.	Y				3						■	
U.S.	Y				9							
Y	Y				6							stream/water side
Y	Y				1, 2		■	■		■	■	drought tolerant
	Y				6							Chelone glabra - native
Y					5							site specific
Y												
Y												alleopathic, aggressive
Y					9							
U.S.*	Y				7							long flowering if deadheaded
	Y											try 'Carillon'
Y										■		semi evergreen
U.S.	Y				8							butterflies! drought tolerant
												excellent groundcover
Y	Y				4							
	Y			•	12							
					7							
					11							
Y					6							
	Y				2							
	Y				3							
Y												delicate
	Y											for purple foliage try 'Amethyst Mist', 'Midnight Burgundy', 'Plum Pudding', 'Chocolate Ruffles', 'Obsidian'
			•		7							for purple foliage try 'Palace Purple'
	Y											
	Y				1							
	Y											
Y	Y				4							tolerates standing water
U.S.	Y				3, 6							

The Plant Systems Approach

Common Name	Scientific Name	Mature Height	Cold Hardiness Zone	Exposure
Herbaceous (Perennials & Grasses) Layer				
Brit-Marie Crawford Ligularia	Ligularia dentata, 'Brit-Marie Crawford'	36 - 48"	5	S, PSh
Cardinal Flower	Lobelia cardinalis	36"	3	Sh, PSh
Canada Mayflower	Maianthemum canadense	3"	4	S, PSh
Ostrich Fern	Matteuccia struthiopteris	48"	3	PSh, Sh
Wild Bergamot	Monarda fistulosa	2 - 3'	3	S
Blue-eyed Mary	Omphalodes verna	2 - 8"	5	PSh, Sh
Cinnamon Fern	Osmunda cinnamomea	24 - 60"	3	PSh, Sh
Hanse Herms Switchgrass	Panicum virgatum 'Hanse Herms'	4 - 5'	5	S
Purple Foliage Switchgrass	Panicum virgatum 'Shenandoah'	36"	4	S
Beard Tongue	Penstemon digitalis 'Husker Red'	24 - 36"	3	S, PSh
Creeping Phlox	Phlox stoloifera	6 - 8"	4	PSh, Sh
Solomon's Seal	Polygonatum commutatum	60 - 72"	3	PSh, Sh
Christmas Fern	Polystichum acrostichoides	24"	3	PSh, Sh
Self Heal	Prunella grandiflora	8 - 12"	5	S, PSh
Black-eyed Susan	Rudbeckia hirta	30"	4	S
Bloodroot	Sanguinaria canadensis	10 - 12"	3	PSh, Sh
Little Bluestem	Schizachyrium scoparium	30"	3	S, PSh
Stonecrop Sedum	Sedum specable	12 - 36"	5	S
Blue-Eyed Grass	Sisyrinchium angustifolium	8 - 10"	3	S, PSh
Goldenrods	Solidago species	18 - 48"	3	S
Lady's Tresses	Spiranthes odorata	12 - 24"	5	S, PSh
Creeping Thyme	Thymus praecox (serphyllum)	2"	5	S
Foamflower	Tiarella cordifolia	6 - 12"	3	PSh
Starflower	Trientalis borealis	4 - 8"	3	PSh, Sh
False Hellebore, Indian Poke	Veratrum viride	36 - 84"	3	S, PSh
Ironweed	Vernonia noveboracensis	36 - 80"	5	S
Labrador Violet	Viola labradorica	6 - 12"	3	S, PSh
Siberian Barren Strawberry	Waldstenia ternata	4 - 6"	3	S, PSh
Golden Alexander	Zizia aptera	12 - 16"	4	S, PSh

Native	Wildlife Value	Outstanding Fall Foliage	Purple Foliage	Prolific Fruit	Plant System Models	Spruce / Fir Forest	Northern Hardwood / Conifer Forest	Oak Pine / Hickory Forest	Beech / Maple Forest	Mixed Pine / Red Oak Woodland	Seaside Association	Comments
			•									constant moisture
Y	Y				4							hummingbirds! Try 'Ruby Slippers' for butterflies
Y								■		■	■	
Y					11							edible fiddleheads
Y	Y											
					10							
Y												
	Y		•									
Y*	Y											
	Y		•									
	Y				4							
Y												spreads quickly
Y					11		■		■			evergreen flowers, spreads slowly if moist
Y	Y											
Y									■			delicate
Y	Y				3							grass, try 'The Blues'
	Y				1							
Y					1							
Y	Y				8			■		■	■	use natives
Y												forms colonies
	Y				8							
Y					10, 11, 12							'Running Tapestry' has purple markings
Y												cool woodlands, delicate
Y					6							moist to wet, poisonous
Y					6							moist, low ground
U.S.	Y		•									
					2, 8							
Y					1							

The Plant Systems Approach 113

The planting plan: designing the plant system and selecting plants

Factors to consider when designing

Now that you've selected a method to create a plant system, it's time to develop a specific design on a planting plan. When designing your plant system and choosing specific plants, consider the following factors:

- The site's **exposure** to sun. *Full sun* means six or more hours of direct sun daily. *Part sun* means less than six hours of direct sun, or long periods of filtered light (dappled shade). *Shade* means little or no direct sunlight daily and/or less than six hours of filtered light each day.

- The presence of **microclimates**, areas where temperature, humidity and exposure vary from the dominant conditions, (e.g., an area where the sun gets trapped by a stone wall that provides additional warmth to the soil).

- **Soil conditions**. Are there any limitations? (Refer to your inventory for soil type, moisture conditions, and other site characteristics identified in your site inventory.)

- The amount of **planting space** and **soil volume** available.

- **Maintenance requirements**. You may want to integrate low maintenance into the design. (See Integrating Low-Maintenance Practices into the Design on page 118 for more information.)

- **Your budget**. (See Designing within a Budget on page 116 and page 117 for more information.)

- **The right plant** for the right place for the right function. For example, if utility wires run overhead, select plants and small trees that will stay below the wires; don't place arborvitaes and tall evergreens under eaves where they might split apart from ice and snow sliding off the roof. Plant broadleaf evergreens such as rhododendrons, hollies, and boxwoods in winter shade where they aren't exposed to drying winds; and plant cold-hardy, disease-resistant shrub roses in wind-protected, well-drained, sunny sites.

> **EXPOSURE**
>
> Exposure is determined by compass orientation, which way a planted area is facing or from what directions it is protected. The exposure influences the light and wind and combined weather impacts the area receives. In other words, it is the differing proportions of sunlight, wind, and shade an area receives. In New Hampshire, winter winds typically blow from the northwest. On summer afternoons, the sun angles low and from the west. Locations with a southern exposure are often warmer in winter and hotter in summer.

Always choose the right plant for the space. **Left:** *This small shrub, Carol Mackie Daphne, Daphne x burkwoodii 'Carol Mackie', and the adjacent perennials will stay below the windows even when the plants reach full size.* **Right:** *This combination of viburnums and small trees is too tall for this space and will require frequent pruning to keep them below the window.*

Determining shape and plant layout

The available space on your site will determine the shape of your plant system. If you are planting alongside a structure, such as a wall, you arrange the plants in a more linear fashion, with staggered centers and the taller plants in the background. In a large, open area, you'd position the tallest plants in the middle.

When placing plants within a planting area, you'll need to consider each of their light requirements. Remember, what begins as an open area where plants receive full sun, over time develops shade pockets which eventually may not allow enough light for some sun-loving plants to survive.

You can intentionally place plants that require part shade so that other plants that can tolerate full sun will help provide the needed shade until the plant system matures.

Selecting the best plants for the site

The Plant-System Models and the Plant Chart group plants by layers and size and provide information on zone hardiness, site requirements, wildlife value, native or nonnative status, some basic plants associated with natural communities, as well as interesting characteristics of each plant. These factors can help you select plants for your system, but the lists have limitations. We have included many of our favorite plants that fit the needs of a variety of site conditions, but many other wonderful plants don't appear on our list. You may want to find out more about the plants on the list, see what a certain plant looks like and find other plant ideas. Appendix D contains many web sites and books that you may find helpful.

Estimate planting bed size and number of plants

Once you have an idea for the shape of the plant system and the plants you want to include, you need to estimate the space you have available. To give you a general idea for the number of plants needed, compare your space to one of the Plant-System Models. Note that the models were designed for spaces of different shapes and sizes. Each model contains several plants that provide a variety of layers, including those that cover the soil.

The number of plants to include in your planting plan is determined by their mature size and the site conditions. For example, if you want to plant three winterberry hollies whose mature size is 8 to 10 feet wide, you will want to give the plants enough room to grow by planting them so the trunk/stems are 9 feet apart. Also, keep plants' centers at half the distance of the mature width away from planting bed edges, sidewalks, steps, pathways, etc. So, an 8-foot x 10-foot-wide plant would be placed 4 to 5 feet away from obstacles such as

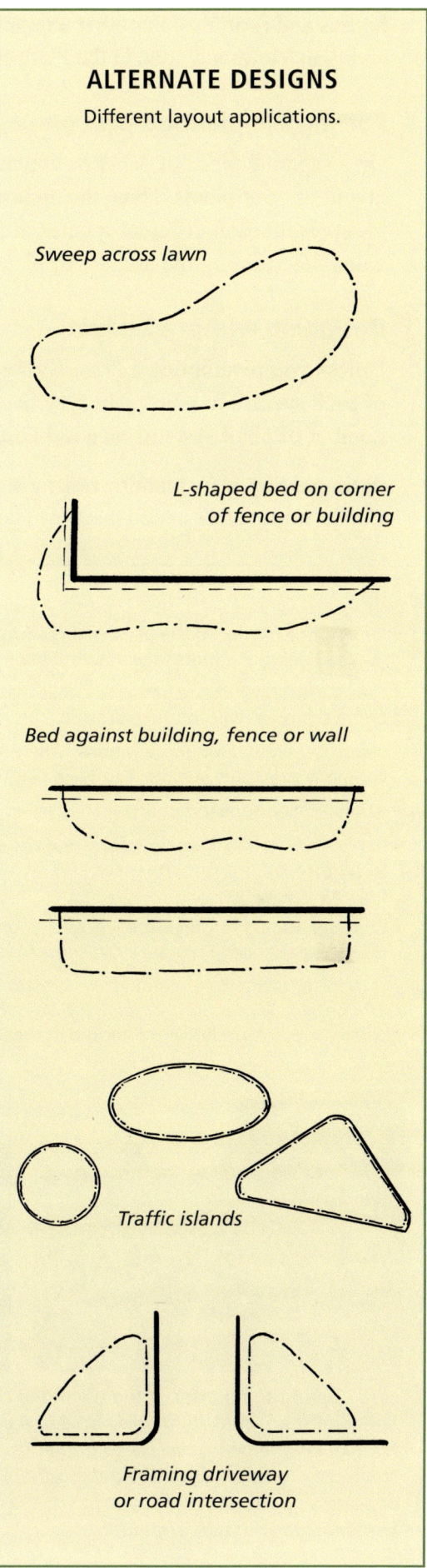

ALTERNATE DESIGNS
Different layout applications.

Sweep across lawn

L-shaped bed on corner of fence or building

Bed against building, fence or wall

Traffic islands

Framing driveway or road intersection

houses and rooflines. For other examples take a look at the Conceptual Elevation, Scale Diagram, and Plan Views included in the Plant-System Models beginning on page 66.

Putting the planting plan on paper

On a separate piece of paper or vellum, use an increased scale of ¼ inch = 1 foot to better visualize the layout of your plants. Draw the approximate outline of your plant-system boundary. Use a different symbol to represent each different species of plant in the plant system. Refer to the plant list for mature size of plants when determining the number of plants needed for the space.

Designing within a budget

Unless you're adopting a Plant-System Model as your own, you may need to increase or decrease the number of each species in your plant system design. If you are creating a large plant system or intend to create a number of plant systems on a tight budget, there are different ways to work with the dollars you have.

A simple way is by planting mostly small plants or seedlings available in the early spring through your County Conservation District and the New Hampshire State Forest Nursery (http://www.dred.state.nh.us/nhnursery/).

DESIGN TIPS

- Curving the border of the plant bed replicates nature more than straight lines and sharp corners and is better habitat for wildlife. Curved lines make spaces seem larger and more distant. Straight lines and sharp edges suggest formality.
- People generally like to gather in areas that provide a feeling of security, created by having a structure behind them, rather than out in the open with nothing around.
- Plants generally look more natural when planted in clumps of 3, 5, or 7. Stagger centers and avoid planting in straight lines. For many examples, see the Plan View diagrams on the Plant System-Models.
- A small space appears confined when its edges are obvious. To modify, use vines or shrubs to soften the straight lines of a fence.
- Cool colors (green, blue, violet) retreat visually, giving the impression of greater space. Warm colors (orange, red, yellow) seem to surge forward, making the space look smaller. When planting warm and cool colors together, use four times more cool colors to balance the warm.
- Consider adding sensory experiences to your design. Include plants of various shapes, textures, and forms to enhance visual and auditory experiences. Fragrance can come from stems and leaves as well as flowers. Edible plants also add to the human experience.

For more information regarding the artistic aspects of design such as balance, contrast, proportion, and form, see *The Perennial Garden-Color Harmonies through the Seasons*, by Jeff and Marilyn Cox. This reference also has an excellent explanation of the golden ratio, the underlying principle in the artistic placement of plants.

Left: Curving the border of the plant bed replicates nature better than straight lines and sharp corners. Berms also add a more natural feel to a landscape.
Middle: People generally like to gather in areas that provide a feeling of security, created by having a structure behind them. **Right:** This plant system has a variety of textures and colors and adds to visual and tactile interest as in this waiting area outside an Italian restaurant.

Commercial landscapers or municipalities can buy plants in bulk from businesses that specialize in providing native species for restoration or mitigation projects such as New England Wetland Plants (www.newp.com), which also sells native seed mixes and upland species. It will take longer for young plants to reach maturity; shrubs will tend to grow faster than trees.

Another option is to phase your plant system in over time, planting the largest material such as a shade tree and building your soil the first year, followed the next year by shrubs and smaller plants.

You could also combine these options, planting one large tree and using seedling stock for shrubs (seedlings come in bundles and are very reasonably priced). These seedlings could be over-planted to start and thinned out as they mature if the extra maintenance is not an issue.

A final option would involve putting in 3 or 4 of the most-costly plants, surrounded by less-expensive perennials and annuals, followed a year later by adding a few more costly plants, moving perennials around to fill any spaces.

THE THREE-YEAR PLAN: AN EXAMPLE OF HOW TO IMPLEMENT AND INSTALL A PLANT SYSTEM OVER 3 YEARS TO ACCOMMODATE BUDGET

Year 1
- *Prep bed—add 2" compost over surface.*
- *Install ornamental rocks.*
- *Install largest plants.*
    - 1 Red cedar
    - 1 Flowering cherry
- *Install filler plants.*
    - 3 Effusa juniper
    - optionals—annuals and/or perennials
- *Cover soil with 3" bark mulch.*
- *Stay off bed and keep well watered.*
- *Leave vegetative litter on in autumn.*

Year 2
- *Select and install more filler plants.*
    - 3 Gray dogwood
    - 1 Virginia creeper
    - 9 Lowbush blueberry
    - 1 'Diablo' ninebark
- *Re-edge bed.*
- *Add 1" mulch or more where mulch less than 3".*
- *Water if less than 1"/week average rainfall, or in drought.*
- *Leave vegetative litter on in autumn.*

Year 3
- *Increase size of bed to accomodate growth of shrubs, if needed, or to add beyond original plan system.*
- *Re-edge old borders, or edge newly created borders.*
- *Add plant material.*
    - 30 Pennsylvania sedge
- *Add herbaceous layer (see suggestions in chart provided).*
- *Add bird feeder, bird bath, bench or ornament.*
- *Check level of bark mulch, making sure it is 3" deep.*

INTEGRATING LOW-MAINTENANCE PRACTICES INTO THE DESIGN

A good common-sense design can help reduce long-term maintenance of your entire landscape. All designed landscapes need some maintenance, but your design choices can help reduce the time needed to maintain the property (or paying someone else to do it) and provide more time for you to enjoy it. Here are some design tips that integrate low maintenance practices:

Preserve existing plants.

Try to preserve or reuse all existing vegetation except invasive species. Augment existing native plants with more natives or other appropriate plants. Plants native to the area often make the best choice, as they have proven that they can handle the site conditions. Natives usually need little or no maintenance and provide an attractive, sustainable landscape that reflects sense of place and supports wildlife.

Create plant systems within lawn areas.

Based on the amount of lawn needed for identified uses, aim to decrease the size of lawn area by increasing the size or numbers of plant systems. For lawn areas you choose to keep, create easy mow lines by designing gradual curves along planting beds instead of sharp angles. For grass pathways, allow enough room for a lawn mower to do the job easily, reducing the need for additional trim work.

Plan for snow plowing and snow removal.

Within parking lots or along sidewalks, large planting beds that encompass a plant system, rather than smaller individual trees, can save time and money. Well-designed planting beds are much easier to plow around than individual plants that have pavement or concrete in between, and large planting beds allow for more soil volume, plant diversity, and increased plant health.

Along the edges of planting beds where snow is likely to pile up, choose perennials that die back in the winter or shrub-like groundcovers that can handle snow loads without becoming damaged (e.g., evergreens such as *Juniperus horizontalis* varieties, Bar Harbor, Blue Rug and Blue Chip; and Russian Cypress, and deciduous, low-growing shrubs such as bearberry, lowbush blueberry, huckleberry, and the cotoneaster varieties 'Lowfast', 'Tom Thumb', and 'Creeping Willowleaf'). Also, remember to choose plants that can handle the road salt that typically comes with snow removal.

This May photo shows a variety of layers and flowering plants that provide early sources of nectar for pollinators increasing diversity while reducing lawn maintenance.

Well designed planting beds within parking lots are much easier to plow around than individual plants that have pavement or concrete in between, and large planting beds allow for more soil volume and plant diversity.

Plant densely and/or choose larger-sized plants to cut back on the need to weed.

In tight spaces choose plants bred to stay smaller than their original parent, such as the Juniperus chinensis, left, and Juniperus horizontalis, right.

Plant densely and/or choose larger-sized plants to cut back on the need to weed.

Incorporating layers of densely spaced plants lessens the amount weeding needed. Selecting larger-sized plants can also help reduce soil exposure and help cut back on weeding. The more space between plants, especially if soil is exposed, the more area becomes available for unwanted plants (weeds) to grow. With layers of "intentional" plants and less exposure to sunlight, the amount of weeding will diminish dramatically. (Remember that young plants may take many years to reach their mature size.)

Select the right-sized plant for the space.

Dense plantings help cut down on weeding, but make sure the plants have enough room to grow. When designing your plant system consider a plant's mature size and choose enough plants so that when they mature, the tips of their leaves just overlap to help block out light underneath. In areas of restricted space, avoid plants that will overtake their neighbors at maturity, necessitating regular pruning. You can still plant your favorite varieties by choosing those bred to stay smaller than their original parent, (e.g. varieties of summersweet such as Compact, Hummingbird, and Sixteen Candles, stay under four feet tall and wide at maturity, whereas their parent plant can grow as tall as 10 feet and 6 feet wide).

Building healthy soils and selecting "problem-free plants" help manage plant diseases and human-induced problems.

Selecting plants promoted as relatively problem-free—especially natives—and using disease-resistant varieties is good common-sense practice. Integrated landscaping relies first and foremost on designing and creating a system of plants, soil, and practices that work together with natural processes. Building the soils in your plant system design helps provide the foundation for healthier plants. Only occasionally will you need to intervene. For example, in the newly established integrated landscaping demonstration site in Grafton County, viburnum leaf beetle became a problem. Landscapers chose the low-impact control strategy of hand-picking the beetles.

Designing for all seasons reduces maintenance and supports wildlife habitat.

Design your plant systems with shrubs and perennials that produce and retain seedheads, fruits, and berries through the winter for birds and other animals. Instead of cleaning up the garden each fall, let the garden put itself to bed. Leaving plants with seedheads standing and dried foliage in place not only provides food for wildlife but adds winter interest for the human eye as plant parts catch snow and ice. Leaving garden cleanup until spring also helps provide winter protection for perennial plants and soils. Plant crowns are protected by a blanket of organic debris, and leaves and plant parts are held in a cage of dried stems left standing. This is especially important in winters of minimal snow cover.

Before you rake it all up, consider that all the so-called yard debris that litters the landscape will decompose as part of the nutrient cycle. Landscape debris is full of nutrients and humus-building components that will feed soil organisms, which are still active in the fall. Thus "litter" becomes a resource, reducing the need to add new mulch every year. Last year's garden debris harbors insects and other invertebrates, which can help ground-feeding migrant birds survive when they return in the spring.

If it just seems too messy, use garden shears to shear back frosted plants without seedheads to 12 inches. Allow the chopped-up stems to fall to the ground and remain in place. Allow at least 12 inches of remaining stems to stand through the winter, their bases capturing and holding windblown leaves, leaving the mulch intact.

- If in doubt about what flowers make good winter food sources for wildlife, experiment. Leave some of each of plant you're less familiar with. You may be pleasantly surprised and entertained.

- Snip annuals at mulch levels, chopping them up into 3-inch to 6-inch pieces and tucking them under existing shrubs or in and around other plants where they can't be seen. Avoid pulling annuals, as this mixes soil into the mulch layer and brings weed seeds to the surface. Leaving annual stems and roots in place reduces the need for weeding in the next season.

- In spring, clip back the remaining stems and leave them at the bases of crowns or take them to the compost bin.

- Apply a ½-inch to 1-inch layer of new mulch to the edge of the bed, without disturbing the original layer.

Leave "litter" in place. Landscape debris is full of nutrients and humus-building components that get pulled deep into the soil to become a resource, reducing the need for adding new mulch every year.

Instead of cleaning up the garden each fall, leave plants with seedheads and dried foliage standing in place, which not only provide food and cover for wildlife but add winter interest for the human eye.

CHAPTER 6

Establishing Plant Systems

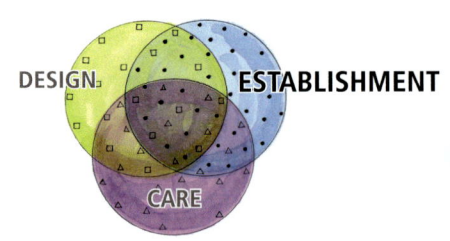

By now you should have one complete plant system designed on a planting plan. The next step is to establish your first plant system as a component of your entire integrated landscape plan, which may contain more than one plant system. This section of the manual takes you through the establishment and care of a plant system.

The ultimate goal is to plant and care for the complete landscape in such a way that plants will thrive, rather than merely survive. The integrated practices that follow will help you establish an ecological and sustainable plant system. When you plant well, you honor your design and lower your maintenance effort and replacement costs.

Protect existing plants

Before making improvements, consider how to protect the valuable features you already have in your plant systems and throughout your landscape.

PROTECTING TREES DURING CONSTRUCTION

Be involved early. Meet on site with all involved in any construction process to discuss the type of work to be completed, and develop strategies for protecting desirable trees, and groupings of existing vegetation.

Protect the Roots:

- Protect the "critical root zones" of desirable trees.

- The radius of the critical root zone is determined by multiplying the diameter of a tree in inches, by 1½–2 feet. In other words, a 10-inch-diameter tree will have a 15–20 foot radius "critical root zone". If possible, don't just protect the "dripline" of the tree.

- The critical root zone should be protected by placing hard fencing around the outer edge of the zone.

- Within this protected zone, there should be no activity, storage or soil compaction.

- Avoid any kind of trenching or soil disturbance close to the trunks of trees and shrubs as cutting, trenching, or soil compaction, may eventually lead to plant decline and death.

- It may not always make sense to protect the full critical root zone especially for roadside vegetation. In these cases, work with others to create the largest "zone of protection" possible.

Protect the Bark:

- If the critical root zone is protected, then bark should be protected. However, sometimes bark still gets damaged during construction and maintenance activities.

- Work with all contractors to be sure everyone understands the importance of bark and the need to protect bark from nicks, scrapes, and gouges.

- Fences and well-defined tree protection zones can help protect bark.

- You may want to additionally mark or flag vegetation that could be in danger of injury from equipment, including trees that may be damaged during routine snow removal.

Protect against changes in grade:

- Changes in grade can be damaging to plant roots.

- Make sure that grade is not changed within identified protection zones.

- You may want to inspect and restore changes in grade that result from normal road maintenance activities such as snow removal and road regrading.

Adapted from *The Citizen Forester*, Dec. 2004, No. 88, Protecting Trees During Construction, Massachusetts Urban Forestry Program.

Lay out your planting bed

Once you've determined the shape and size of the planting bed on paper use a garden hose, clothesline, or flagging tape and stakes to lay out the area. This will serve as the outline of your bed. Refer to your design and move the hose around until you have the approximate shape of the bed. If you plan to locate the bed in a lawn area, consider your foot traffic and flow. Use stakes with colored ribbons of flagging tape to see heights and flows of the design from the outside in. This is also a good time to think about safety, before you put a shovel into the ground, call DIG SAFE System Inc. toll free at 1-888-344-7233. They will help you locate any underground utilities before any digging takes place.

Use a garden hose, clothesline, or flagging tape and stakes as the outline of your bed. Refer to your design and move the hose around until you have the approximate shape of the bed.

You may need to remove existing lawn or other vegetation. If you want to keep some of the plants within an area, try to work around them without having a heavy impact on their root systems, which can extend underground way beyond the spread of the above ground plant.

Saving large trees when creating a plant system underneath

Choose seedlings or plants with smaller rootballs rather than larger plants that will disturb more of the existing tree's roots. Near the trunk where roots are very large, use groundcovers that have very small root systems and can be tucked in among the large tree roots.

When digging a hole under an established tree, try to avoid chopping off the existing tree roots. When you do find large roots, use the combination of pushing roots aside by a few inches and moving the planting hole over a few inches to accommodate space for both tree roots and a small plant. The best scenario is not to hurt roots at all, but when necessary, it is better to cleanly cut off a small feeder root than to damage a large woody anchor root.

Removing existing small plants

When small plants aren't going to be saved and are outside of a tree's critical root zone, there are three ways we suggest to remove them: tilling the area, smothering the vegetation, or using a combination of the two. The quickest method is to use a rototiller to turn up the plants and rake them out. The downside of this method is that you can churn up thousands of latent weed seeds that may be exposed to more light and germinate. However, adding a light layer of mulch after planting can help curb some of this germination. Repeated tilling once every four to six weeks is a very effective method for removing vegetation though it does take more time. (Be aware that this method may actually encourage the propagation of some perennial species from roots and rhizomes.)

Smothering existing vegetation also takes time, but is effective. Turf takes about 6 to 8 weeks to eliminate; other herbaceous and woody plants may take longer. Use a heavy material that blocks light and won't blow away. Plastic sheeting needs to be heavily secured as it easily takes off in a light breeze.

The most effective method is to both till the soil and then cover it to help smother any left over weeds and seeds. Tilling the soil first before covering speeds up the process, as the existing vegetation will break down faster.

Note: Pernicious invasive plants can be more difficult to eliminate. Consult the following resources:

- New England Wildflower Society's website on invasive plant publications with links to many resources: www.newenglandwild.org/protect/invasive-plant-publications.html
- Center for Invasive Species and Ecosystem Health: www.invasive.org
- *NH Guide to Upland Invasive Species,* 2010, by NH Dept. of Agriculture Markets and Food, Plant Industry Division

Preparing the soil for planting

A thorough analysis of the soil will largely dictate the design, implementation, and care of your landscape. The time you've already spent learning about your soil will pay off as you create a planting bed that will nurture your plants and give them the best start possible towards long-term health. If you haven't spent time learning about your site specific soil, we suggest that you review the chapter on soil before you move further ahead with establishing a plant system.

For new plant systems, following your soil test results and preparing the whole planting bed allows you to improve the soil over the entire rooting area. If adding amendments such as lime or compost, till the area six to eight inches deep to incorporate the amendments, making sure to stay outside the critical root zones of existing plants. Use common sense and avoid applying amendments on a steep slope or within 25 feet of any water body.

If planting individual trees or shrubs among existing plantings don't add organic amendments such as peat moss or compost to the backfill. Instead, if you want to add amendments, amend the whole planting bed.

Select healthy plants

Once the planting bed is ready, it's time to purchase your plants. Buy nursery-grown plants from reputable, local dealers who may propagate the plants they sell or buy them in from regional sources. Avoid wild collecting, as it disrupts plant communities and can cause their demise. Rarely do plants collected from the wild survive the ordeal.

Some plants have higher survivability rates if planted in the spring. Evergreens such as rhododendrons and conifers should be planted early, because they are highly susceptible to winter "burn" (desiccation) if roots haven't grown out into the soil before the ground freezes, especially if they have full-sun and/or wind exposure. Some species of deciduous trees also have better survivability when planted in spring rather than fall—oaks, gingko, beech, and birch, to name a few.

Woody shrubs and trees are generally purchased in containers or as balled-and-burlapped nursery-grown plants. Perennials are readily available as container-grown plants or may be mail-ordered as bare-root dormant plants. Each holding method has advantages and disadvantages.

Balled-and-burlapped plants

Larger-size plants dug in the spring for market often come balled-and-burlapped or "B&B," meaning the rootball is wrapped in burlap and tied. B&B trees and shrubs are best planted early in the season or in the fall (September to early October). While they have great "holdability" on top of the ground, they suffer a lot of root damage in the digging process. When selecting B&B stock, be sure the ball of soil is solid and well-tied. A broken, loosely-tied ball frequently suggests dried or broken roots, or both. Flat-bottomed and cracked rootballs are signs of rough handling, which also breaks roots. Desiccated, scorched, wilted, or dull leaves may indicate that the rootball has been allowed to dry out. Avoid plants with these problems.

Balled & burlapped trees and shrubs are best planted early in the season or in the fall; containerized plants can be planted any time the ground isn't frozen.

When purchasing containerized plants, tip the plant on its side and gently pull it out from its container to examine the root system as container-bound plants may have encircling (girdling) roots. Soil or other planting media should be visible between and among the roots.

Bare-root plantings aren't only for seedlings anymore. One- and two-inch-diameter trees are now also being planted as bare-root stock and available for community plantings.

Containerized plants

An advantage of purchasing containerized plants is that they can be planted any time the ground isn't frozen. When selecting containerized plants be aware that rapid growth and finite soil volume inside the container may have caused root-bound plants and encircling (girdling) roots. Neither problem is evident until the plant is removed from the container. Tip the plant on its side and gently pull it out from its container to examine the root system. Soil or other planting media should be visible between and among the roots. With a root-bound plant, you'll see an almost solid mass of roots. Good root systems have many small roots, white, and buff-brown in color.

It's also possible to encounter the opposite problem: not enough roots. Some trees and other types of plants occasionally reach market before they've had a chance to become fully established in a container. Root loss due to environmental extremes (heat, cold, moisture) in the container can also create poor root systems, or even kill containerized plants' roots.

Bare-root plants

These are young trees or shrubs that were field grown then harvested in late fall or sometimes in early spring without soil (bare-root) and stored in a cooler until shipped in early spring. They must be planted while still dormant in the early spring, before warm spring weather arrives (in New Hampshire around April 30). This is when the environmental conditions are favorable: days are slowly providing more light, the earth is cool and moist, but warming, and the spring rains can be abundant. Bare-root shrubs and trees have good survival rates if planted quickly and correctly but may take longer to recover from transplant shock than containerized or B&B material. Bare-root plantings allows for an inexpensive way to plant large numbers and to increase biodiversity on your property.

Bare-root plantings aren't only for seedlings anymore, one and two-inch-diameter trees are now also being planted as bare-root stock and available for community plantings. This is a fairly new technique developed by Cornell University. Please note that with this method trees must be planted within 24 hours of being dug.

Once the plants arrive on site, place them in a shaded location and water well to prevent stress. Don't place plants on hot asphalt and don't let containers and balled-and-burlapped plants dry out. Get plants in the ground as quickly as possible after delivery.

Selecting healthy trees

When selecting trees, look for straight trunks and branches spaced evenly up the stem. Avoid trees that have two leaders (main stems) and those in which the leader has been destroyed. Trees with multiple or missing leaders tend to lose their upward-directed growth.

Some ornamental trees and most fruit trees consist of a top (scion) grafted onto a rootstock. There will be a swelling on the lower trunk where the scion meets the rootstock. This is called the graft union. Grafts are particularly prone to cold damage and may exhibit signs of splitting or abnormal swelling. Avoid a tree with these characteristics. When planting a grafted tree, keep the graft union 2-3 inches above the soil surface.

Avoid trees with visible signs of damage such as broken branches, wounds, injured bark, or discolored areas on branches and trunks. Vigorous trees should have several inches of new twig growth from the previous year. If the tree is in leaf, check for evidence of insects or diseases. Avoid such trees, since these signs are symptoms of stress. Avoid weedy pots or rootballs, an indication that plants have been sitting unattended for a long time. Encircling or girdling roots should also be avoided.

Once the plants arrive on site, place in shade and water well to eliminate stress. Don't place plants on hot asphalt and don't let containers and B&B material dry out. Get plants in the ground as quickly as possible after delivery.

Planting

Placing plants

Set the plants out using your plant system design as a guideline. Don't forget to give plants enough room to grow over their lifetime, by placing plants at least half their mature width away from the center of another plant.

Plants may also be "faced" at this time, turning their best sides towards the primary viewing spot. Step back and observe them from several different angles, including from first- and second-story windows within the building. Adjust as needed until the placement pleases you.

When purchasing a grafted tree, check the graft to make sure there are no signs of splitting or abnormal swelling. When planting, keep the graft union two to three inches above the soil surface.

Plant by order of size

Install plants using proper planting procedures for annuals, perennials, shrubs, and trees as described below. Begin by planting your largest materials first, remembering to check various views (from inside your home/building, from the street, along the driveway, etc.). Start with trees. Plant shrubs next, followed by vines, woody groundcovers, and then herbaceous materials. The largest herbaceous materials (i.e., ornamental grasses) are followed by other smaller perennials, then annuals. Bulbs are planted around and between the above-mentioned plants.

Remove tags and labels

Remove any tags and labels before planting, when they are easy to reach. They not only clutter the visual beauty of newly-planted landscape plants but can constrict the cambium layer of plants, leading to premature death as stems grow. If a label is needed for identification purposes, tuck it under the mulch beside the base of the plant where it can be retrieved to refresh your memory. Your design plans and sketches also provide a record of plant materials.

Plant at proper depth

Planting trees and shrubs at the proper depth is critical to their survival. Generally, plants should be placed at the same depth as they were previously growing. This is not always easy to determine. First, identify the correct depth and expose the trunk flare, the point at the base where the trunk widens and the roots begin to branch from the trunk. Remove any soil that covers the trunk flare. To determine the proper depth of the planting hole, measure the distance between the bottom of the rootball to the bottom of the trunk flare and dig the hole no deeper than this measurement. It is crucial that the bottom of the rootball sit on undisturbed soil to prevent settling over time. If the bed is too deep, even with additional soil, the rootball will settle and sink deeper into the hole. Don't dig or cultivate the bottom of the planting bed, as this may also cause the rootball to settle. Trees and shrubs planted too deep send their roots upward, which can cause roots to eventually encircle the plant and girdle it.

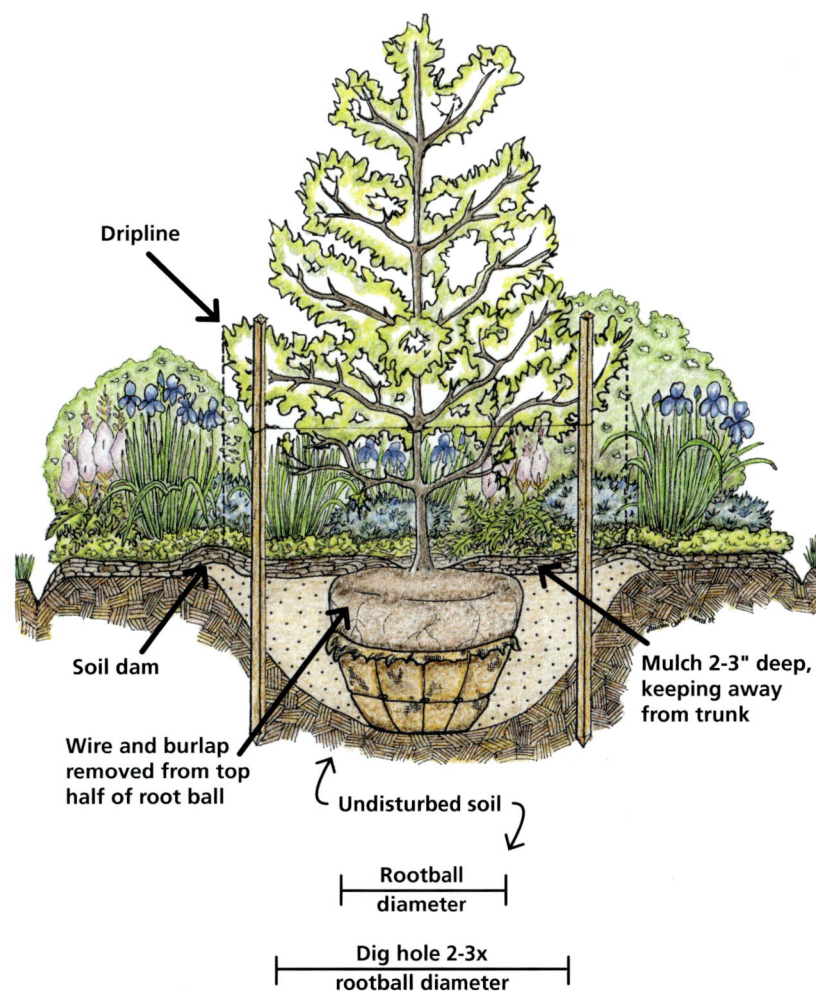

Root distribution

Contrary to popular belief, most roots don't grow deep underground. In fact, most tree roots stay within the top 12 inches of soil. These roots expand outward from the tree or shrub as soil conditions permit. In the right conditions, the root system can grow outward 2-4 four times the diameter of the plant's canopy.

Within a planting bed that hasn't been tilled, dig a hole 2-3 times wider than the rootball. The wider the better! The loosened soil creates more air space for oxygen and water, fostering healthy root growth in the top 12 inches of soil.

Establishing Plant Systems

When carrying the plant, lift and move the tree or shrub carefully by the rootball and keep the rootball intact. Get extra people (strong friends) if you need help lifting, handling or adjusting the tree, as the rootballs can be extremely heavy. To prevent damage to the rootball don't let the tree drop to the ground at any time.

Planting balled-and-burlapped (B&B) trees and shrubs

For B&B trees and shrubs the goal is to protect the rootball from breaking apart or crumbling.

1. Move the plant to the edge of the planting hole.

2. Before placing in the planting hole, cut 2/3 down around the diameter of the wire basket using heavy duty wire cutters. (This is for easy access to the sides of the wire basket that you won't have once it is sitting in the planting hole.) To keep the rootball intact, don't try to remove the top 2/3 of the basket or burlap at this time.

3. Ease the ball gently down the side of the hole, working with gravity.

4. Position the plant in the hole.

5. With your wire cutter, reach down and make additional cuts to the top two thirds of the basket so it can be opened up and lifted up off the ball. Take a utility knife and reach down as far as possible in the hole, cutting the burlap and removing as much as possible leaving the bottom third of the burlap sitting in the bottom third of the wire basket.

6. Remove all ropes, strapping, and strings and any plastic used to package the rootball.

7. Backfill the top half of the hole with soil.

8. Water the soil to remove any air pockets and to firmly set the soil. (A five-gallon bucket works well; a slow hose is even better.)

9. Add the remaining soil to the planting hole. Make sure the top of the rootball and the root flare (the point on the stem where the uppermost roots are connected) is at the surface of the planting bed and doesn't get buried with soil. Don't put extra soil on top of the rootball. Planting too deep is the cause of many plants' demise.

10. Construct a shallow, donut-shaped soil dam at the edge of the rootball to allow water to infiltrate where it can do the most good.

11. Water slowly and deeply right after planting.

12. Stake trees only in extreme conditions, in areas subject to windy conditions. Most B&B or container trees don't need staking as the rootball is heavy enough to anchor the tree. If necessary, provide the support to the lower third of the tree. Staking keeps the rootball stable so roots can grow out into the surrounding soil. Tie the trunk loosely so it can move in the wind, which strengthens it and increases growth. Fasten the trunk to stakes with flexible material such as wide straps or fabric that won't cut into the tree. (The traditional wire-and-garden hose method isn't recommended, because as the tree moves, the wire can cut through the hose and eventually into the tree.) Remove stakes and ties after the first year.

13. Add two or three inches of mulch to the planting area. Pull the mulch a few inches back from the base of the tree to prevent moisture from building up on the trunk.

Planting containerized trees and shrubs

1. Remove each plant from its container and inspect the roots. If they are matted or have roots circling around the container, slice the rootball in three or four places from top to bottom with a sharp knife, slicing about an inch deep.

2. Then make an "X" across the bottom of the rootball. Pull on the loosened/cut roots to tease them out of their circular patterns. Loosening the root structure of container plants in this way is extremely important. Failure to do so may result in girdling roots, slow plant growth and serious stress over time.

3. Prune cleanly any dead or crushed roots.

4. Set the plant in the hole and distribute the roots evenly.

5. Follow steps 7-13 in the section above.

6. Note that container-grown plants generally need more frequent watering during the establishment period.

Planting bare-root tree seedlings, perennials and groundcovers

It is critical that plants remain dormant and that roots never dry out before planting. Keep roots damp and covered. You may also soak bare-root plants in a bucket of water overnight before planting, but don't leave roots sitting in water for longer than that. Dig a hole as wide as the longest roots.

1. Keep the flare of the stem at ground level and distribute the roots so they fan out from the trunk while you place soil around them.

2. Place bare-root plants that don't have a taproot on a mound of soil in the center of the planting hole.

3. If roots are broken or damaged, use sharp by-pass pruners to make clean cuts that promote callus development and growth of new roots from the cut areas.

4. Don't amend soil with compost, lime, fertilizer, or anything other than the soil you dug from the planting hole. Backfill the hole with removed soil to the flare of the plant stem.

5. Water each plant well after planting and shape a saucer or ring of soil around the base to help contain water. Bare-root plants may be more susceptible to drying out because they have so few roots at first. Keep them well-watered for the first year, then water as needed during dry weather.

> **STAKING PERENNIALS AND ANNUALS**
>
> Choosing short or tall sturdy varieties of perennials and annuals reduces or eliminates the need for additional support; however you may still want to include some plants that do tend to flop over in wind or rain. Keeping these plants upright gives pollinators better access to blossoms and nectar. To reduce the staking chore, place these plants in locations that protect them from wind and rain, against a fence or building, or within a densely planted hedge. It also helps to plant them among other tall plants; the hedge-like effect supports tall stems and helps buffer the impact of strong wind.
>
> If you do have plants that need extra support, stake them in early spring to avoid damaging tubers or fleshy-rooted plants such as dahlias and iris. Installing stakes early, also gives foliage time to grow, eventually obscuring the stake.
>
> Choose a stake based on the mature height of the plant, the exposure, and the strength of prevailing winds. Set the stake one to two feet deep to help ensure success. Chemical-free, rot-resistant stakes will last for many years. White oak, metal fence posts, and concrete reinforcing rods cut to desirable lengths are examples of stakes with surfaces that weather to blend in over time. You can also use stems of some of the larger ornamental grasses as staking material, as well as twigs and saplings with branch stubs left on.

Establishing Plant Systems

Planting containerized perennials, groundcovers and other herbaceous material

Plant the perennials, groundcovers, and annuals in single-species groupings, rather than scattering individual specimens throughout the planting bed. Clumps of three, five and seven work well, and massing a single color is pleasing to the eye, as long as you maintain diversity in the overall system.

Plant groundcovers around the bases of shrubs; once they have become established the groundcovers will spread to fill in the planting bed, decreasing the area to be mulched. As with all plants, calculate the mature size of all herbaceous plants to determine proper spacing, and plant staggered on center. Plant densely on slopes to prevent erosion.

Dig a planting hole wider than the soil volume in the container but not any deeper than the plant sits in the pot. If roots are pot-bound, pull them apart before planting. Water in well. Mulch with 1-2 inches of organic mulch, keeping mulch away from the crowns or stems.

Spring bulbs may provide nectar and pollen sources for wildlife in the early spring and serve as a plant-system layer.

Planting bulbs

Spring bulbs provide nectar and pollen sources for wildlife in the early spring. Their flowers deliver a welcome burst of color after a long winter. Bulbs can be planted as a plant-system layer. They also can add a sweep of diversity in a lawn or meadow. Don't forget to explore interesting fall bulbs, too.

For more impact and interest, plant bulbs in groups of 7, 8, or 12, or in large sweeps. It's quicker to plant in a large hole or trench than individual holes. Rake back the litter layer and save it to mulch the bed later. You can plant bulbs close together for more impact when flowering. Generally, three times the bulb height is a good rule of thumb for how deep to plant, but if you're not sure, follow label recommendations for the bulbs you purchase or consult references. Water well at planting time and mulch the planting bed with an inch or two of organic mulch, or replace the litter layer you previously removed.

Water! Water! Water!

Watering is the most important aftercare for all newly installed plants, and it's very common to underwater. Water deeply and infrequently to encourage plants to root deeply. Frequent, shallow watering encourages roots to stay near the surface where they are more apt to dry out.

For the first week after planting, water daily, then every other day for the next two weeks. Continue to water twice a week during the first growing season (until the ground freezes), gradually backing off to once a week in the fall.

How much? A good guideline: add a little more than half a gallon per square foot of soil surface under the dripline twice a week, which delivers an inch of water each week to the root area. For new trees, apply 2-3 gallons of water per inch of trunk diameter (measured at the base) each time. Trees may need additional water during dry periods for the first 3 to 4 years after plantings, while smaller plants are normally established within a year and shouldn't need additional water unless there is severe drought.

A decorative rain gauge or even a simple coffee can help determine if supplemental watering is needed.

Adjust watering frequency according to the weather. A rain gauge will help determine watering needs. If overhead sprinklers are used, a can or pie plate with a rock in it, set in the path of the sprinklers, is a good way to tell when an inch has been applied. High temperatures and winds increase the water needs of plants and cause soils to dry out rapidly. For newly installed plants, water every other day during hot, dry periods. Cool, rainy weather reduces the need for water.

The impact of rainfall also needs to be taken into account. It takes about one-quarter inch of rain to get through the canopy of trees and shrubs. It can take one-half to three-quarters of an inch to penetrate through two inches of dry mulch. In a one inch rainfall event only about one quarter inch of water reaches the topsoil in the above example. Light precipitation may need to be supplemented with additional watering.

Permanent irrigation isn't necessary or recommended. Once established, a sustainable and ecological plant system adapts to the conditions of its environment including periods of heavy rain and dry conditions. In fact, permanent irrigation can interrupt this process. Permanent irrigation also consumes energy and wastes water. Temporary drip irrigation may be helpful for newly-planted systems, but should not be used once plants are established. Also, keep foot traffic to a minimum to reduce compaction of soil to allow water and air to reach plant roots. Once you've established a plant system that's suited to your region and the specific conditions on the property, you'll be rewarded with a landscape that not only enhances biodiversity but also conserves water and energy—including your energy.

Corrective pruning

Well-chosen plants from reputable nurseries will have minimal pruning needs. Follow the three Ds for pruning at planting time: Prune only dead, diseased, or damaged tissues. Pruning cuts, even those well done, demand energy from the plant to compartmentalize or wall off those injuries at a time when you want the plant to establish root growth. Also, because the leaves serve as the source of energy for root establishment and growth, leaving the shoots intact will benefit the plant.

Give small plants at least a year (one full growing season) to make new growth, lengthen stems and roots, and gain overall vigor before doing any structural pruning. Once the plants are well established, use minimal corrective pruning to guide the plant's growth over a period of years. In addition to the three Ds, look for the crossing stems or rubbing branches, inward growth, and competing terminals.

Fruit trees require more than corrective pruning; each species, and sometimes cultivars within a species, has specific pruning requirements for good production. Check the UNH Cooperative Extension fact sheets at http://extension.unh.edu/Pubs/PubsHG.htm#HG_Svt for information on caring for fruit trees.

Larger trees take longer to become established as roots need to return to a normal mass for the size of the tree. Once trees are well established, they may need pruning to develop a good structure

Never "top" a tree (lop off its top to decrease its size or change its appearance). This practice distorts the tree's natural habit and aesthetics and leaves a large wound, making the plant more susceptible to disease and insect attack.

Proper Pruning Principles

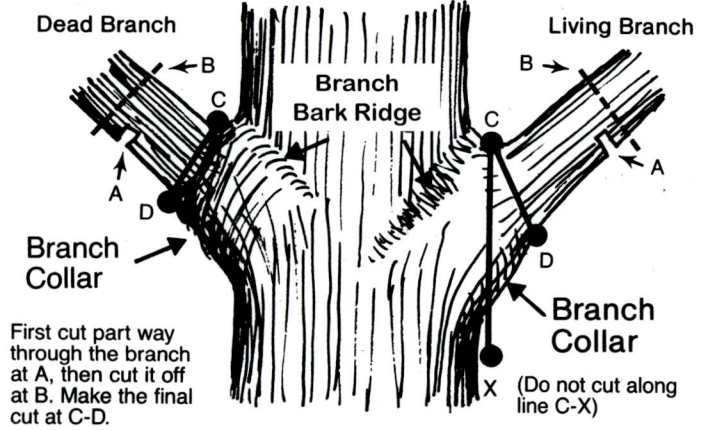
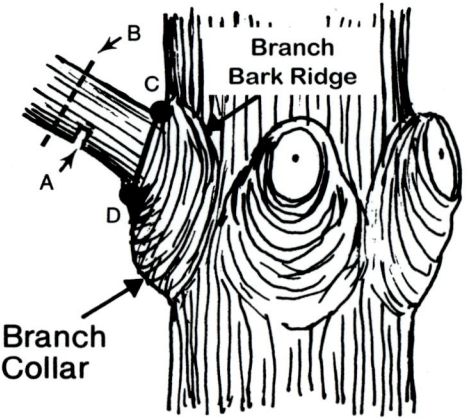

Hardwoods

Thanks largely to the work of Dr. Alex L. Shigo and other scientists at the USDA Forest Service's Northeastern Forest Experiment Station in Durham, NH, much is now understood about a tree's natural system of defense against infections from wounds. Based on this knowledge, these methods of making pruning cuts are recommended to help

Conifers

work *with* rather than against a tree's natural tendency to wall off injured tissues and prevent the spread of decay. In these illustrations, final cuts should be made from points C to D. Do *not* cut along the C-X, which is simply an imaginary vertical line to help you locate C-D.

for long-term health. Different tree species require different pruning strategies. Learning proper pruning techniques is important for continued plant health. Poor pruning practices can result in disease and insect problems that weaken or even kill plants. To learn more about this important topic, see Appendix D.

Edge the planting bed

Once you've finished planting, but before applying mulch, cut an edge to define the boundaries of the landscape bed and any other area, such as turf, patio, walkway, etc, to help reduce maintenance. The most typical edge is between a landscape bed and lawn. In this situation the edging severs and prevents any turf roots from growing into the bed, lessening the chance that lawn plants get established and compete with the landscape plants. A simple cut-in edge that has a slight curve to it can look attractive and graceful as opposed to an edge with many curves that can be distracting and busy. Avoid installing plastic edging, bricks, or other materials to create a boundary. A simple, cut-in edge is all that is needed to define a boundary. Edging materials aren't necessary, can add to the cost, and tend to be less attractive, as they interrupt visual flow and draw the eye to the structural edging rather than the overall landscape. They also tend to heave upward, as the ground freezes and thaws.

A simply cut-in edge that has a slight curve to it can look attractive and graceful. Avoid installing plastic edging, bricks, or other materials to create a boundary.

Cut-in edges can be done vertically or diagonally, using a half-moon-shaped sod cutter or a border spade. A diagonally-cut edge has a few benefits worth mentioning, though it takes a little more skill to perfect. It doesn't cut the adjacent turf roots off as abruptly as a vertical edge does, allowing the established turf roots more room to grow and expending less energy callusing over the cut roots. As a result, turf stays healthier along a diagonal edge than along a vertical edge.

Cover bare soil

Bare soil promotes weed-seed germination, loss of organic matter by wind and rain, loss of water by drying soil, compaction of topsoil by rain splash, and reduction of habitat for valuable soil organisms. The denser the groundcover layer, the less mulch you'll need and the less weeding you'll have to do over time.

Provide 2-3 inches of mulch to cover and protect exposed soil and suppress weeds. Don't apply more than 2-3 inches of mulch, though, as roots need to obtain air and water. Thick applications of mulch and mounds of mulch piled around the base of a trunk or stem ("volcano mulching") encourage plant roots to grow upward into the mulch for air and water rather than outward into the soil. Mulch thickness can vary around plants: up to 3 inches around trees and shrubs, and as thinly as one half to one inch around annuals. Mulch should never touch the stems of plants. It should be pulled away from the base to prevent moisture buildup, which can attract insects and promote disease.

Dense ground covers such as this lamium and variegated Solomon's seal prevent weeds from germinating, offer greater biodiversity and interest than lawn areas and, with their greater surface area and textures, capture water droplets to reduce runoff.

Thoughts on lawns and mowing

Most landscapes incorporate some lawn/turf area where people have a green space to gather, picnic, and play. Manicured lawns appeal to humans, but a monoculture of non-native grasses has little biodiversity and attracts less wildlife. While we don't discourage lawns, we do encourage you to consider carefully how much lawn you need and how you will maintain it.

Avoid thick applications of mulch and "volcano mulching," that encourages plant roots to grow upward into the mulch for air and water rather than outward into the soil.

Non-native grasses are often kept green with applications of fertilizers and pesticides that can be quite toxic to wildlife (such as amphibians and wetland inhabitants) when they run off lawn areas into water bodies. Many non-native grasses also need heavy irrigation. We encourage you to shift your perception of what is "appealing" and reduce the size of manicured lawns on your property. Use grass mixes well-suited to the site that will proliferate and spread. Try low-mow dwarf grass varieties, groundcovers, or stands of Dutch white clover instead. For a more thorough understanding of healthy lawns, see the resources in Appendix D.

Consider wildlife when mowing your lawn. Frog mortality from mowing can be high, especially when metamorphs (young frogs emerging from their tadpole phase) are coming out. Turtles will use open, well-drained soils (including lawns) for laying eggs. We can usually avoid an adult turtle when mowing, but hatchlings are obviously much smaller and could be overlooked. Learn about turtle-hatching dates in your area, and be on the lookout for nesting areas. Why not take a walk around before you mow, and find, and move any visible creatures?

Correct application of mulch thickness can vary around plants: up to three inches around trees and shrubs, and as thin as one half to one inch around annuals. Mulch should not touch the stems of plants.

TYPES OF MULCH

The best mulch for your landscape comes from your own property. Grass clippings, pine needles, chopped or shredded leaves, and wood chips all make good mulches, recycle waste materials on site, and save money. Cover crops such as spring oats planted in late summer or early fall will hold bare soil and the residue will act as mulch in spring, when you can plant right through the matted remains.

Dyed "decorator mulches" come in various colors from orange to purple, most of which don't blend in well with the natural landscape. Wood mulches are expensive, often trucked in from far away, and can contain shredded pressure-treated wood, pallets, and construction debris. Chemicals used in pressure treatment leach into the soil and are known to be harmful to microorganisms and people.

Bark mulch lasts longer than wood mulch and returns more nutrients to the soil. It can be purchased from local sawmills and landscape supply outlets. Using the by-products of a local industry is the next best thing to recycling your own waste materials for mulch. Buying locally also reduces the cost and energy used in shipping, as well as preventing the chance of bringing in non-native pests.

Avoid using non-degradable mulches such as black plastic or landscape fabric. Occasionally they may be warranted for temporary smothering of tough perennial weeds, but otherwise they may actually end up creating more work than they save! When weed seeds germinate on top of landscape fabric or plastic, their roots grow down through it, making removal very difficult. Impermeable plastic can impede rainfall infiltration, interfere with air exchange in the soil, and prevent wet soils from adequately drying out. It's also very difficult to install bulbs, annuals, and other plants when you have to cut through these plastic ground covers. Use organic mulches instead, which have the benefits of adding nutrients and feeding microorganisms.

Practices to reduce mortality and injury to wildlife include delaying mowing (try every two to three weeks instead of every week during times of slower growth). Raising mower blades will provide more habitat for small creatures, and save water, time, and fuel. Leave your grass clippings on the lawn to decompose and recycle nutrients and water back to the turf area.

In midsummer, a mowing height of 3 inches helps prevent drought injury to lawns. Lawns go semi-dormant and turn brown during hot, dry periods if they aren't irrigated; however, they generally make a full recovery once temperatures cool. Healthy soil of at least 6 inches deep helps maintain a healthy lawn with minimal added water. Weeds, though not appreciated by everyone, bring needed minerals up from the subsoil, add biodiversity, and can remain green in the hottest and driest of weather. Bluets, violets, pussy-toes, hawkweeds, wild strawberries, and self-heal left in nicely-shaped patches, can provide visual pleasure, attract butterflies and beneficial insects, and can be mowed after bloom.

Groundcovers can serve as an alternative to a high-maintenance lawn.

132 *Establishing Plant Systems*

CHAPTER 7

Caring for Sustainable Plant Systems

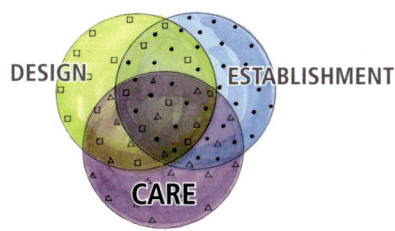

In our extremely fast-paced culture, we look for convenience in our lifestyles and have latched onto the idea of low-maintenance landscapes. The appeal of a beautiful yard surrounding our home, or the manicured look of a commercial property with the promise of little effort, seems as easy to achieve as a wrinkle-free shirt.

While not impossible to achieve, low-maintenance landscapes should use an integrated approach that requires front-end planning in the design and establishment of the plant systems. As a general rule, the more planning carried out initially, the less maintenance needed over time.

Sustainable plant systems are growing, living dynamic communities of organisms under the strong and ever-changing influence of environmental factors such as precipitation, temperature, soil conditions, and human activities. Even with the best practices, care and maintenance are under the influence of uncontrollable factors.

A lower-maintenance landscape

Weather is unpredictable, bringing droughts, floods, spans of sub-zero cold with little or no snow cover, or a warm fall and an early spring, all of which affect plant health. Animal populations also fluctuate in response to plants and weather. Mole tunnels, vole and mice damage, and deer munching on our prize shrubs are part of the pulse of interconnected life in our landscapes. Even the best design and best maintenance plans promising a low level of involvement and expense are at the mercy of the greater rhythms of nature. A certain amount of acceptance and flexibility regarding our landscapes can prime us for the more deliberate and disciplined tasks of maintaining them.

The ecologically-based maintenance practices that follow are part of integrated landscaping and will help plant systems thrive rather than merely survive over the years. You may find some of these practices different from those you use now. For a comprehensive list of practices see Appendix F.

We suggest you try altering one practice at a time, incorporating new practices over time. Take on those you feel most comfortable with and get started. Like life, landscapes evolve over time. We can't stop them from changing but we can learn to adjust to the changes.

Weed management

Understanding the best practices in weed management is one of the most important aspects of reduced landscape maintenance. Weed management, "weeding," can be defined simply as the removal of undesired plants growing in competition with desired ones. Even more simply, let's define a weed as "a plant out of place." Many so-called weeds are useful, beautiful, and interesting when they grow elsewhere. As you learn more about the wild plants in your surroundings, you might even choose to retain a particular weed or weed community as an important part of your landscape planning.

Eliminating weed-seed sources is a key factor in achieving a low-maintenance landscape. Removing weeds while they are small is the best practice, the smaller and sooner, the better. Small weeds pull more easily, quickly, and with the least disturbance of the soil. As a weed is removed, soil clinging to the roots is dislodged and falls onto the surface. Within the soil pulled up from below lurk latent seeds waiting

Use the two-handed method when pulling weeds to minimize the exposure of weed-seed-latent soil to light.

> **BEST WEEDING PRACTICES**
>
> - Small to medium weeds: Use the two-handed method shown at left.
> - Medium to large weeds: Move surrounding mulch back a few inches so tip of spade or trowel can penetrate earth to dislodge the weed. Gently shake soil from the root while it is still partially in the ground.
> - Annual weeds: Annual weeds die at the end of the growing season. Annuals such as lambs quarters, yellow rocket, and amaranth, can be snipped at the ground with pruners. This allows the roots to decompose in place, adding organic matter to the soil without disturbing it. As the roots decompose they establish pathways for rainwater and air. Dormant weed seeds in the soil aren't brought to the surface where exposure to light initiates germination.
> - Biennial and perennial weeds: Biennial weeds such as primrose and thistle produce seeds during their second year of growth. First-year biennials show themselves as tight rosettes growing close to the ground. Perennial weeds such as dandelions and ground ivy produce seeds each year. Remove both biennial and perennial weeds when you first spot them, using the techniques above. Any fragment of root left in the soil can generate a new plant; make sure to get the roots completely out. Because of their deep taproots, biennials, and perennials often accumulate many minerals. So as long as they are not in seed, leave these pulled-up plants, with their roots, hidden underneath other vegetation to decompose.
> - When removing a weed with roots intact, don't allow soil to be cast over the top of existing mulch. Once the soil is gently knocked off of a weed's root system, smooth the area down and cover the disturbed area with mulch.
> - Some weeds such as the invasive purple loosestrife should not be hand-pulled to avoid the "starfish effect" that may occur when their easily broken roots regenerate into many plants after removing the original stem. See Appendix D for more information on removing invasives.

for the presence of light to germinate. There can be hundreds of weed seeds in a handful of soil churned up with the best of intentions.

To help lessen the amount of soil disturbance and seed germination when pulling weeds, use the two-handed method. Hold the soil and mulch in place with one hand at the base of the weed being pulled, and simultaneously dislodge the soil clinging to the weed's roots as it is pulled upward between the thumb and forefinger. This two-handed method is just as quick, but with less disturbance of soil and weed seed germination in later weeks. Place immature weeds under existing vegetation to decompose onsite, increasing organic matter.

It's essential to remove weeds before they go to seed, and best to pull them when they are small. Mature weeds that have formed seedheads, weeds with signs of diseases, or weeds with invasive root systems need to be removed from the planting bed rather than left to decompose.

Insects and plant diseases

From an integrated landscaping perspective, an outbreak of disease or "pest" populations reflect stresses within the larger system. Investigating the causes instead of fixing the symptoms allows plants and animals to fend for themselves, thereby taking advantage of nature's inherent checks and balances. In turn, you can establish a tolerable threshold of damage.

Using pesticides to remove plants, animals or diseases perceived as undesirable may also kill populations of associated creatures. A pesticide application may result in other unintended consequences that disturb the self-adjusting balance of the natural system.

Selecting relatively problem-free plants and using disease-resistant varieties is good common sense practice, yet the bigger picture relies first and foremost on a healthy system. Natural systems are remarkably resilient; they offer great examples of what is needed to maintain overall health.

Artificial fertilizers, insecticides, herbicides, and fungicides may take care of a perceived problem in the short term but can have an overall negative, long-term impact on present and future communities.

Pesticides can also contaminate nearby water bodies. Very small amounts of some chemicals can have large impacts on water quality. Many microscopic animals such as water fleas and aquatic insect larvae are highly susceptible to even very low concentrations of some pesticides. Loss of these organisms can affect the efficient cycling of nutrients throughout the system, as well as the health of fish populations and other aquatic life.

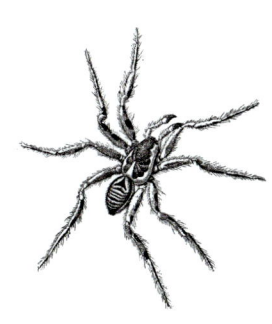

Managing Plant Stressors

There may be times when your plant system does need help. Insects and diseases may emerge to cause unanticipated threats. For example, recent outbreaks of hemlock woolly adelgid continue to threaten eastern hemlocks, and the viburnum leaf beetle is becoming a problem with many species of viburnums. Use an Integrated Pest Management (IPM) approach from the start.

Inspect plants regularly, focusing on high-value or highly visible plants. Try to identify problems early. Make sure you've identified the real cause of a plant problem before taking action. It may require some research on the insect or disease to determine what strategy will work best. Always give natural parasitoids and predators a chance to suppress the problem.

Can you remove the plant damage and/or pest organism by hand, by pruning, or with a jet of water? Look for cultural solutions to disease problems: improve air circulation around plants, conserve water in the soil to reduce seasonal drought stress, plant resistant varieties. If a plant continuously has problems, perhaps replacing it with a less problematic plant is the best strategy.

Through the seasons

Dividing plants

Plants that rarely need dividing have lower maintenance requirements, but won't cover the ground as fast. Perennials that do need division such as daylilies, iris, and astilble, help increase the quality and quantity of plants and their blooms. When plants do need division, use these "new plants" to create large, single-species sweeps. Such sweeps serve as better visual anchors than a hodge-podge of single plants of different species. Large groupings provide more flowers, nectar, and pollen for wildlife that prefer working one plant species at a time. Division stresses plants, as they use energy to counter and acclimate to new sites. Provide adequate shade and water while recently divided plants recover.

> **THE STERILE GARDEN**
>
> *A plant that has fed nothing has not done its job. Somehow along the way we have come to expect perfection in our gardens. . . . Today gardeners are so concerned about the health of their plants that they run for the spray can at the first sign of an insect. Ironically, a sterile garden is one teetering on the brink of destruction. It can no longer function as a dynamic community of interacting organisms, all working smoothly to perpetuate their interactions. Its checks and balances are gone. Instead, the sterile garden's continued existence depends entirely on the frantic efforts of the gardener alone.*
>
> — Douglas Tallamy, *Bringing Nature Home*

Dragonflies keep other insects in check.

Ladybug preys on aphids.

Dead-heading

When flowers dry up and seedheads form, it may appear from a human point of view that a plant's seasonal life cycle is complete. The urge to remove "unsightly" seedheads and get plants to re-bloom is common. However, deadheading interrupts natural cycles and stimulates the production of more blooms, requiring additional energy to replace the top growth, and the fading flowers still harbor varying amounts of pollen and nectar useful to other life forms. By allowing spent flower heads to remain, diverse relationships between plant and animal cycles are encouraged. Seeds that mature can also lead to spring seedlings you wouldn't get with dedicated deadheading. Leave "dead-heads" hidden beneath foliage on the floor of the garden to feed soil life and create humus.

Spent flowers and stems tucked beneath plants feed soil life and create humus over time.

Limit seasonal cleanup

Leaving natural debris in the landscape instead of raking beds and pulling annuals decreases labor and contributes to a healthy system. When left in place, the plant debris, full of nutrients and humus-building components, begins to decompose and over time is pulled deep into the earth by soil organisms. Twigs, leaves, and chopped-up stems decompose more readily than bark mulch, while adding to the humus layer, and reducing the need for additional mulch every year. Limited raking in planting beds minimizes the unintended mixing of soil into the mulch layer. This reduces the need for weeding next season.

When we think of autumn we may think of the dramatic color of our trees, but look around for interesting "understatements" too.

Landscape beds have more winter interest and are aesthetically pleasing when plants are left standing to catch snow and ice. They also harbor valuable seedheads, fruits, and dried berries for birds and other animals into and through the winter, when they need it most. Last year's leaves and other winter debris harbor insects and other invertebrates, which can help ground-feeding migrant birds survive when they return in the spring.

Tips for cleanup

- Leave frosted plants standing in the garden if they have seedheads. Shear back the top 12 inches of others with garden shears at 3-4 inch intervals, letting the chopped up stems fall to the ground. Allow at least 12 inches of remaining stems to stand through the winter, as their bases capture and hold windblown leaves. Leave mulch intact.

Winter interest for people and wildlife.

- Snip annuals at mulch level, chop up into 3-6 inch pieces and place under existing shrubs, or between the stem-protruding crowns (with the exception of diseased plants which should be removed).
  Note: Diseased plants need to be removed. Do not compost diseased plant tissue.

- In spring, clip back remaining stems and either leave them at the base of plants or add to compost.

- In spring, if desired, apply one-half to one inch of mulch (making sure the mulch layer does not exceed 3 inches) to the edge of the bed without disturbing the original layer.

Winter protection

Healthy plant systems need little assistance when it comes to surviving the winter season. Follow nature's lead, which is effective and resource-savvy, especially when preparing for winter. Nature covers and insulates the ground level with a layer of litter, inviting more life to stay put while adding nutrients, minimizing temperature extremes, and reserving moisture levels. A blanket of fall leaves protects the previous season's accumulation of organic matter, which can be blown or washed away during winter, especially in times of little or no snow cover.

If lower maintenance is your goal, there is no need to choose plants that require winter protection such as cages or products to help prevent desiccation. Keep in mind, "the right plant for the right place for the right function."

Re-edging beds in the spring

Re-edge beds each spring on the original edge without increasing the bed size. Start by pushing mulch back from the work area. Push soil from the trench gently up onto the planting bed without mixing soil in with mulch. Step away and look at your edge to see if it is smooth and graceful. Pull mulch back to cover exposed soil. Increase bed size only if you need to accommodate the growth of trees and shrubs. Transplant groundcovers that spill over the edge to areas missing lower layers of vegetation.

Re-edge beds each spring to separate lawn from planting beds.

SEASONAL CALENDAR FOR WILDLIFE HABITAT PLANTINGS AND STRUCTURES

This sample calendar shows suggested seasonal actions to consider in maintaining a wildlife habitat area.

December-February
- Keep all bird feeders cleaned and filled.
- Keep water source free of ice.
- Clean out old nests from bird nest boxes.
- Put up new bird-nesting boxes.
- Build bat boxes, bird boxes and feeders.
- Start planning spring projects.

March-April
- Check all structures for winter damage.
- Check around pond for damage or areas where rubber liner is exposed.
- Check nesting boxes once a week for bird nesting activity.
- Keep all bird feeders cleaned and filled until the end of March.
- Take down bird feeders at the end of March (bears are coming out of hibernation); thoroughly clean and store.

April-May
- Reinstall pump in pond.
- After bird migrations in April, cut standing dead perennials and let fall in place.
- Plant new gardens with shrubs and perennials for wildlife food and cover.
- Monitor nest boxes.
- Keep water source clean and filled.

June-August
- Water and weed beds and garden plots (as needed).
- Repaint, re-stain, or repair all wooden structures (as needed).
- Keep birdbaths clean and filled; scrub to remove algae.
- Mow fields after August 1.

September-November
- Thin and plant new bulbs, corms, and tubers.
- Cover pond with mesh or netting to keep leaves out.
- Clean out nesting boxes.
- Begin filling bird feeders in mid-late November.
- Keep water source clean and filled.

Wildlife activity around your site will fluctuate as the area develops. Certain species will meet their habitat needs in an early-growth vegetated area, while others will benefit from a mature plant community.

Care and maintenance tips for future years

Expand the landscape bed over time. As woody plants, such as shrubs and trees, grow, expand the edge of the bed to accommodate their new size. For perennials and groundcovers, divide and fill in open spots, move extras to another plant system, or join a plant swap. You can let nature take its course or choose to take a more active role. For example, move sun-loving perennials to the outer edge of the bed or to another garden and introduce shade-loving plants in their place, as the plant system matures.

Stay alert for potential new invasive species. As mentioned earlier, invasive species can migrate into your landscape from neighboring properties. By learning to identify them you can remove them early before they become a problem. However, in future years it is likely that new invasive species will become part of the Northeast's landscapes. Stay on top of emerging problems. (See Appendix D.)

Consider wildlife habitat as ongoing work. Wildlife activity around your site will fluctuate as the area develops. Certain species will meet their habitat needs in an early-growth vegetated area and others will benefit from a more mature planting. Allow your habitat to be a work in progress, adding additional plants or structures over time. You may wish to keep a log of the wildlife activity on your site, listing birds that feed and nest, for instance, or amphibians you observe.

Healthy plant systems grow and change over time

As natural landscapes grow and change over time, so will plant systems. Changes may occur suddenly and dramatically by the force of nature like an extreme weather event or they may evolve slowly as plants grow, mature, and compete for resources. Instead of trying to stop change, or "fix it," embrace the changes you see. Go back occasionally and see if your planting systems incorporate the integrated landscaping principles.

As plant systems mature, some plants will thrive while others may not. While you observe the landscape, you'll see plants that move toward the sun and others that stay in the shadows. Don't rush to make changes; see what the system does on its own. You'll be in for some interesting and pleasant surprises.

GARDENS THAT MAKE A DIFFERENCE

But now, for the first time in its history, gardening has taken on a role that transcends the needs of the gardener. Like it or not, gardeners have become important players in the management of our nation's wildlife. It is now within the power of individual gardeners to do something that we all dream of doing: to make a difference. In this case, the 'difference' will be to the future of biodiversity, to the native plants and animals of North America and the ecosystems that sustain them.

Douglas Tallamy, *Bringing Nature Home*

This viburnum seedling, discovered in a 15-year-old, now heavily shaded, plant system, provides an unexpected but welcome addition.

138 *Caring for Sustainable Plant Systems*

By following nature's lead, as this maturing plant system at the Blaisdell Memorial Library in Nottingham, NH, demonstrates, vibrant and low maintenance spaces are created and become models for others.

Now, get up and get out!

Whether you've read this manual cover-to-cover or just skimmed through it, step outside right now and begin looking at your surroundings in a new way. You might begin by trying to find a feature of your existing landscape you hadn't noticed before: the play of light and shadow on the ground below the old crabapple tree, a fleet of dragonflies flitting around a planting bed, or the way a layered planting area pleases the eye.

Can you see parts of your existing landscape that already follow nature's lead? Can you think of one small change you could make toward a more integrated landscape?

If you have plants that already provide food for wildlife, could you add a few more to create layers to provide wildlife cover, as well?

If you see an area of exposed soil, could you protect it with mulches and ground covers?

Is there an invasive plant species you could remove and replace with your first plant system?

By following nature's lead, you can make changes in your own outdoor space that really matter to the world around you, from the smallest unseen participants, such as microorganisms, to the larger players, including us. In the process, the landscape can become a model for others. Every small step taken leads toward a more integrated approach. As vibrant, useful yards and landscapes connect to one another, across neighborhoods and public spaces, the positive impacts will benefit the natural landscape, the air, water and soil, and all of the life that ultimately depends on it.

APPENDIX A

BEST BETS: Woody Plants
Favorite native woody plants for mid-Atlantic butterflies and moths

Common Name	Plant Genus	Number of Butterly/Moth Species Supported
Oak	Quercus	534
Black cherry	Prunus	456
Willow	Salix	455
Birch	Betula	413
Poplar	Populus	368
Crabapple	Malus	311
Blueberry	Vaccinium	288
Maple	Acer	285
Elm	Ulmus	213
Pine	Pinus	203
Hickory	Carya	200
Hawthorn	Crataegus	159
Spruce	Picea	156
Alder	Alnus	156
Basswood	Tilia	150
Ash	Fraxinus	150
Rose	Rosa	139
Filbert	Corylus	131
Walnut	Juglans	130
Beech	Fagus	126
Chestnut	Castanea	125

BEST BETS: Herbaceous Plants
Favorite native herbaceous plants for mid-Atlantic butterflies and moths

Common Name	Plant Genus	Number of Butterly/Moth Species Supported
Goldenrod	Solidago	115
Aster	Aster	112
Sunflower	Helianthus	73
Joe Pye, Boneset	Eupatorium	42
Morning glory	Ipomoea	39
Sedge	Carex	36
Honeysuckle	Lonicera	36
Lupine	Lupinus	33
Violet	Viola	29
Geranium	Geranium	23
Black-eyed susan	Rudbeckia	17
Iris	Iris	17
Evening primrose	Oenothera	16
Milkweed	Asclepias	12
Verbena	Verbena	11
Beardtongue	Penstemon	8
Phlox	Phlox	8
Bee balm	Monarda	7
Veronica	Veronica	6
Little bluestem	Schizachyrium	6
Cardinal flower	Lobelia	4

Source: *Bringing Nature Home,* Douglas Tallamy; http://bringingnaturehome.net/

APPENDIX B

PLANT LISTS
Select Listing of Replacement Plants that describe attributes found in Invasive Species (Including Wildlife Value, Aesthetic Summer and Fall Foliage, Prolific Flowers, and Fruit)

Outstanding Fall Foliage - Tree Layer

Common Name	Scientific Name
Amur Maple	Acer ginnala
Paperbark Maple	Acer griseum
Japanese Maple	Acer palmatum
Red Maple	Acer rubrum
Sugar Maple	Acer saccharum
Shadblow, Serviceberry	Amelanchier canadensis
Allegheny Serviceberry	Amelanchier laevis
Autumn Brilliance Serviceberry	Amelanchier x. grandiflora 'Autumn Brilliance'
Cole Serviceberry	Amelanchier x. grandiflora 'Cole'
Pagoda Dogwood	Cornus alternifolia
White Flowering Dogwood	Cornus florida
Cornelian Cherry Dogwood	Cornus mas
Wada's Memory Magnolia	Magnolia x. 'Wada's Memory'
Black Gum	Nyssa sylvatica
Sourwood	Oxydendrum arboreum
Callery Pear	Pyrus calleryana
Scarlet Oak	Quercus coccinea
Pin Oak	Quercus palustris

Outstanding Fall Foliage - Shrub and Small Tree Layer

Common Name	Scientific Name
Regent Serviceberry	Amelanchier alnifolia 'Regent'
Red Chokeberry	Aronia arbutifolia 'Brilliantissima'
Black Chokeberry	Aronia melanocarpa
Silky Dogwood	Cornus amomum
Gray Dogwood	Cornus racemosa
Rockspray Cotoneaster	Cotoneaster horizontalis
Nikko Deutzia	Deutzia gracilis 'Nikko'
Dwarf Bush-Honeysuckle	Diervilla lonicera
Heart-Leaved Disanthus	Disanthus cercidifolius
Redvein Enkianthus	Enkianthus campanulatus
Large Fothergilla	Fothergilla major
Dwarf Huckleberry	Gaylussacia dumosa 'Bigeloviana'
Pallida Chinese Witchhazel	Hamamelis mollis 'Pallida'
Oakleaf Hydrangea	Hydrangea quercifolia
Little Henry Sweetspire	Itea virginica 'Little Henry'
Virginia Creeper (vine)	Parthenocissus quinquefolia
Low Grow Fragrant Sumac	Rhus aromatica 'Low Grow'
Flameleaf Sumac	Rhus copallina
Staghorn Sumac	Rhus typhina
Red Berried Elderberry	Sambucus pubens
Lowbush Blueberry	Vaccinium angustifolium
Highbush Blueberry	Vaccinium corymbosum
Arrowwood Viburnum	Viburnum dentatum
Doublefile Viburnum	Viburnum plicatum tomentosum
Blackhaw Viburnum	Viburnum prunifolium
American Cranberry Viburnum	Viburnum trilobum
Compact American Cranberry Viburnum	Viburnum trilobum 'Compacta'

Purple Foliage - Tree Layer

Common Name	Scientific Name
Amur Maple	Acer ginnala
Japanese Maple	Acer palmatum
Crimson Frost Japanese Birch	Betula platyphylla 'Crimson Frost'
Royal Frost Japanese Birch	Betula platyphylla 'Royal Frost'
Forest Pansy Eastern Redbud	Cercis canadensis 'Forest Pansy'
Grace Smoke Bush	Cotinus coggygria 'Grace'
Purple Fountain Beech	Fagus sylvatica 'Purple Fountain'
Copper Beech	Fagus sylvatica 'Purpurea'
River's Purple European Beech	Fagus sylvatica 'Riversii'
Rohani Purple Beech	Fagus sylvatica 'Rohanii'
Spaeth Purple Beech	Fagus sylvatica 'Spaethiana'
Wada's Memory Magnolia	Magnolia x. 'Wada's Memory'
Cardinal Tea Crabapple	Malus hupehensis 'Cardinal'
Pink Princess Crabapple	Malus 'Pink Princess'
Pink Spires Crabapple	Malus 'Pink Spires'
Prairiefire Crabapple	Malus 'Prairiefire'
Velvet Pillar Crabapple	Malus 'Velvet Pillar'
Wildfire Tupelo	Nyssa sylvatica 'Wildfire'
Blireana Plum	Prunus x blireana
Mt. St. Helen's Flowering Plum	Prunus cerasifera Mt. St. Helen's
Newport Flowering Plum	Prunus cerasifera 'Newport'
Thundercloud Plum	Prunus cerasifera 'Thundercloud'
Canada Red Chokecherry	Prunus virginiana 'Schubert'

Purple Foliage - Shrub and Herbaceous Layer

Common Name	Scientific Name
Brunette or Hillside Black Bugbane	Actaea racemosa
Gaiety or Chocolate Chip Bugleweed	Ajuga reptans
Royal Purple Smokebush	Cotinus coggygria 'Royal Purple'
Chocolate Joe Pye Weed	Eupatorium rugosum 'Chocolate'
Weeping Purple Beech	Fagus sylvatica 'Purpurea Pendula'
Red Obelisk Beech	Fagus sylvatica 'Red Obelisk'
Expresso Spotted Cranesbill	Geranium maculatum 'Expresso'
Hocus Pocus Hardy Cranesbill	Geranium pratense 'Hocus Pocus'
Coral Bells, foliage types	Heuchera foliage types: 'Amethyst Myst', 'Midnight Burgundy', 'Obsidian', 'Palace Purple'
Brit-Marie Crawford Ligularia	Ligularia dentata, 'Brit-Marie Crawford'
Candymint Crabapple	Malus 'Candymint'
Pink Princess Crabapple	Malus 'Pink Princess'
Origanum laevigatum	Origanum laevigatum 'Rosenkuppel'
Beard tongue	Penstemon digitalis 'Husker Red'
Diablo Ninebark	Physocarpus opulifolius 'Diablo'
Summer Wine Ninebark	Physocarpus opulifolius 'Summer Wine'
Black Beauty Elderberry	Sambucus nigra 'Black Beauty'
Guincho Purple Elderberry	Sambucus nigra 'Guincho Purple'
Cutleaf European Elderberry	Sambucus nigra 'Laciniata'
Midnight Wine Weigela	Weigela florida 'Midnight Wine'
Wine and Roses Weigela	Weigela florida 'Wine and Roses'

Prolific Fruit - Tree Layer

Common Name	Scientific Name
Japanese Maple	Acer palmatum
Eastern Flowering Dogwood (sporadic)	Cornus florida
Cornelian Cherry Dogwood	Cornus mas
Kousa Dogwood	Cornus kousa
Wada's Memory Magnolia	Magnolia x. 'Wada's Memory'
Cardinal Tea Crabapple	Malus hupehensis 'Cardinal'
Pink Spires Crabapple	Malus 'Pink Spires'

Prolific Fruit - Tree Layer

Common Name	Scientific Name
Prairiefire Crabapple	Malus 'Prairiefire'
Black Gum	Nyssa sylvatica
Chokecherry	Prunus virginiana

Prolific Fruit - Shrub and Herbaceous Layer

Common Name	Scientific Name
Doll's Eyes	Actaea pachypoda
Red Baneberry	Actea rubra
Wild Sarsaparilla	Aralia nudicaulis
Bearberry	Arctostaphylos uva-ursi
Jack-in-the-pulpit	Arisaema triphyllum
Blue-bead lily	Clintonia borealis
Bunchberry Dogwood	Cornus canadensis
Rockspray Cotoneaster	Cotoneaster horizontalis
Black Crowberry	Empetrum nigrum
Wintergreen	Gaultheria procumbens
Dwarf Huckleberry	Gaylussacia dumosa 'Bigeloviana'
Canada Mayflower	Maianthemum canadense
Partridgeberry, Checkerberry	Mitchella repens
Solomon's Seal	Polygonatum commutatum
Beach plum	Prunus maritima
Low Grow Fragrant Sumac	Rhus aromatica 'Low Grow'
Staghorn Sumac	Rhus typhina
Native Roses	Rosa spp. (R. virginiana, carolina, palustris)
Black Beauty Elderberry	Sambucus nigra 'Black Beauty'
Mapleleaf Viburnum	Viburnum acerifolium
Hobblebush Viburnum	Viburnum alnifolium
Wild Raisin, Witherod Viburnum	Viburnum cassinoides
Arrowwood Viburnum	Viburnum dentatum
Linden Viburnum	Viburnum dilatatum
Nannyberry Viburnum	Viburnum lentago
Doublefile Viburnum	Viburnum plicatum tomentosum
Blackhaw Viburnum	Viburnum prunifolium
American Cranberry Viburnum	Viburnum trilobum
Compact American Cranberry Viburnum	Viburnum trilobum 'Compacta'
Lowbush Blueberry	Vaccinium angustifolium
Highbush Blueberry	Vaccinium corymbosum
Cranberry	Vaccinium macrocarpon
Lingonberry	Vaccinium vitis idea majus
Mountain Cranberry	Vaccinium vitis idea minus

Flowering Tree Layer

Common Name	Scientific Name
Red Maple	Acer rubrum
Shadblow, Serviceberry	Amelanchier canadensis
Allegheny Serviceberry	Amelanchier laevis
Autumn Brilliance Serviceberry	Amelanchier x. grandiflora 'Autumn Brilliance'
Cole Serviceberry	Amelanchier x. grandiflora 'Cole'
Forest Pansy Eastern Redbud	Cercis canadensis 'Forest Pansy'
Pagoda Dogwood	Cornus alternifolia
Eastern Flowering Dogwood	Cornus florida
Cornelian Cherry Dogwood	Cornus mas
Grace Smoke Bush	Cotinus coggygria 'Grace'
Common Witchhazel	Hamamelis virginiana
Wada's Memory Magnolia	Magnolia x. 'Wada's Memory'
Candymint Crabapple	Malus 'Candymint'
Cardinal Tea Crabapple	Malus hupehensis 'Cardinal'
Pink Princess Crabapple	Malus 'Pink Princess'

Flowering Tree Layer

Common Name	Scientific Name
Pink Spires Crabapple	Malus 'Pink Spires'
Prairiefire Crabapple	Malus 'Prairiefire'
Velvet Pillar Crabapple	Malus 'Velvet Pillar'
Sourwood	Oxydendrum arboreum
Newport Flowering Plum	Prunus cerasifera 'Newport'
Thundercloud Plum	Prunus cerasifera 'Thundercloud'
Canada Red Chokecherry	Prunus virginiana 'Schubert'

Flowering Shrub and Herbaceous Layer

Common Name	Scientific Name
Brunette or Hillside Black Bugbane	Actaea racemosa
Bugleweed	Ajuga reptans
Regent Serviceberry	Amelanchier alnifolia 'Regent'
Red Chokecherry	Aronia arbutifolia 'Brilliantissima'
Black Chokeberry	Aronia melanocarpa
Blue False Indigo	Baptisia australis
Pigsqueak	Bergenia cordifolia
Boxwood	Buxus macrophylla 'Wintergem'
County Wicklow Scotch Heather	Calluna vulgaris 'County Wicklow'
Gold Haze Scotch Heather	Calluna vulgaris 'Gold Haze'
Martha Herman Scotch Heather	Calluna vulgaris 'Martha Herman'
Springtorch Scotch Heather	Calluna vulgaris 'Springtorch'
Pink Turtlehead	Chelone lyonii
Tall Tickseed	Coreopsis tripteris
Silky Dogwood	Cornus amomum
Gray Dogwood	Cornus racemosa
Royal Purple Smokebush	Cotinus coggygria 'Royal Purple'
Slender Deutzia	Deutzia gracilis
Fringed Bleeding Heart	Dicentra eximia
Dwarf Bush-Honeysuckle	Diervilla lonicera
Woodland (yellow) foxglove	Digitalis grandiflora
Redvein Enkianthus	Enkianthus campanulatus
Chocolate Joe Pye Weed	Eupatorium rugosum 'Chocolate'
Large Fothergilla	Fothergilla major
Expresso Spotted Cranesbill	Geranium maculatum 'Expresso'
Hocus Pocus Hardy Cranesbill	Geranium pratense 'Hocus Pocus'
Daylilies	Hemerocallis species
Coral Bells	Heuchera micrantha 'Palace Purple'
Annabelle Hydrangea	Hydrangea arborescens 'Annabelle'
Little Henry Sweetspire	Itea virginica 'Little Henry'
Othello, Brit-Marie Ligularia	Ligularia dentata 'Othello', 'Brit-Marie'
Beard tongue	Penstemon digitalis 'Husker Red'
Diablo Ninebark	Physocarpus opulifolius 'Diablo'
Self Heal	Prunella grandiflora
Staghorn Sumac	Rhus typhina
Mertyann Japanese Spirea	Spirea japonica 'Mertyann'
Miss Kim Lilac	Syringa patula 'Miss Kim'
Lowbush Blueberry	Vaccinium angustifolium
Highbush Blueberry	Vaccinium corymbosum
Arrowwood Viburnum	Viburnum dentatum
Blackhaw Viburnum	Viburnum prunifolium
American Cranberry Viburnum	Viburnum trilobum

APPENDIX C

INVENTORY WORKSHEETS

Integrated Landscaping Inventory Worksheets

1. Diverse forms of life live and work together interdependently.

A. Record the existing vegetation on the property, to the best of your ability. (Circle plants native to region.) Include:

Trees:
- Emergent from Canopy
- Overstory/Canopy
- Understory

Shrubs

Vines

Herbaceous plants (non-woody):

Wildflowers

Perennials

Annuals

Groundcovers

Vines

Grasses

Other ground coverings such as:
- Ferns
- Mosses
- Lichens

List any invasive plant species

B. Estimate the percentage of native species.

C. What cover, food, and water sources (i.e., wildlife habitat) does the site provide? (Place a check mark in appropriate boxes.) A useful tool is *A Landowner's Guide to Inventorying and Monitoring Wildlife in New Hampshire*, by Malin Ely Clyde with Darrel Covell and Matt Tarr of UNH Cooperative Extension. (See Appendix D.)

- ❑ Natural water sources
- ❑ Bird baths
- ❑ Feeders
- ❑ Flowers, nectar sources
- ❑ Fruits, seeds, nuts
- ❑ Insects
- ❑ Evergreen trees or shrubs
- ❑ Perching areas
- ❑ Travel corridors and flyways
- ❑ Burrows
- ❑ Cavities
- ❑ Dead or partially dead trees (snags) and woody debris
- ❑ Nest boxes
- ❑ Rock walls or rock piles
- ❑ Brush piles
- ❑ Tall grass or meadow
- ❑ Other

D. Make a list of wildlife currently on the property. Include evidence of tracks, scat, nests, food parts, actual sightings, etc.

    Type   **Sign (live sighting, nest, scat, food remains, etc.)**   **Location**
    Mammals
    Birds
    Reptiles
    Amphibians
    Invertebrates/insects/spiders

E. Can you identify existing native plants or plant communities that could attract various species of wildlife?

F. Are there any unique habitats or rare or endangered plants or animals on the property or nearby?
(Check with your local conservation commission. In NH, consult the NH Wildlife Action Plan or the NH Natural Heritage Bureau.)

2. Soils are covered and protected from the impacts of excessive wind, sun, and rain.

A. What vegetation layers currently exist? (Look back at your answers in 1A. to answer this question.)
- ❑ Canopy (overstory) trees
- ❑ Understory trees
- ❑ Shrubs
- ❑ Herbaceous plants (non-woody stems)
- ❑ Groundcovers
- ❑ Decomposing litter layer

B. What layers are missing?

C. Is soil currently protected from wind, sun, and rain? How so? (plant litter, applied mulch etc.)

D. Are there any exposed or eroded soils?

E. What are the natural mulches covering the soils currently? How do they differ from area to area?

F. Which direction do the prevailing winds come from?

G. Is there a need to buffer strong winds because of any wind damage to plants, structures, or soil erosion due to wind?

3. Rainfall is filtered, conserved, and available when needed.

A. What watershed drains the rainfall that hits your property? If you're not sure, consult a topographical map, which will show the elevations of your property and the surrounding area, so you can locate the nearest water source that your property drains to.

B. Estimate the amount of impervious surface or low-permeability surfaces on the property. (Surfaces that don't allow fluids to pass readily through them such as pavement, concrete sidewalks, roofs, hard-packed gravel, etc.)

    0%   10%   25%   50%   75%   100%

C. Estimate the percentage of lawn currently (or anticipated) in the landscape.
   0%   10%   25%   50%   75%   100%

D. Identify relatively flat areas. If you need flat surfaces for outdoor activities such as a patio, recreational area or small lawn, could you use existing flat areas?

E. How are lawn areas used now?

F. How much lawn will you need for the above activities?

G. Identify steeply sloping areas. Are these sparsely or heavily vegetated? Can you add plants there? Is erosion present? Can any of these areas tolerate a walkway accessible to a wheelchair (if on public property, is it compliant with the Americans with Disabilities Act?)

H. Do sources of runoff originate on or off the property? Where? When? Are there times of excess flow (heavy rainstorms) or seasonal impacts (snowmelt)?

I. Can you collect or reuse runoff water?

J. If you see examples of soil erosion, can you identify the cause (e.g. runoff from roofs, steep slope, roads)?

K. Is there surface water present on the site? Natural or man-made? If so, what type:
   Salt water body
   Lake
   Pond
   Stream or River
   Wetland
   Vernal Pool (a seasonal body of standing water that typically forms in the spring and dries up in summer, vernal pools are free of fish, providing important breeding habitat for many species such as frogs, salamanders and turtles.)

L. What types of wildlife use these wet areas?

M. Can you find evidence of water pollutants on the property or nearby such as contamination from road salt, high nutrient levels from manure piles, etc.?

N. Estimate the water quality (certain aquatic animals or invertebrates can be indicators of water quality, for more information see the following Web site: www.epa.gov/superfund/students/clas_act/spring/critter.htm)
   Excellent   Good   Poor

O. Where does your drinking water come from?
   Private well   Community well   Municipal well   Municipal supply from water body

P. Where does the wastewater from your home go?
   Private septic system   Community septic system   Municipal sewer system   Other

4. Soil organisms are fed by the cycling and recycling of all nutrients.

A. Is plant litter left on the soil to provide food for decomposers and future plant growth? Yes or No

B. Are there evergreen plants or shrubs in the landscape that can be used to hide weeds that have been pulled or plant litter like twigs, so they can decompose naturally? Yes or No

C. Are there indications of animal life in your soil (e.g. ant hills, earthworm castings, insects, carcasses, spiders)?

D. What were the results of any soil testing? (See Appendix D.)

E. What was the result of percolation testing?
- ❑ water drains very slowly
- ❑ water drains gradually
- ❑ water drains fast

F. Are any fertilizers currently used on the property? What type and for what purpose?

5. Fertility reserves are held within humus in the upper layers of soil.

A. Are there any areas where soil is exposed?   Yes or No

B. Are there areas of:
- ❑ Shallow soils
- ❑ Exposed bedrock

C. Do you estimate the presence of enough organic material and humus (the dark layer of partially formed soil, just under the plant litter) for soil to stay moist, cool and alive? Yes or No

D. Do you find plants or animals present that indicate wet soils (alder, cattails, red maple, black gum, spotted turtle, or other wetland species)?

E. Are there areas of soil that show evidence of not being disturbed for many years? For example, areas of vegetation that have been undisturbed for 40 years or more. These soils are likely to be in excellent condition, likely supporting a diverse soil community and should be left intact and protected during any construction.

6. Diversity builds over time and keeps plant insects and diseases in check.

A. Estimate the number of different plant species on site.

B. As best as possible, identify the types of natural plant communities on your property (such as old pasture, wetland, young forest, mature pine forest, etc.)

C. Can you recognize any invasive species on the site? (See Appendix A.)

D. If the property's vegetation is a product of disturbance, and/or dominated by invasive species, is it possible to determine what plant community occupied the site prior to disturbance?

E. Do you find evidence of plant/animal diseases or insect problems on the property?

F. Are there any chemicals used on the property to control insects or diseases? If so, what?

7. The subsoil provides inorganic compounds required for living and nonliving processes.

A. Do you see evidence of soil compaction from heavy machinery or snow storage? Are there areas where soil may be compacted by heavy equipment in the future that need to be fenced off?

B. Can you find areas to store topsoil during construction where soil could be placed on a level surface and covered with a tarp to prevent runoff?

C. What is the plant hardiness zone for the site? (See Appendix F.)

D. Can you identify existing site conditions (low, wet, or excessively sandy soils) that may require plants tolerant of specific conditions?

E. What is the average precipitation? (For a map, go to: http://www.currentresults.com/Weather/US/average-annual-state-precipitation.php.)

F. Does the property have microclimates, that is, areas where the temperature, humidity and exposure vary from the dominant conditions due to slope aspect, wind movement, snow drift, frost pockets, air drainage, and/or heat reflection/storage? (Hint: look for species that may indicate the presence of microclimates.)

G. Are there sources of heavy air pollutants on the property? Yes or No

H. Does heavy traffic or vehicles idling by or near the property pose an air-quality concern? Yes or No

I. Is the property downwind from incinerators or other industrial smoke stacks? Yes or No

J. Is the property subject to high-elevation ozone? Yes or No

K. In general, what is the average air quality of the property?
   Excellent   Good   Fair   Poor

8. Subsoil provides inorganic compounds required for living and nonliving processes.

A. List practices currently used to maintain the landscape (such as mowing, weeding, and/or fertilizing).

B. Is plant debris removed from the property, taken off site, or composted onsite? Do you compost? Would you consider trying it? (See Appendix D.)

C. Can you find ways to leave plant residue on the property during spring and fall clean-up to help build soil, organic matter, recycle nutrients and reduce waste?

D. Are grass clippings collected or allowed to remain on lawns after mowing?

E. How often is the lawn mowed? How high is the mower set?

F. Is there a diversity of plant species on site to allow for a diversity of root systems?

9. Plant systems are dynamic and will change over time.

A. What areas of the site currently receive full sun, partial sun, and little to no sun during the growing season?

   Full sun: _____

   Part sun: _____

   Little to No sun: _____

B. For past plantings, have you considered the mature size (height and width) of the plants? Will plants crowd each other out? Will trees shade out other plants? Are there any overstory trees planted under power lines?

C. Do existing plants need regular pruning to contain their size? If so, consider transplanting these plants to a location where they can grow to their natural size and shape.

D. Are trees and other plants in good health, structurally sound and aesthetically pleasing? Do any need to be thinned, transplanted or removed? Can any of them be relocated to other parts of the landscape? You may want to seek the advice of an arborist or other landscape professional. (See Appendix D.)

E. Are existing plants appropriately located? Do they frame views? Consider plants for fall and winter interest as well as those that look good during summer.

F. Can you identify existing plants of historical significance?

G. Which vegetation should you retain in your new plan?

10. Humans experience health-promoting sensory, intellectual, emotional and spiritual stimulation, opportunities for learning, and insights into the wonder of complex natural processes.

A. What can you learn about the history of the site?

B. What season(s) provide the most favorable views?

    Winter   Spring   Summer   Fall

C. What season(s) offer the most unfavorable views?

    Winter   Spring   Summer   Fall

D. Do you see obstructions that need to be removed? If they are plants, can they be relocated elsewhere on the property?

E. Describe the noise levels on the property and their sources (air traffic/auto/barking dog/nearby industrial site?)

F. Identify sources of pleasant and unpleasant smells.

G. Are there any streetlights or signs on the property or nearby?

H. Can you identify needs for more or less screening?

I. Note the view from the windows in each room of the home, office, school or other building located on this property (for example, kitchen, bedroom, offices, computer lab, dining area, etc.).

    Room   View:

_____

_____

_____

_____

J. Are there any notable sensory experiences? What are the sources?

K. Are there any anticipated changes that will or may occur in the short/long term?

L. Can you identify areas that could serve as a quiet space for reading or reflecting?

APPENDIX D

ADDITIONAL RESOURCES

UNH Cooperative Extension

Education Center

http://extension.unh.edu/FHGEC/FHGEC.htm

Toll free number: 1-877-EXT-GROW (1-877-398-4769)

The Family, Home & Garden Education Center at UNH Cooperative Extension in Manchester provides practical solutions to everyday questions for the citizens of New Hampshire. It is staffed by professionals and intensively trained volunteers available to answer your questions about gardens, lawns and landscapes, household food safety and food preservation, water quality, integrated pest management, tree planting and care, backyard livestock and more. The center is staffed 9 a.m. to 2 p.m. Monday through Friday and Wednesday evenings 5 p.m. to 7:30 p.m. Email your questions to: answers@unh.edu.

County Extension Offices

http://extension.unh.edu/Counties/Counties.htm

Belknap
Belknap County Complex
625 Main St., 3rd Floor, Suite 1
Laconia, NH 03246-2900
Phone: 603-527-5475

Carroll
73 Main Street
Conway, NH 03818
Phone: 603-447-3834

Cheshire
800 Park Avenue
Keene, NH 03431
Phone: 603-352-4550

Coös
629A Main Street
Lancaster, NH 03584-9612
Phone: 603-788-4961

Grafton
1930's Nursing Home Building, 1st Floor
3855 Dartmouth College Highway, Box 5
North Haverhill, NH 03774-4909
Phone: 603-787-6944

Hillsborough
329 Mast Road
Goffstown, NH 03045
Phone: 603-641-6060

Merrimack
315 Daniel Webster Hwy
Boscawen, NH 03303
Phone: 603-796-2151

Rockingham
113 North Road
Brentwood, NH 03833-6623
Phone: 603-679-5616

Strafford
268 County Farm Road
Dover, NH 03820-6015
Phone: 603-749-4445

Sullivan
24 Main Street
Newport, NH 03773
Phone: 603-863-9200

New Hampshire Fish and Game Department

Fish and Game's state headquarters and four regional offices include staff of the department's Public Affairs, Marine and Inland Fisheries, Wildlife and Law Enforcement divisions. These dedicated employees spend countless hours studying, protecting and educating the public about New Hampshire's natural resources to ensure their presence for use and enjoyment by current and future generations.

Headquarters – NH Fish and Game Department
11 Hazen Drive
Concord, NH 03301
Phone: 603-271-3211

North Country (Region 1)
629B Main Street
Lancaster, NH 03584
Phone: 603-788-3164

Lakes Region and Central N.H. (Region 2)
PO Box 417
New Hampton, NH 03256
Phone: 603-744-5470

Southeastern N.H./Seacoast (Region 3)
225 Main Street
Durham, NH 03824
Phone: 603-868-1095

Southwestern N.H. (Region 4)
15 Ash Brook Court
Keene, NH 03431
Phone: 603-352-9669

Recommended Reading and References

BIOMIMICRY

Benyus, Janine M. *Biomimicry: Innovation Inspired by Nature.* HarperCollins, 2002 (ISBN: 0-06-053322-6) www.biomimicry.net

McDonough, William, and Michael Braungart. *Cradle to Cradle: Remaking the Way We Make Things.* North Point Press, 2002 (ISBN: 0-865-47587-3)

COMMUNITY AND URBAN TREES AND FORESTS

The Citizen Forester. *Protecting Trees During Construction.* No. 88, Dec. 2004, Massachusetts Urban Forestry Program

Beresford-Kroeger, Diana. *Arboretum America: A Philosophy of the Forest.* University of Michigan Press/Regional, 2003 (ISBN: 0-472-06851-7)

Trowbridge, Peter J., and Nina L. Bassuk. *Trees in the Urban Landscape: Site Assessment, Design, and Installation.* John Wiley & Sons, Inc., 2004 (ISBN: 0471392464)

COMPOSTING

Make a New Garden Without a Rototiller. extension.unh.edu/FHGEC/docs/rototill.htm

Worming Your Way to Rich Black Compost. http://extension.unh.edu/news/2006/05/worming_your_way_to_rich_black.html

DIAGNOSTIC AND TESTING SERVICES

UNH Cooperative Extension, Plant Biology Department
Spaulding Life Science Center, Rm G28
38 College Road
Durham, NH 03824
phone: 603-862-3200

Cornell Nutrient Analysis Laboratory. http://cnal.cals.cornell.edu/

Bug Finder. www.insectidentification.org

Soil Testing Service, www.extension.unh.edu/Agric/AGPDTS/SoilTest.htm

Insect Identification - Arthropod Identification Center, www.extension.unh.edu/Agric/AGPDTS/IDform.pdf

Plant Diagnostic Laboratory, www.extension.unh.edu/Agric/AGPDTS/PlantH.htm

ECOLOGY AND THE NATURAL WORLD

Alden, Peter. *Field Guide to New England*, National Audubon Society 1998. (ISBN: 0-679-44676-1)

Daily, Gretchen, C. *Nature's Services, Societal Dependence on Natural Ecosystems.* Island Press, 1997 (ISBN: 1-559-63476-6)

Ecological Landscaping Association, www.ecolandscaping.org

Leopold, Aldo. *A Sand County Almanac and Sketches Here and There*. Oxford University Press, USA, 1987 (ASIN: B000OKDPL2)

Thomashow, Mitchell. *Ecological Identity: Becoming a Reflective Environmentalist*. MIT Press, 1996 (ISBN: 0-262-70063-8)

GARDENING, LANDSCAPING, AND PERMACULTURE

American Horticultural Society. *American Horticultural Society Gardening Manual*. Dorling Kindersley, 2000 (ISBN: 0-7894-5952-3)

Beresford-Kroeger, Diana. *A Garden for Life: The Natural Approach to Designing, Planting, and Maintaining a North Temperate Garden*. University of Michigan Press/Regional, 2004 (ISBN: 0-472-03012-4)

Diekelmann, John, and Robert Schuster. *Natural Landscaping: Designing with Native Plant Communities*. University of Wisconsin Press, 2002 (ISBN: 0-299-17324-0)

Ellis, Barbara W. Rodale's *Illustrated Encyclopedia of Gardening and Landscaping Techniques: Chemical Free*. Rodale Press, Inc., 1990 (ISBN: 0-87857-898-6)

Henderson, Carrol L. *Landscaping for Wildlife*. Minnesota Department of Natural Resources, 1987 (ISBN: 9999529941)

Howard, Louise E. *The Earth's Green Carpet*. Rodale Press, 1947 (ASIN: B0007E1ZN0)

Jacke, Dave, and Eric Toensmeier. *Edible Forest Gardens* (Vol. 1&2). Chelsea Green, 2005 (ISBN-10: 1890132608 & ISBN-13: 978-1890132606)

Marinelli, Janet. *Stalking the Wild Amaranth: Gardening in the Age of Extinction*. Henry Holt and Company, Inc., 1998 (ISBN: 0-805-04415-9)

Northeast Organic Farming Association's Landscape Standards (NOFA), www.nofa.org

Reed, Sue. *Energy-Wise Landscape Design: A New Approach for Your Home and Garden*. New Society Publishers, 2010 (ISBN: 0-865-71653-6)

Shapiro, Howard-Yana, Ph.D., and John Harrisson. *Gardening for the Future of the Earth*. Bantam Books, 2000 (ISBN: 0-553-37533-4)

Shaw-Ernest, Ruth. *The Naturalist's Garden*. Globe Pequot, 1993 (ISBN: 1-56440-135-9)

GEOGRAPHICAL INFORMATION

NETSTATE.COM - Includes average precipitation within each state.
http://www.netstate.com/states/index.html

INSECTS

Baskin, Yvonne. *Under Ground: How Creatures of Mud and Dirt Shape Our World*. Island Press, 2006 (ISBN: 1597261181)

Grissell, Eric. *Insects and Gardens: In Pursuit of a Garden Ecology*. Timber Press, Inc., 2006 (ISBN: 0-88192-768-6)

Tallamy, Douglas W. *Bringing Nature Home.* Timber Press, 2009 (ISBN: 0-88192-992-8)

The Xerces Society. *Attracting Native Pollinators: The Xerces Society Guide to Conserving North American Bees and Butterflies and Their Habitat.* Storey Publishing, 2011 (ISBN: 1- 60342-695-4)

INVASIVE SPECIES

Alternatives for Invasive Ornamental Plant Species. http://www.ct.gov/caes/lib/caes/documents/special_features/nativealternatives.pdf

Invasive Plant Atlas of New England. http://nbii-nin.ciesin.columbia.edu/ipane

Invasive Plant Information. www.nhinvasives.org

NH Guide to Upland Invasive Species, 2010. NH Dept. of Agriculture Markets and Food, Plant Industry Division.

State List of Invasive Species. http://www.invasivespeciesinfo.gov/unitedstates/state.shtml

LAWNS AND LAWN CARE

Bormann, F. Herbert, Diana Balmori, and Gordon T. Geballe. *Redesigning the American Lawn: A Search for Environmental Harmony.* Yale University Press, 2001 (ISBN: 0-300-08694-6)

Daniels, Stevie. *The Wild Lawn Handbook: Alternatives to the Traditional Front Lawn.* John Wiley & Sons, Inc., 1997 (ISBN: 0-02-862004-6)

Franklin, Stuart. *Building a Healthy Lawn: A Safe and Natural Approach.* Storey Books, 1988 (ISBN: 0-88266-5189)

Northeast Farmers Association (NOFA). *The NOFA Organic Lawn and Turf Handbook.* http://www.organiclandcare.net/store/nofa-organic-lawn-and-turf-handbook

Tukey, Paul. *The Organic Lawn Care Manual.* Storey Books, 2007 (ISBN: 1-158017-649-6)

PLANT SELECTION & NATURAL COMMUNITIES

Cullina, William, and New England Wildflower Society. *Guide to Growing and Propagating Wildflowers of the United States and Canada.* Houghton Mifflin Co., 2000 (ISBN: 0-395-96609-4)

Cullina, William, and New England Wildflower Society. *Native Trees, Shrubs, and Vines: A Guide to Using, Growing, and Propagating North American Woody Plants.* Houghton Mifflin Co., 2002 (ISBN: 0-618-09858-5)

Leopold, Donald Joseph. *Native Plants of the Northeast: A Guide for Gardening and Conservation.* Timber Press, Inc., 2005 (ISBN: 0-88192-673-6)

Neal, Cathy, Margaret Hagen, and Leslie van Berkum et al. *Best Plants for New Hampshire Gardens and Landscapes.* UNH Cooperative Extension, 2003 (ISBN: 0971967520)

New England Wetland Plants, www.newp.com

New Hampshire State Forest Nursery, www.dred.state.nh.us/nhnursery

Roberts, Edith A., and Elsa Rehmann. *American Plants for American Gardens.* University of Georgia Press, 1996 (ISBN: 0-8203-1851-5)

Sperduto, Dan, and Ben Kimball. *The Nature of New Hampshire: Natural Communities of the Granite State.* University Press of New England, 2011 (ISBN: 978-1-58465-898-6)

University of Connecticut Plant Database, www.hort.uconn.edu/Plants

PRUNING

Gilman, Edward F. *An Illustrated Guide to Pruning.* Thomson Delmar Learning, 2002 (ISBN: 0766822710)

Pruning Central-Leader Apples Video. UMass Fruit Advisor, 02/12/07. http://www.youtube.com/watch?v=qx7ndnTeUME

Pruning Deciduous Shrubs, www.extension.unh.edu/Pubs/HGPubs/PrunDec.pdf

Pruning Evergreens, www.extension.unh.edu/Pubs/HGPubs/PrunEverg.pdf

Pruning Shade Trees, www.extension.unh.edu/Pubs/HGPubs/prunshad.pdf

RAIN GARDENS

University of Rhode Island Cooperative Extension, www.uri.edu/ce/healthylandscapes/raingarden.htm

University of Wisconsin, Cooperative Extension. Rain Gardens: A How-to Manual for Homeowners. www.clean-water.uwex.edu/pubs/pdf/home.rgmanual.pdf

SOCIAL VALUES OF NATURAL SYSTEMS

Kuo, Frances E., and William C. Sullivan, Drs. "Environment and Crime in the Inner City: Does Vegetation Reduce Crime? *Environment and Behavior.*" Vol. 33, No. 3, 343-367, Human-Environment Research Laboratory University of Illinois, Urbana-Champaign, 2001

Louv, Richard. *Last Child in the Woods: Saving Our Children from Nature-Deficit Disorder.* Algonquin Books of Chapel Hill, 2005 (ISBN: 1565123913)

Society for the Protection of New Hampshire Forests, NH's Changing Landscape, www.spnhf.org

SOIL INFORMATION AND TESTING

ATTRA National Sustainable Agriculture Information Service, www.attra.ncat.org

Center for Integrated Agricultural Systems, University of Wisconsin-Madison, Building Soil Organic Matter with Organic Amendments. 2002. www.cias.wisc.edu

Fred Magdoff and Harold van Es. *Building Soils for Better Crops*, 2000, Sustainable Agriculture Network. www.sare.org

Soil Foodweb, Inc, www.soilfoodweb.com

UNH Cooperative Extension, Soil Tests, Soil Test Form On-Line Development Page www.ceadmin.unh.edu/soils/form/index.cfm

Understanding Your Soil Test Results, www.extension.unh.edu/Pubs/HGPubs/Soiltest.pdf

USDA Natural Resources Conservation Service Web Soil Survey, http://websoilsurvey.nrcs.usda.gov

"Soil Biology and Land Management." Technical Note No. 4: 1996, USDA Natural Resources Conservation Service. www.soils.usda.gov/sqi

WETLANDS, WATER QUALITY AND SEPTIC

NH Department of Environmental Services (NHDES) Shoreland Protection Act, www.des.nh.gov

Subsurface Systems Bureau - State-approved Septic placement plan, www.des.state.nh.us/ssb

Water Quality - Organisms as indicators, www.epa.gov/superfund/students/clas_act/spring/critter.htm

Neal, Catherine, Jeff Schloss, and Stan Swier et al. *Landscaping at the Water's Edge: An Ecological Approach.* UNH Cooperative Extension, 2007 (ISBN: 978-0-9719675-6-4)

WILDLIFE AND HABITAT — LANDSCAPING, MONITORING, AND ENHANCEMENT

Alden, Peter, and National Audubon Society. *National Audubon Society Field Guide to New England.* Knopf Publishing Group, 1998 (ISBN: 0679446761)

America's Wildlife Resource – an online field guide, www.enature.com

Benyus, Janine M. *The Field Guide to Wildlife Habitats of the Eastern United States.* Simon & Schuster Trade, 1989 (ISBN: 0-671-65908-1)

Clyde, Malin Ely, Darrel Covell, and Matt Tarr. *A Landowner's Guide to Inventorying and Monitoring Wildlife in New Hampshire.* UNH Cooperative Extension, 2004 (ISBN: 0-9719675-5-5)

DeGraaf, Richard M., and Mariko Yamasaki. *New England Wildlife: Habitat, Natural History, and Distribution.* University Press of New England, 2000 (ISBN: 0-87451-957-8)

Druse, Ken, with Margaret Roach. *The Natural Habitat Garden.* Clarkson Potter, 1994 (ISBN: 0-517-58989-3)

Landau, Diana, and Shelley Stump. *Living with Wildlife: How to Enjoy, Cope with, and Protect North America's Wild Creatures around Your Home and Theirs.* Sierra Club Books, 1994 (ISBN: 0-87156-547-1)

Martin, Alexander C., Herbert S. Zim, and Arnold L. Nelson. *American Wildlife & Plants: A Guide to Wildlife Food Habits.* Dover Publications, 1989 (ISBN: 0-486-20793-5)

NH Wildlife Action Plan, Rare and Endangered Plants and Wildlife, www.nhfg.net/Wildlife/wildlife_plan.htm

Picone, Peter M. *Enhancing Your Backyard Habitat for Wildlife.* Connecticut Dept. of Environmental Protection, Wildlife Division, 1995 (ASIN: B0006QFR5G)

Schneck, Marcus. *Your Backyard Wildlife Garden: How to Attract and Identify Wildlife in Your Yard.* Rodale Press, 1992 (ISBN: 0-87596-129-0)

Taylor, James, Thomas Lee, and Laura F. McCarthy. *New Hampshire's Living Legacy: The Biodiversity of the Granite State.* NH Fish & Game Dept. 1996 (ISBN: 0-9652156-1-X)

U.S. Department of Agriculture, Wildlife Services, www.aphis.usda.gov/wildlife_damage

APPENDIX E

Selecting Woody Plants for Shoreland Landscapes

The plants listed are those that occur near water in their natural habitats, including lowland and upland plants. See column on vegetative buffer zones. They are recommended for use in multi-layered plant systems. Some of these plants may be uncommon and difficult to find in a nursery, but many are readily available. Choose plants that are suitable for your site conditions, soils, sun exposure, and cold hardiness zones.

Source: Neal, Catherine, Jeff Schloss, and Stan Swier et al. *Landscaping at the Water's Edge: An Ecological Approach.* UNH Cooperative Extension, 2007 (ISBN: 978-0-9719675-6-4)

Common Name	Scientific Name	Mature Height	USDA Cold Hardiness Zone
Under 3'			
Bog Rosemary	Andromeda polifolia	1 - 2'	2
Bearberry	Arctostaphylos uva-ursi	1'	2
Leatherleaf	Chamaedaphne calyculata	1 - 3'	2
Bunchberry	Cornus canadensis	6 - 9"	2
Bearberry Cotoneaster	Cotoneaster dammeri	12 - 18"	5
Rockspray Cotoneaster	Cotoneaster horizontalis	2 - 3'	5
Rose Daphne	Daphne cneorum	6 - 12"	4
Slender Deutzia	Deutzia gracilis	2'	5
Dwarf Greenstem Forsythia	Forsythia viridissima 'Bronxensis'	1 - 2'	5
Creeping Wintergreen	Gaultheria procumbens	6"	3
Little Henry Sweetspire	Itea virginica 'Little Henry'	2 - 3'	5
Sheep Laurel	Kalmia angustifolia	1 - 3'	2
Bog Kalmia	Kalmia polifolia	3'	2
Coast Leucothoe	Leucothoe axillaris	2 - 4'	5
Creeping Mahonia	Mahonia repens	10 - 18"	5
Paxistima	Paxistima canbyi	1'	3
Gro-Low Fragrant Sumac	Rhus aromatica 'Gro-Low'	2'	3
Lowbush Blueberry	Vaccinium angustifolium	1 - 2'	2
American Cranberry	Vaccinium macrocarpon	4 - 6"	2
3'-6'			
Mountain Cranberry	Vaccinium vitis-idaea var. minus	4 - 8"	2
Regent Serviceberry	Amelanchier alnifolia 'Regent'	4 - 6'	3
Summersweet Clethra	Clethra alnifolia	3 - 8'	4
Sweetfern	Comptonia peregrina	3 - 5'	2
Spike Winterhazel	Corylopsis spicata	4 - 6'	5
American Hazelnut	Corylus americana	3 - 9'	4
Dwarf Bush Honeysuckle	Diervilla lonicera	3 - 5'	3
Atlantic Leatherwood	Dirca palustris	3 - 6'	3

KEY

Vegetative Buffer Zone(s)	Native & Wildlife Value	Soil	Sun	Comments and Cultivars (cvs.)
LL=Lowland transition	Y=Yes	WD=well-drained	PS=partial sun	Sp=spreading
SL=Shoreland		W=wet (bog)	S=full sun	EG=evergreen
UPL=Upland		A=acidic	Sh=shade	
		M=moist		

Vegetative Buffer Zone(s)	Native	Wildlife Value	Soil	Sun	Comments and Cultivars (cvs.)
SL	Y		W A	S PS	EG, Sp, cvs. 'Montana', 'Angustifolia', 'Compacta', 'Grandiflora'
UPL	Y	Y	A	S PS	EG, Sp, salt tolerant, does well in very poor soils
SL	Y		W A	PS	EG, cvs. 'Nana', 'Cascade' and 'Tiny Tim' under 3' tall
LL UPL	Y	Y	M A	PS Sh	Sp, excellent groundcover
UPL			WD	S	EG, Sp, good bankcover, very fast
UPL			WD	S	Sp, good bankcover
UPL			M WD	PS Sh	EG, fragrant flowers
UPL			WD	S	cv. 'Nikko' recommended for compact growth form
UPL				S	Sp, groundcover type forsythia
LL	Y		M A	Sh PS	EG, Sp, groundcover
LL	Y		M	S PS Sh	This is a compact cv.; others are listed in 3-6' height class
SL LL UPL	Y		A W or M	PS	EG, Sp, does well in poor soils, poisonous to livestock
SL LL	Y		W A		
LL			A M WD	Sh	EG, choose small cvs. for this size class
UPL			A M WD	Sh PS	EG, Sp, groundcover
UPL			M WD	S PS	EG, tolerates high pH
UPL	Y		A WD	S PS	Sp, other cvs. get much larger; good fall color
LL UPL	Y	Y	A		Edible blueberry, does well in very poor soils
SL LL	Y	Y	M A	S	EG, Sp, edible cranberry
LL	Y	Y	M A	S	EG, Sp, edible Ligonberry
LL UPL	Y	Y	M WD A	S PS	Sp, edible berries; other cvs. are larger
SL LL	Y	Y	M A	S PS	Fragrant, salt tolerant; nice cvs. include 'Hummingbird', 'Sixteen Candles', 'Compacta', 'Ruby Spice'
UPL	Y	Y	WD	S PS	Sp, does well in poor dry sandy soils
UPL			M WD	S PS	
UPL	Y	Y		S PS	Sp, edible nuts
UPL	Y			S PS	Sp, very tough plant
SL LL	Y		W	Sh	

Common Name	Scientific Name	Mature Height	USDA Cold Hardiness Zone
3'-6'			
Dwarf Fothergilla	Fothergilla gardenii	3 - 4'	5
Huckleberry	Gaylussacia sp.	3 - 5'	3
Smooth Hydrangea	Hydrangea arborescens	3 - 5'	3
Oakleaf Hydrangea	Hydrangea quercifolia	3 - 6'	5
Inkberry	Ilex glabra	3 - 6'	5
Common Winterberry	Ilex verticillata 'Red Sprite'	3 - 5'	4
Virginia Sweetspire	Itea virginica	3 - 5'	5
Sweetgale	Myrica gale	3 - 4'	1
Rhodora	Rhododendron canadense	3 - 4'	2
Pinxterbloom Azalea	Rhododendron periclymenoides	4 - 6'	4
Meadowsweet	Spirea latifolia	3 - 5'	3
Steeplebush	Spirea tomentosa	2 - 4'	3
Common Snowberry	Symphoricarpos albus	3 - 6'	3
Red Chokeberry	Aronia arbutifolia	6 - 10'	4
6'-9'			
Black Chokeberry	Aronia melanocarpa	5 - 10'	3
Sweetshrub	Calycanthus floridus	6 - 9'	4
Silky Dogwood	Cornus amomum	6 - 10'	4
Red-Osier Dogwood	Cornus sericea	8 - 10'	2
Large Forthergilla	Fothergilla major	6 - 9'	4
Vernal Witchhazel	Hamamelis vernalis	6 - 10'	4
Common Winterberry	Ilex verticillata	6 - 10'	3-4
Northern Bayberry	Myrica pensylvanica	6 - 10'	3
Mountain Holly	Nemopanthus mucronata	6 - 10'	4
Common Ninebark	Physocarpus opulifolius	5 - 10'	2
Roseshell Azalea	Rhododendron prinophyllum	2 - 8'	3
Pinkshell Azalea	Rhododendron vaseyi	5 - 9'	4
Swamp Azalea	Rhododendron viscosum	6 - 9'	4
Swamp Rose	Rosa palustris	6 - 8'	4
Elderberry	Sambucus canadensis	6 - 12'	3
Wild Raisin Viburnum	Viburnum cassinoides	6 - 10'	3
Arrowwood Viburnum	Viburnum dentatum	6 - 9'	2
10'-15'			
Buttonbush	Cephalanthus occidentalis	8 - 15'	5
Gray Dogwood	Cornus racemosa	10 - 15'	3b
Chinese Witchhazel	Hamamelis mollis	10 - 15'	5

Vegetative Buffer Zone(s)	Native	Wildlife Value	Soil	Sun	Comments and Cultivars (cvs.)
UPL	Y		M WD A	S PS	Excellent fall color
UPL		Y	WD A	PS	EG, Sp, edible berries
LL UPL	Y		M WD	S PS	Sp, cvs. include 'Annabelle', 'Grandiflora', 'White Dome'
LL			M WD	S PS	
LL	Y	Y	M A	S PS	EG, Sp, avoid sites with winter sun, wind exposure, many cvs. include Compacta', 'Viridis', 'Nigra', Red Sprite
SL LL	Y	Y	M A	PS S	Compact cv., others listed in 6-9' class; plant with male pollinator
SL LL	Y		W or M	S PS Sh	Fragrant flowers; 'Henry's Garnet' recommended
SL	Y	Y	W	S	Aromatic
SL LL	Y		M A	PS Sh	Deciduous azalea
UPL	Y		WD	PS	Deciduous azalea; try cvs. 'Album', 'Roseum'
LL UPL	Y		M WD	S	Sp
SL LL	Y		M	S PS	
SL LL		Y		S PS Sh	Sp, fills in large areas, adaptable to many conditions
LL UPL	Y	Y		S PS	Sp, cv. 'Brilliantissima' has beautiful red fall foliage
LL UPL	Y	Y		S PS	Sp, cv. 'Autumn Magic' has good fall color and compact form
LL UPL				S PS	Fragrant, adaptable to many conditions.
SL LL	Y	Y	M	PS	
SL LL	Y	Y	M	S PS	Sp, colorful winter twigs
SL LL UPL	Y		M A	PS S	Excellent fall color
SL LL	Y	Y	M	S PS	Sp, late winter flowers
SL LL	Y	Y	M A	S PS	Sp, many improved cvs., plant with male pollinator
FAC	Y	Y	WD	S PS	Sp, salt tolerant, does well on poor soils
SL	Y	Y	M		Sp, forms thickets
UPL	Y		WD	S PS	Tough plant; new purple-leaved cvs.popular; 'Nanus' is dwarf form
UPL	Y			PS Sh	Deciduous azalea, toelrates high pH, dry open woods
LL			M A	PS Sh	Deciduous azalea
SL	Y		W	PS Sh	Deciduous azalea
SL	Y	Y	W	S	
SL LL UPL	Y	Y		S	Sp, 'Aurea' has yellow foliage, Sambucus nigra 'Black Beauty' has dark foliage; edible fruit; tolerates wet or dry soils
SL LL	Y	Y		S PS	
LL UPL	Y	Y	WD	S PS	Sp, many new cvs. selected for berry set and fall color
SL	Y	Y	W	S PS	
SL LL	Y	Y	M	S PS	Sp, fills in large areas
LL UPL				S PS	Fragrant, very early spring flowers; cv. 'Pallida' has excellent fall color

Appendix E: Shoreline Plant Chart

Common Name	Scientific Name	Mature Height	USDA Cold Hardiness Zone
10'-15'			
Panicle Hydrangea	Hydrangea paniculata	10 - 20'	3
Spicebush	Lindera benzoin	10 - 12'	4
Rosebay Rhododendron	Rhododendron maximum	5 - 15'	3
Purpleosier Willow	Salix purpurea	8 - 15'	3
Highbush Blueberry	Vaccinium corymbosum	6 - 12'	3
Blackhaw Viburnum	Viburnum prunifolium	12 - 15'	3
American Cranberrybush Viburnum	Virburnum trilobum	8 - 12'	2
Striped Maple	Acer pensylvanicum	15 - 20'	3
Speckled Alder	Alnus rugosa	15 - 25'	4
Downy Serviceberry	Amelanchier arborea	15 - 25'	4
Shadblow Serviceberry	Amelanchier canadensis	10 - 20'	3
Allegheny Serviceberry	Amelanchier laevis	20 - 25'	4
White Fringetree	Chionanthus virginicus	15 - 25'	4
Pagoda Dogwood	Cornus alternifolia	15 - 25'	3
Corneliancherry Dogwood	Cornus mas	20 - 25'	4
Common Witchhazel	Hamamelis virginiana	20 - 25'	3b
Sweet Azalea	Rhododendron arborescens	8 - 20'	4
Flameleaf Sumac	Rhus copallina	10 - 20'	4
Pussy Willow	Salix spp.	10 - 20'	3
25'-45'			
Eastern Redcedar	Juniperus virginiana	20 - 40'	3b
Black Spruce	Picea mariana	30 - 40'	3
Hophornbeam	Ostrya virginiana	30 - 40'	3b
American Hornbeam	Carpinus caroliniana	25 - 35'	3b
Eastern Redbud	Cercis canadensis	20 - 30'	5
Sweetbay magnolia	Magnolia virginiana	15 - 30'	5
Kousa Dogwood	Cornus kousa	25 - 35'	5
Red Mulberry	Morus rubra	30 - 45'	5
Over 45'			
Red Maple	Acer rubrum	40 - 60'	3b
Yellow Birch	Betula alleghaniensis	50 - 70'	3
River Birch	Betula nigra	40 - 70'	3b
Atlantic White Cedar	Chaemaecyparis thyoides	40 - 50'	4
Green Ash	Fraxinus pennsylvanica	50 - 60'	2b

Appendix E: Shoreline Plant Chart

Vegetative Buffer Zone(s)	Native	Wildlife Value	Soil	Sun	Comments and Cultivars (cvs.)
LL UPL			M WD	S PS	Many cvs. available including 'Pink Diamond' and 'Limelight'
SL LL	Y	Y	W or M	S PS	Fragrant
LL UPL	Y		M A WD	PS Sh	EG, avoid winter exposure
SL			W	S PS	Sp, good for bank stabilization; 'Nana' a compact cv.
LL UPL	Y	Y	M A WD	S PS	Edible blueberry
UPL		Y	WD	S PS	Good in dry soils
LL UPL	Y	Y	M WD	S PS	Cv. 'Wentworth' recommended for fruits for jellies, 'Alfredo' for fall color and compact form
LL UPL	Y		M WD	PS	
SL LL	Y		M	S	
LL UPL	Y	Y	M WD A	S PS	
SL LL	Y	Y	M A	S PS	Sp
SL LL	Y	Y	M A	S PS	
LL		Y	M	PS S	Silky white flowers, large blue berries
UPL	Y	Y	M WD A	PS	
UPL		Y	WD	PS S	Very early yellow flowers, red fruit
LL UPL	Y		M	S PS	Flowers late fall, fragrant
LL	Y		M A	PS Sh	Deciduous azalea
UPL	Y			S	Sp, forms large colonies, red fall foliage
SL LL			M	S PS	For nice catkins use S. caprea or S. chaenomeloides; the native S. discolor is not as good, subject to canker
UPL	Y	Y	M WD	S	EG, tolerates poor dry conditions
LL	Y		M	S	EG
UPL	Y	Y	M WD	S PS	
LL	Y		M	PS Sh	
LL UPL	Y		M	PS S	Cold hardiness depends northern seed source
LL	Y		M A	PS	EG, avoid winter exposure; large fragrant flowers
UPL		Y	WD A	PS	Good substitute for flowering dogwood, white flowers on hardiest vars.
LL		Y	M		
SL LL	Y		M A	S PS	Many cvs. selected for good fall color, some are more hardy than others
LL	Y	Y	M	S PS	
LL UPL			M	S PS	Recommended over paper birch for landscape use due to pest resistance; 'Heritage' most popular cv.
SL LL	Y		W or M	S	EG
LL UPL	Y			S	Tolerates many soil conditions; use seedless cvs. near lawns and walkways

Appendix E: Shoreline Plant Chart

Common Name	Scientific Name	Mature Height	USDA Cold Hardiness Zone
Over 45'			
American Larch	Larix laricina	40 - 80'	2
American Sweet Gum	Liquidambar styraciflua	60 - 80'	5
Dawn Redwood	Metasequoia glyptostroboides	50 - 100'	5
Black Gum	Nyssa sylvatica	30 - 50'	4
American Plane Tree	Platanus occidentalis	75 - 100'	4
Swamp White Oak	Quercus bicolor	50 - 60'	4
Pin Oak	Quercus palustris	60 - 70'	4
Eastern Arborvitae	Thuja occidentalis	40 - 60'	2

APPENDIX F

Landscape Practices Aligned with the Ecological Principles

These landscape practices are directly linked to the processes of nature and the biodiversity found within our landscapes. By supporting one, you support the other.

1. Diverse forms of life live and work together.

- Bring in fruit, flowers, seed heads by planting diverse, native plant species.
- Heavily stud with natives, about 80% of overall plantings.
- Provide structure, both horizontal and vertical.
- Promote nesting/shelter/cover.
- Leave litter layer for invertebrates and insects.
- Build diverse litter layers to protect and conserve a diversity of microorganisms. Use on-site resources for mulch and compost.
- Allow some perennials and grasses to stand above snow height for winter food.
- Plant sources of nectar, pollen, and larval food for pollinator complexes.
- Plant evergreens for extreme low temperature and protection from wind.
- Design outdoor lighting use for minimal disruption to nocturnal species.
- Limit tree care to safety issues: leave old, large, dying, and dead trees, when possible.

2. Soils are typically covered and protected by structural layers.

- Provide all structural layers where appropriate. Add what's missing to ensure that landscapes include the following:
  - ✓ Upper canopy
  - ✓ Lower canopy
  - ✓ Tall shrubs
  - ✓ Short shrubs
  - ✓ Vines
  - ✓ Diverse litter layer
  - ✓ Herbaceous layer: grasses, forbs, ephemerals, ferns
  - ✓ Woody, herbaceous ground covers
  - ✓ Thallophytes such as lichens and mosses
  - ✓ Thick "O" horizon
- Plant a mix of evergreen and deciduous plants to ensure soil coverage in winter.
- Soften edges of interface between woods and lawns by "stair stepping" vegetation.
- Provide living fences and hedgerows.
- Create windbreaks to protect soils and habitat from excessive drying.
- Keep native plantings along yard perimeters intact, including front yards.
- Connect to natural linkages, corridors, and greenways throughout the neighborhood.

Vegetative Buffer Zone(s)	Native	Wildlife Value	Soil	Sun	Comments and Cultivars (cvs.)
LL	Y		M WD A	S	
LL			M	S	
SL LL			M	S	
LL	Y	Y	M A	S PS	Excellent fall color
LL	Y		M	S	Very large, messy - plant only in naturalized areas
SL LL	Y	Y	M A	S	
LL UPL	Y	Y	M A	S	
LL UPL	Y	Y	M WD	S	EG; cvs. 'Techny', 'Nigra' 'Emerald' for cold climates

- Save large trees, especially those with cavities, and trees that provide mast.
- Reduce the size of lawns and other simplified, less diverse ecosystems.

3. Rainfall is filtered and conserved until needed.

- Minimize impervious surfaces.
- Keep water on site by increasing infiltration and storage (i.e., large dead wood, all structural layers).
- Use plants to slow the flow.
- Plant densely and leave litter to mitigate rains, winds, and drying sun.
- Use diverse leaf forms and diverse root systems to clean rain and hold onto soil sediments, respectively.
- Trace erosion back to source and fix using plants to reduce velocity and increase evapotranspiration.
- Design for increased dry conditions by including some drought-tolerant plants.
- Maximize shoreland buffers.

4. Soil feeds plants and plants feed soil.

- Always cover soils to prevent erosion and leaching unless providing small areas for bird dusting or turtle egg-laying habitat. Cover stored soil piles.
- Gain an understanding of current soil structure and conditions to help with species selection, plant health, and soil development.
- Leave litter on, including woody materials, to add and replace organic matter over time, especially ramial chipped wood (RCW).
- Run on-site litter through a chipper-shedder for mulch, bringing in less bark.
- Tuck weeds, which are full of nutrients, under plants to decompose in place (remove seed heads first).
- Shear dead standing perennials into 2-inch pieces, letting them fall to litter layer, increasing habitat and organic matter.
- Improve soil by using cover crops prior to planting an area.
- Practice 'no-till' where possible by using sheet mulching to protect soils.
- Regenerate soils to "better than you found them" conditions.
- Investigate the use of bio-char, ramial chipped wood, and making on site compost teas to improve soil and plant growth over time.

5. Humus is microscopic, yet essential for fertility and soil structure.

- Break up larger sticks into smaller pieces and leave on site; tuck under plants if necessary.
- Leave larger logs and coarse woody debris to decompose in place.
- See practices listed in no. 4, above.

6. Diversity builds over time to spread risks and to ensure natural checks and balances.

- Build predator populations, such as wasps, hornets, spiders, birds, amphibians, reptiles, and small mammals.
- Build in insectary plants for parasitoid wasps.

- Build trophic levels, from soil biology and invertebrates to bigger animals.
- Provide native plants for herbivorous insects because 96% of all bird species depend on insects during reproduction.
- Prevent predation by domestic cats. Keep trash and open compost piles covered.
- Be aware of barriers to wildlife passage, such as curbing, solid stone walls, terraces, fences, large open expanses of turf, and impervious surfaces. Build in access, openings, and crossings.
- Use bridges with natural stream beds of sand and gravel to allow natural flow to occur.
- Provide perches and flyways for birds and some insects.
- Use water to attract wildlife, such as a birdbath, water feature, or pond. Water sources are important all year, including shallow running water and wet gravel and pebbles. Edges allow wildlife to come and go.
- Design in and around:
  - ✓ **Compositional diversity,** such as snags with nesting cavities, large dead wood, rocks and boulders, and undisturbed soils.
  - ✓ **Structural diversity,** such as vegetative layers, age structure, and successional patches.
  - ✓ **Functional diversity,** such as niches, food webs, species interactions, soil microbes, and fungi.
- Have about 80% native plants as a backbone in your landscapes.
- Use disease-resistant cultivars and varieties when possible.
- Remember, there is no good and bad in nature; everything is food for everything else.

7. Plants supply clean and fresh air above and cool shade below.

- Leave litter on to help regulate temperature swings in soil level.
- Do not overmulch; 2 to 3 inches is enough.
- Avoid compacting soils.
- Design and stay on pathways through meadows and woodlands to avoid compaction.
- Know that roots die in place, adding organic matter and air channels into soil layers.
- Cool, moist soils enhance root growth and mycorrhizal fungi.
- Add missing layers to increase 'air-conditioning.'
- Practice only necessary and correct pruning.
- Create micro-climates with boulders and logs for moisture storage and habitat.

8. The subsoil provides on-site inorganic compounds.

- Take advantage of the practice of burrowing animals, such as ants, moles, and turtles laying eggs, as well as large tap-rooted plants, as they bring minerals to the upper levels where they can be cycled into the soil food web.
- Cover newly exposed soils with diverse mulches.
- Use diverse plants with varied root systems.
- Always take a soil test when applying off-site amendments.

9. Landscapes are dynamic and change over time.

- Look at succession with a selective eye.
- Give woody plants enough room according to their mature size.
- Fill in with herbaceous grasses, ground covers, and clumping and spreading perennials.
- Let seedlings establish where wanted, weed out and reuse others.
- Transplant seedlings to enhance other areas.
- Allow landscape beds to fill out while decreasing lawn areas over time.
- Watch how species composition changes, as habitat succeeds and changes over time.
- Remove opportunistic and invasive species when small.

10. Humans have a need for beauty, choice, and interest in the landscape, including a sense of place and history.

- Get people out and involved in nature and in their landscapes.
- Maintain and enrich sense of place.
- Look to surrounding lands for clues on native species usage, and land features that may be mimicked in your landscape.
- Respect and enhance historical artifacts in the landscape.
- Include features for people that heighten their experience and time spent in the landscape.
- Benefit both humans and wildlife with four-season and winter interest, as well as a continuation of color and bloom.
- Demonstrate that aesthetics and ecology in the landscape are not mutually exclusive!

APPENDIX G

USDA HARDINESS ZONE MAP

Approximate range of average annual minimum temperatures throughout New England. Use this USDA zone map as a general guide when shopping for plants. Each property has its own microclimates, so know your site.

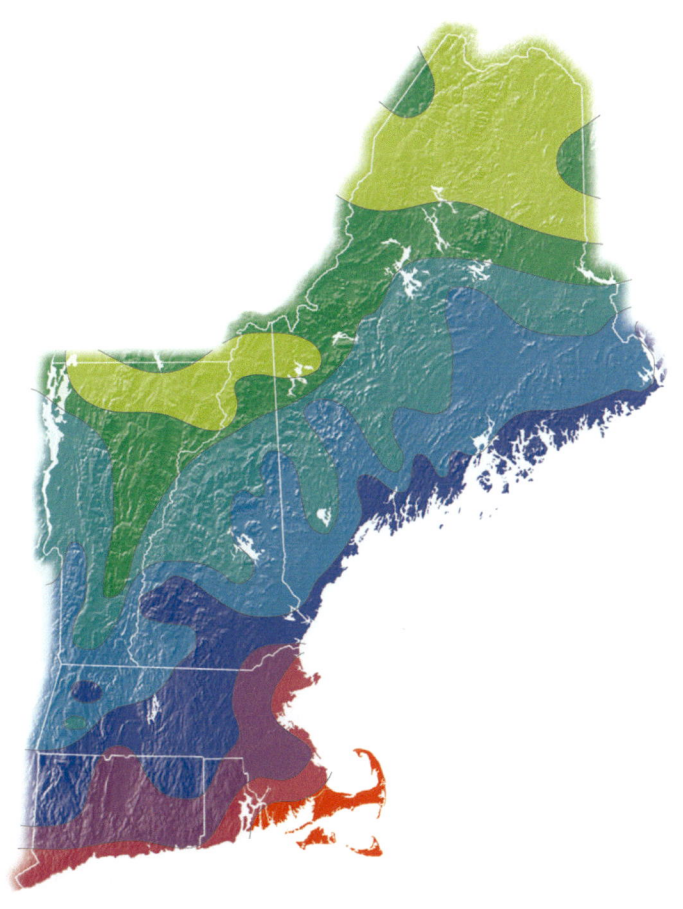

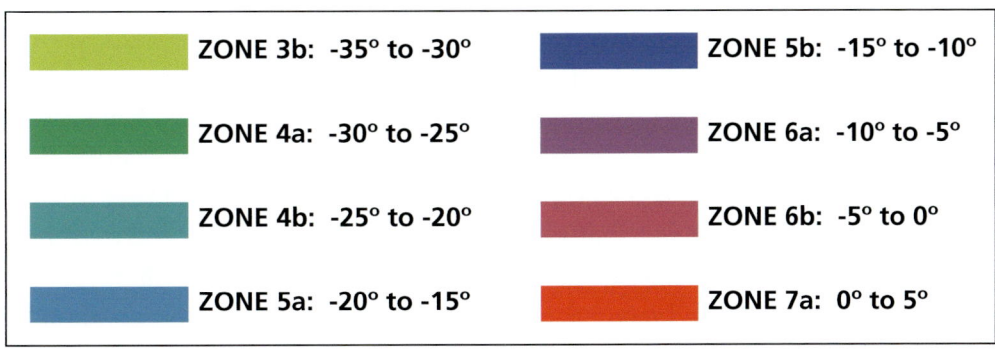

Source: People, Places & Plants Magazine.

Appendix G: USDA Hardiness Zone Map **167**

ABOUT THE AUTHORS

Lauren Chase-Rowell, an advocate of earth-centered living, integrates the art and science of interior and exterior design using permaculture and simple living practices. She has degrees in entomology, horticulture technology, and a specialized master's degree in education, "Integrating the Arts in Learning." She holds two certifications in permaculture design and education, and is a certified landscape professional with the NH Landscape Association. She taught sustainable landscaping at UNH for 14 years, and is a 2001 graduate of the NOFA Organic Landcare program. Lauren's businesses, Outdoor Rooms Permaculture Landscape Design Services and Chop Wood Carry Water Permaculture, provide her clients with highly functional and aesthetic landscapes integrated into local, natural systems. Lauren is a coauthor and illustrator of *Landscaping at the Water's Edge: An Ecological Approach.* She balances working, farming, family, and community in Nottingham, NH.

Mary Tebo Davis is an Urban and Community Forestry Educator for UNH Cooperative Extension. With degrees in environmental conservation and environmental education, she shares her passion for teaching about the natural world with volunteers and communities. She has been recognized for her innovative and creative partnerships and program accomplishments—establishing Manchester, NH's first green roof and the Natural Resources Stewards Program that teaches and engages volunteers and college students to sustain ecosystems in their communities. Mary is a coauthor of *Landscaping at the Water's Edge: An Ecological Approach.* She lives in Strafford, NH, where she loves to "play in the dirt," walk in the woods, and pick berries on Blue Job Mountain with her family and friends.

Katherine Hartnett is a geographer who works on reducing the ecological footprint of the built environment. In 1995, she helped found The Jordan Institute, a non-profit center for efficient land- and energy-use practices. Kate now works on integrated design and development projects. Since 1992, she has collaboratively designed, and lived in, two energy-efficient active and passive solar homes (www.nhsea.org), and co-manages a 150-acre tree farm. She's also working on a high-performance renovation of a 1910 home in Berlin, reducing energy use by half so far. Kate's work on this book fulfilled a desire to help develop and share a landscaping approach that follows nature's lead.

Marilyn Wyzga has been a practicing artist and teaching naturalist for 30 years. She created and coordinates Homes for Wildlife, the NH Fish and Game Department's award-winning schoolyard habitat program, and convenes the NH Children in Nature Coalition, an organization she helped establish. Marilyn's appreciation for native plants led her to pursue postgraduate studies with the New England Wildflower Society. She has applied her design skills to interpretive and educational exhibits, children's theater, and most recently to landscaping for wildlife, beginning with her own backyard. Marilyn was honored with the New England Wildflower Society's Education Award, and recognized as the Wildlife Society's Conservation Educator of the Year. She credits her parents' bold experiment in family camping with her lifelong love of the outdoors, and her mother for her appreciation of growing things.